StartUP SOAR C

Successful Outcomes by Adapting to Resiliency

author: Ray Garcia

publisher: Buoyant Capital, NYC, U.S.

website: http://buoyant.cc

microblog: http://startup-soar-coaching.tumblr.com

2nd Edition available in print and ebook formats.

This edition is for mentors, coaches, and teachers to use to train the next generation of entrepreneurial leaders to create value through new venture formation. An abridged version is available titled "StartUp your Future", which is to be read by the entrepreneur being coached or mentored. If they are highly self motivated they could use this book in place of the abridged version but I suggest that they do so with a mentor or peer team that will help them maintain the motivation to get through all the exercises and chart out a journey for their businesses.

Table of Contents

Start UP SOAR Coaching by Ray Garcia

Table of Contents

Table of Contents

Table of Contents

Table of Contents

Table of Contents

Introduction

Start-up now, get inspired to create a high impact international business, make a difference by putting ideas into action, and produce a return on investment with your talents.

Entrepreneurs gain satisfaction by using their talents to produce new wealth for both society and themselves. In a modern world, employment choices typically fit established institutional norms. A "good" job in a government bureaucracy or a large corporation, with its abundance of restrictive policies, may not provide much work satisfaction despite the employment benefits and stability. If you have ever thought, dreamed, imagined, or fantasized about starting a business, or being part of a company doing creative work with a purpose, then you have started to connect with your entrepreneurial spirit.

This book is for anyone who wants to better understand the entrepreneurial approach. It originated from the first entrepreneurship course I taught at the University of Pisa from 2011 through 2014 and is based on over 15 years of experience as an entrepreneur of venture backed technology companies. The course was designed for PhD researchers and MBA students looking to expand their work opportunities beyond their traditional prescribed paths into institutions and corporations. This material is not only for academic researchers, it assumes that entrepreneurship is latent in all people. Traditionally, we are taught not to aim for self-employment through entrepreneurship during the years of primary education. Anyone with an advanced education, self-motivation, ambition, a vision for how to improve the world, a good attitude, and a willingness to take on the challenge of actively exploring entrepreneurial pursuits, should be able to follow the material and put it to use in their own efforts. If you currently own or are working in a company and want to innovate and expand the business, this book might be of value in inspiring you to grow a high impact international business by leveraging the business you are already doing. Read it to prepare for the journey and put the concepts into action; do not be a passive reader. Start-up now, get inspired to create a high impact international business, make a difference by putting ideas into action, and produce a return on investment using your talents.

Audience

This book is for anyone who is looking to create economic value by adopting the mindset of an entrepreneur. It is used for the entrepreneurship course at the University of Pisa for PhD researchers and MBA students looking to explore options beyond their traditional prescribed paths into institutions and corporations. The course material and video lectures are available on-line for those with an ambition to create value that may change the world. In the entrepreneurial journey, they gain the satisfaction of using their talents to produce new wealth for society and themselves.

In a modern world, employment choices typically fit established institutional norms. The government bureaucracy, or the large corporation with its abundance of policies, in other words, a "good" job, with benefits and stability, may not provide much work satisfaction. Modern societies treat these jobs' as rewards, a prize, or an entitlement for following the rules of modern society. This default work path misdirect the talented and ambitious away from the paths that are most creative, impactful, challenging, and possibly most attuned to a need for purposeful work. Entrepreneurs produce new value for society by contributing to the wealth of their communities and themselves. If you have ever thought, dreamed, imagined, or fantasized about starting a business, or being part of a company that is doing purposeful work and making a difference, then you have started to connect with your inner entrepreneurial spirit.

This book's content originated from a course on entrepreneurship given to PhD Researchers who wanted to commercialize their research. They needed exposure to business to understand whether this was feasible for their research. The material is not particular to PhD researchers, instead it assumes that entrepreneurship is latent in all people. We are programmed not to aim for becoming an entrepreneur as a first choice during our many years of education. Yet anyone with an advanced education, self-motivation, ambition, a vision for how to improve the world, a good attitude, and a willingness to take on the challenge of actively exploring entrepreneurial pursuits, should be able to follow the material and put it to use in their own efforts.

If you currently own or are working in a company and want to innovate and expand the business this book might be of value in inspiring you to think about growing a high impact international business by leveraging the business you are already doing.

If you are just curious about business, wanting to understand what entrepreneurs think about and why, then this book might provide insights. Read it to prepare for the journey and put the concepts into action; do not be a passive reader.

How to use this book

Read or scan the book fast to form a mental map outline of entrepreneurship and put it into practice as soon as possible. Each subtopic will take years for the reader to understand and master. Many excellent books address detailed explanations of each subtopic. They are of four types: academic, specific to a sector, how-to mechanics, or success stories of managing an existing business. These books omit the challenges of starting a new venture from an idea to how to think about the journey. They do not provide a mixture of techniques that may fit the enormous variety of business situations the entrepreneurs will be faced with in the future. This omission in other books makes it hard for the ambitious entrepreneur to absorb the details and mechanics of business since they lack a way of thinking about the journey. I call this the pre-entrepreneur stage, the personal startup phase where someone is trying to gain a sense of the journey before they fully commit to self-directed learning that will last a life time.

INTRODUCTION

The criticism of MBA programs is that entrepreneurship courses use existing company cases and do not focus on what an entrepreneur does from the start of a business. The new ventures are trying an innovation never sold in the market, and the entrepreneurs may not have prior experience with business. First time technology entrepreneurs face these conditions. These are valuable lessons to learn by doing so they can be applied broadly to any new venture. Business texts are primarily of two types, authored by entrepreneurs from experience, or authored by academics as a traditional course textbook. With rare exception, one will find a practicing entrepreneur who is a trained active teacher, who has written a book that is useful for practitioners and students. This book is my attempt to fill this gap.

This book's premise is that reading about business is not enough; one needs to put it into action. The book intends for the reader to carry it with them, read a little, act on the concept, observe other businesses, and build up to launching a business. While this print version is the complete text, it was written for the e-book format which omits the reference material, is low cost and allows for immediate distribution. The e-book is easy to carry and use for inspiration and guidance throughout the entrepreneurial learning journey. The book accompanies a fully interactive in-classroom course used to jolt the aspiring entrepreneurs into action, with the expectation that most of the learning will take years of real world business practice. The topics of the book provoke active learning that comes from interacting with others in discussions of various challenges and exercises included at the end of the book. To support active learning, on-line tools complement the book, such as a LinkedIn.com group for discussion and a micro-blog with links, references, and book recommendations. This book assumes the reader, turned entrepreneur, is learning using on-line resources. The original book draft included images, charts, graphs, exercises, and references that were all removed in favor of providing these on-line. The book tries to be a timeless guide. Reference it as a terrain map not as a set of travel directions between the start and stop and restarts of your entrepreneurial journey.

Preface

While on a business trip to Italy in 2006, with my business partner, Giovanni Battistini, we visited Professor Paolo Ferragina PhD at the University of Pisa. We were looking to solve a complex technical problem for our entrepreneurial venture, Zonebee, and through our pursuits to find the best minds to solve it, we found the Computer Science Department at the University of Pisa. Paolo Ferragina's research in information retrieval algorithms are at the forefront of scientific breakthroughs. These are sponsored research programs by Yahoo and Google. All search engine companies would have great interest in accessing discoveries in this particular field of research.

In our first meeting, Paolo Ferragina was curious why two entrepreneurs would be in Pisa, Italy talking to researchers. He said that his sponsors would review his research and recognize it as scientifically interesting then ask, "What is the business model that makes money." For a researcher who just made another breakthrough discovery in computer science, this was an odd question. Was it not enough to have been the first to solve a complex mathematical problem encoded in a computer algorithm to advance human knowledge? From that spark of an encounter, these fundamental questions started a dialogue of hundreds of emails between us. We were sorting through the mission of a doctoral program at the university. We asked ourselves whether university doctoral programs needed to be complemented with the possibility of commercializing research beyond what the technology transfer office already did. If so how might the additional support be provided? Would anyone else care?

While Giovanni Battistini and I did not find our technical solution during that trip to Pisa, Italy, we did eventually find a solution from a University in Poland. What our trip did was trigger new entrepreneurial activities that did not start until years later. We both recognized that within the corridors of research departments of major universities are latent entrepreneurs, without a commercial context for their research or opportunity to see a path beyond the confines of their academic pursuits. They were likely unaware of that question "what is the business model and how does it make money?"

Since our first meeting, Paolo Ferragina has patented several inventions based on his research and is seeking commercial licensing opportunities. He took on the innovation challenge of extending the doctoral programs at one of the oldest universities in the world, the University of Pisa, the place of Galileo, the beginning of the scientific method, and a university steeped in history and tradition, and not a place where innovating education is likely to naturally happen. In 2010 the new Rector, Prof. Massimo Mario Augello, nominated Paolo Ferragina as Vice Rector for Innovation and Research. In 2011 the University of Pisa PhD Plus program was launched. The PhD Plus program is a means of providing opportunity for PhD candidates at the University of Pisa to explore opportunities for commercializing their research, to motivate them to think in business terms, and be ready to answer the question, "what is the business model?" They setup the PhD Plus program leveraging the assets of the university and dispensed with the traditional classroom lecture format. In its place, I helped them to construct a program that would borrow from entrepreneurial initiatives in U.S. universities to recast it into a European context.

In 2006, the European Union commission issued a mandate to universities across Europe. Two of the mandates in particular gave the impetus for the Pisa PhD Plus program; first, to integrate entrepreneurial mind-set into the curriculum of universities to foster the commercialization of scientific and technical research, second, to drive economic development through new venture creation by supporting entrepreneurs who start-up businesses. Both of these mandates broadly apply to businesses and the citizens of the Euro Zone, a call to action, a recognition that without entrepreneurship the Euro Zone may not continue to thrive in the face of rapid competition from the rest of the globe. The promise of a European Union is based on the benefits of an economic block and increased commerce. For this to be realized, a dynamic entrepreneurial drive must be fostered across the population. For the next generation of highly educated youth, mid-career professionals, and family businesses, entrepreneurship is a necessity embodied into their ambitions, and infused into the future expectations of this population.

Entrepreneurship in the European Union context is, by proximity and diversity, both international and high impact. A new venture needs to consider the entire E.U. market. It must figure out how to find the best value resources and manage them across the largest market accessible. An E.U. venture has the challenge of delivering products to customers across languages and culture. It has the advantage of the Eurocurrency removing the complexities of foreign currency exchanges within the Euro Zone. While these present formidable challenges, E.U. ventures that are able to compete in its market are better prepared to sell into a global market.

The United States produced an enormous number of innovations in the last thirty years leading to productivity gains and global expansion of its largest corporations. The computer industry alone created new economic zones in several regions of the U.S. of which the Silicon Valley branded region, spanning from San Jose to San Francisco, is just one of many. New York experienced a major turnaround during this period, from urban decay and flight of the middle class to the suburbs to becoming a first class international city at the center of the latest wave of a new-networked economy. To compete globally the top twenty countries try to copy similar rapid economic development in their regions by adopting the policies that fuel the new economy ecosystems. They study the emergence of entrepreneurship as a driver of the economy. The fundamental ingredient in economic development starts with the people who have entrepreneurial ambitions; without this, no amount of economic government policy will create another Silicon Valley regional brand, or be an attractive city for large talented migration as has been New York since its founding. Each region has its own unique characteristics that contribute to economic dynamism which need to emerge from its population recognizing entrepreneurship as a worthy effort, a preferred choice over working as a civil or institutional servant or corporate employee.

Family businesses are at the core of many of the European countries' economies. They mostly remain small, insular, using local suppliers and selling to local buyers, which limits the commercial impact. Most of these family businesses are not international and do not use the latest technology advancement that lead to competitive productivity. The tradition of family businesses throughout Europe provides fertile grounding for developing and gaining basic business skills. When combined with advanced research in science, engineering, technology, and design, this tradition may produce potential for extraordinary economic comparative advantages.

The goals of the PhD Plus program and this book are threefold: first, new venture creation using research work of the PhD students; second, industry innovation through commercialization of research, and; third, to make an impact on society while doing satisfying work. These goals are not exclusive to PhD students nor do they need the individual be the inventor or researcher. We do want the participant in the program to have insight, views, or perspective, to generate business concepts using a range of acquired innovations.

Prologue

This book is used in a university advanced academic course. That course has a nontraditional format that is activity oriented training, akin to an artist studio and not the typical business case method class. It omits examples, case studies, and stories, in favor of letting the entrepreneur discover these first through their own actions then afterwards reading the storybooks about how others did it. I have never found reading a business book full of entertaining stories of much use in my own businesses, mostly because of the lack of context and application of specifics to the situation. Abstracting the patterns from sparse information in a story can lead to false conclusions and prescriptions. They are useful as a teaching aid to help remember a key idea. Learn the concepts by practicing them in real situations and create your own context and examples to learn from.

The global technology entrepreneurial community has developed its own business training through the informal intensive startup incubator and accelerator programs. This handbook adopts the emerging model for entrepreneurial training: inspire ambition, understand the basic concepts, gain a few rudimentary skills, sketch out a model of the business, act it out through storytelling, get feedback, refine it, enroll a team, engage customers, co-create the market, create the product, get sales, get funding to grow. Entrepreneurship needs practice, practice, practice. It is action oriented – reading about business it is not enough. The book recognizes this, addresses the reader using the first person form, and uses short dense blog style passages to get the essence of the concepts conveyed. It does not go into details of the mechanics, these are left to the entrepreneur for self-directed study using the on-line resources and references. Each book section builds on the previous points, but reading it in your preferred order is fine. The aspiring entrepreneur finds the value by reconstructing the journey in whatever order works for them. The book is written from experience and not from academic research. Research has supported many of the concepts, yet it remains largely a subjective topic and thus for the entrepreneur to interpret in their context. There are no simple prescriptions for learning entrepreneurship successfully other than to learn by doing it and having the meta-cognition to understand how to self-direct the learning by collaborating with a team.

The best a teacher can do is to suggest exercises, provide space to practice, guide the learning process, raise awareness, recommend sources to research, elicit the intrinsic motivations, reveal what is possible, give examples and demonstrations, and mentor. The teachers acting as a coach will tap into the entrepreneurs funds of knowledge, raise the bar of expectations, disclose gaps in knowledge and experience, remove excuses, demand performance, convert the simulations into reality. The committed coach invest in their students' potential, make themselves available to those who continue to try an entrepreneurial venture, and act as a mentor to the students so they make a difference with their efforts. No book can accomplish all this within the limits of the medium; this book is simply a guiding structure to aid the entrepreneur in their pursuit. If you are reading this book without taking the course, it will be of value if you make use of the complementary on-line material and you create a support team that includes a coach who can mentor you through the entrepreneurial journey. Entrepreneurs do not sail across an ocean alone. They use a crew, maps, and navigation aids in their explorations.

The chapters cover the foundations of entrepreneurial mind-set, the acquired traits, and aspirations that persist in acting on the ambition to start a new venture. To fully grasp the basic concepts one only needs to develop the obsession and drive to reclaim their self-determination for creating economic value for themselves and society. These chapters were a series of lessons given in the PhD Plus course that make up a dialogue between the entrepreneur and the provocations to jolt the students into action.

The Entrepreneurial Spirit chapter covers topics that help one understand what an entrepreneur is and to start to identify themselves as one, by recognizing that entrepreneurship is a disposition, attitude, and outlook on the prospects for making an impact with the work one does.

The Ideas to Execution chapter challenges the entrepreneurs into understanding how to think of concepts, what myths exist about ideas that prevent one from producing hundreds of business ideas and to help the aspiring entrepreneur gain insight into the reality of ideas and what can be done with them.

The Business Structure Formation chapter provides a simple framework to guide the entrepreneur to uncover common issues with creating a business and determining how to put ambitions into action. The framework is a representation of the basic components that all businesses have. The business concepts in this framework, and the innovations, are provoked to show how the components in the structure work together.

The Social by Design chapter gets to the essence of all business, the people who form it, make it a reality, and the social interactions that create the environment where business emerges from a concept to reality. It explains why social networking matters and where to gain the most value from it. These concepts are the basis for how an entrepreneur learns to market and sell their products. In this chapter one learns why entrepreneurship means leading others into the entrepreneurial journey.

The Funding Bootstrap chapter covers the one question that aspiring entrepreneur's start with, where will they get the money to work on their business. What are the sources and how does one tap into them. The guidance is not what a new entrepreneur wants to hear but it is the reality of how most businesses get started. It discusses how to think about money, basic financial literacy, and covers a few of the main topics that all new entrepreneurs need to learn.

The book closes with a short section on Business Lore, the patterns that one can observe in business and products that come from design. The latest solution touted for hard problems is "design thinking." After the chapters is a set of simple exercises that one can use to get started; these can be done while or after reading the book. The exercises are part of project work in the intensive course. Do these exercises multiple times, like building up muscle you do them repeatedly making them harder as time goes on to gain strength to take on weight, increase speed and endurance.

The course and handbook are inspirational yet practical. It is action oriented and includes exercises that are patterns for how to think and act like an entrepreneur, and in doing so, one can absorb a new behavior that will create expanded opportunities for starting a business. The material provides an outline of many topics that an entrepreneur needs to be familiar with, practice, and gain mastery by doing. The book omits specifics of legal and accounting practices and while it references the U.S., it has a global view of the techniques and topics being applicable to all entrepreneurs.

The book includes methods for self-directed learning to build on the course material and provides a website and LinkedIn group to support the exercises. The website includes the original course presentations, which are an abbreviated version of the material in this book. The website also includes videos, suggested readings, case analysis, discussion forum, and presentations from readers, when they provide them, for comment and feedback.

The goal of the PhD Plus program was to expose researchers to entrepreneurship career options. We have a longer-term objective that guides the program; to spin-off or start-up ventures based on university research by getting the commercialization funded through winning business plan competitions, attracting seed stage investment, and licensing the intellectual property to corporations for the development of new products and services. In our first year, we made progress towards this objective with several businesses receiving modest grants to explore the commercialization of their research. In the second year, we added an intensive course in entrepreneurship for the MBA students and combined the MBA class with the PhD researchers with excellent outcomes. We demonstrated that we could indeed bridge the gap between academic research and commerce when providing a common language familiar to all business students and easy for researchers to quickly gain.

The Entrepreneurial Spirit

A dream needs to overcome fear, irrationality, and failure to become reality.

A question an entrepreneur often reflects on is, "Why am I compelled to be an entrepreneur?" It comes from a fertile imagination. How life might be better, if some aspect of existence was improved? The entrepreneur has a deep desire to be creative in work. Much of these thoughts are just idle dreams. Eventually a few thoughts become ideas that are so strongly compelling that I suspend my inner critic and start to do something about the idea. I have to overcome my fears, act on impulse and find that I am failing a lot. The dreams start to take shape and become real. I experience the frustration of trying to think through every problem and not being able to predict a given outcome, followed by a sense of discovery, an opportunity is revealed, and a feeling that by continuing to try, the odds are increasing that progress will be made.

A personal reflection and a struggle to understand what drives one to impossible challenges, leads to the recurring question, can I become my own dream? Can one bring others along, and when that dream becomes a reality will that reality have created value? It is the elevated sense of meaning that comes from driving towards the next challenge, ever harder, scarier, with the reward being the next challenge.

The entrepreneurial spirit means a fundamental emotional and activating principle determining one's character in the pursuit of producing new economic value. Pursuing excellence, mastery, the application of skills to useful endeavors, with a purpose, is what entrepreneurs do.

Embracing the reality of entrepreneurship requires overcoming fear of failure, and understanding irrational decision-making. Personally, my dream of having self-determination through entrepreneurship was realized by acting on my desires to form a company. Yet, the reality of starting and running a company was different than what I imagined.

Topics in this chapter are:

1. A world of opportunities, it takes having a perspective to see them.

2. What are entrepreneurs and how can one recognized them?

3. Entrepreneurial action and thinking that gets it all started.

4. What can go wrong? You have to get over it.

5. What is business knowledge anyway?

A World of Opportunities

Human Economic Activity

When someone is trying to understand how entrepreneurs succeed, they often start with the question "Are entrepreneurs made or born?" The nature versus nurture question is often the first barrier that an aspiring entrepreneur faces. They consider whether they have what it takes, as if one needs special magical qualities to succeed or try. The belief that you have to be born an entrepreneur serves to keep people from trying. A cynical view would be that entrepreneurs want everyone else to think they have a mysterious natural force that made it so they can pursue their ambitions and others could not. This cynical view would easily remove competition for entrepreneurs by making it the exclusive domain of the naturally gifted. If one is born in a country that is having a civil war, or they have a physical or mental chronic condition, or other challenging circumstances, these will not make it easy to succeed as an entrepreneur. Neither does it make it easier to work for a company as an employee. It may be that if one is born with challenging circumstances, the need to become an entrepreneur is greater since it may be the only alternative and done out of economic necessity.

If one takes the position that entrepreneurship is a natural economic state of all, to whatever degree that may be, then why is it not in the realm of everyone's pursuits? Is it possible that we start as entrepreneurs and nurtured to be employees and subservient to large institutions? The school systems are oriented towards training people to work in government and corporations and provide little preparation for surviving outside institutional workplaces.

All humans have the capacity to create; some create greater value than just for their own needs, and others' are conditioned to function within the status quo. The latent creativity we possess is revealed in our entrepreneurial spirit, -- be it out of need or choice. The desire of creating something of value is easy for anyone to intuitively understand and relate to as a common human activity.

In the developed world of advanced economies the view is – "When everything is predictable you figure out how to fit into that expected or conditioned reality." In the developing world the view is – "When nothing is certain you act to create a reality." The populations of the developing world are larger than in the countries of the advanced economies. The developing world is likely to represent the state of what humans do naturally, shape their existence with what is at hand, be resourceful to survive, create value for others to thrive, be entrepreneurial out of need.

A neighbor plans to go back to Iraq to live and start a business someday. What is normal to him is to run his own business. He is from northern Iraq, a Kurdish town of about 50,000 people. He feels related to all the towns' citizens, and therefore they make up his extended family. He lives a decent life in U.S., owns a home, has a car and a steady job. Yet he remains unsatisfied since he has not started a business since coming to the U.S. over ten years ago. His reason for not starting a business is that he does not have family in the U.S. What is normal for people in the U.S. – a steady job – is not normal to him. Without starting a business, he feels like he has not accomplished anything in life. Thus, he speaks of returning to his homeland someday and fulfilling his ambition of starting his own business. In the U.S., this is a common view among the immigrant populations. By the second generation, the children aspire to work for a big company instead of starting their own businesses and lose the natural drive to be an entrepreneur.

The World Market

If all humans are naturally entrepreneurial, it means they are trying to create economic value daily for survival and to have their communities thrive. The flow of economic activity from these entrepreneurs is to make things and service others, buy things and sell what they create. What does this world market look like? It consists of people trying to make a living. The conditions under which the worlds' population lives vary greatly. They are changing quickly and converging to a global norm that may be increasingly available in the 21st century.

The rich have accumulated enormous wealth. The conditions of historical poverty have improved dramatically in the last 100 years putting many people into a relative middle class existence. This is not an advanced economy view of the middle class, a large segment of the world population has improved their daily life conditions to be better than they were 100 years ago. The rate of this change is increasing and in the last 50 years commerce progressed from largely regional to its global span today. In the last 25 years, in China alone, millions of people have risen out of relative poverty creating a new market for entrepreneurs. Reflecting on one's own entrepreneurial hopes, can you think of a business that would address the entire world market, something that every person may want or need to have or do?

Market Distribution

The entire world market is approximately 7 billion people and growing each year with current estimates at 9 billion by 2050. With a high concentration of 2% of the population owning 50% of the wealth, the top eight largest economies are countries consuming resources at an inequitable rate to support their consumerist lifestyle. These numbers reflect the wish for comforts of material possessions and the trend is that more of the world population wants to own a car, phones, computers, eat beef, and increase their carbon footprint, so the latent market is much greater than that which has so far acquired the skewed consumption habits.

Of 6 billion people who have per capita annual incomes of 1,000 to 12,000 dollars, they average at least an 8th grade education. The affluent live in urban cities. They are likely to have access to media, be it newspaper, TV, or radio, and a high percentage will have a phone, a computer, or mobile phone, with the 2 billion most affluent having over 90% chance of owning a mobile device, and the rest having 50% chance of owning one.

The top twenty economies are countries producing 85% of worlds' economic activity and make up a powerful bloc of trading partners. This is an enormous opportunity when one considers the scale of the global problems, and the promise of technology to address them. Anyone who is fortunate to live in one of these twenty countries and exploits the education system and economic force is able to seize large-scale opportunities in the future. The continuing need to support basic issues of sustaining life, food, water, energy, health, transportation, communications, commerce, and governance, are improved by science and technology in a modern world. The range of solutions still needs improvement to support the entire global population. All aspiring entrepreneurs have huge opportunities for value creation, and the economic rewards that come with it, if they realize the range and scale of problems, and the variety of places and circumstances where they could offer a solution.

The developing world has many people but scarce financial capital resources. The number of human resources are enormous and when made productive can perform marvels using rudimentary techniques as shown in the wonders of the ancient world. These techniques persist today; watch basic building construction in India using human resources instead of earth moving equipment. People power still has a potential to move mountains and dam rivers. The advances in technology have made it possible to attack larger scale problems. Since financial capital remains scarce in the developing world it relies on people power as the dominant force for progress.

Even with the enormous differences between the advanced and developing economies, the penetration of mobile, personal computers and broadband communications is significant and driving change in the world. Historically, communications connectivity and increased transportation logistics capability has contributed to the growth of productivity. With the wide scale adoption of the mobile phone, it is easy to observe how it has helped to bridge rural communities into larger economic activity. With ease of communications comes ease of coordinating transportation and thus increased economic activity.

If we were to consider the mobile phone as one of many modern technology innovations that are within reach of most of the world population, could it change the world in a significant way? The example of how mobile phones may have contributed to facilitating political activism and the dramatic changes in several governments in recent years is an early indication of its potential impact. If one considers that combining technology with human capital, it may set in motion action by entrepreneurs to affect change. Free markets that entrepreneurs can create value in is an exciting future, yet scary for those controlling institutional forces who want to maintain the status quo. It is embraced by anyone who no longer wants to be the subject of the state institutions of control and desire freedom to pursue their entrepreneurial aspirations. People are compelled to act to force change and innovate their governments and stagnant economies. When will the revolution of entrepreneurs start?

The world population is quickly migrating to the cities and creating new cities, both cities within cities and suburban areas that surround the central old city. This increase in urban density is an efficient use of resources and creates opportunities for entrepreneurs to access large segments of people easily, rather than transporting product or delivering services to places that are difficult to reach. It is possible for an entrepreneur to sell globally through these urban populations where there is a local, accessible regional, and global market that connects the major mega-cities. These mega-cities have rural populations migrating to them, they have a continued migration from poor to rich countries, in particular to the major cities. This may have the impact of changing the identities of nations by introducing many cultural influences to places that were previously homogenous. All these changes create spaces of opportunity for entrepreneurs.

Major challenges remain for entrepreneurs starting businesses in these cities. Some of the massive problems are: public health issues, 44% of people in rich countries have cars contributing to large global problems, political unrest, global financial market instability, lack of good governance. All these issues contribute to limiting a truly open global market. Yet, for entrepreneurs, these challenges are opportunities to make a difference and create real value.

While tech entrepreneurs in advanced economies have influenced greatly the penetration of communications technologies, the global reality is that 5% of the worlds' population speaks English, another 5% speaks Spanish with 36% of the population living in China or India and a large segment speaking Mandarin or Bengali. The global entrepreneurs are still an exception and likely an elite group of fortunate talent that might consider doing something good for the rest of the planet. This is expanding rapidly and soon the entire global market may become available to everyone with the global tech community bridging the cultural divides.

Where are the markets?

Entrepreneurs want to find markets with density of buyers, locations where it is easy to find labor and easy to distribute product. Physical distance adds logistical costs for communications technologies that require expensive infrastructure to connect the locations. The growth of urban centers and migration from rural to urban has created the mega-city, places of enormous problems and opportunities.

Mega-cities with populations greater than ten million and incomes greater than 12,000 USD per capita income include Los Angeles, New York City, Paris, Tokyo, Osaka. Those with less than 12,000 per capita income include Mexico City, Rio de Janeiro, Sao Paulo, Buenos Aires, Moscow, Istanbul, and less then 4k in income are Cairo, Lagos, Karachi, Delhi, Mumbai, Kolkata, Dhaka, Beijing, Shanghai, Manila.

Mega-cities of over 10 Million are what many in the advanced economies have come to assume are the dominant economic centers. The list above is less than 5% of the worlds' population, it is a strong indicator of what the world will be like in the future: a higher concentration of people in urban environments. New mega-cities will emerge in the next 40 years as populations continue to migrate into the urban cities away from the rural villages. If the world population increases by two billion people, they will not be living in rural villages – they will live in new cities they build.

We can guess at the population rates, consumption of resources within a range of statistical probability. We are good are predicting trends with facts. When faced with uncertainty, we are fearful of making decisions. We cannot predict what these billions of people will do, where they will live, what they will think, or how they behave; therefore, we have much uncertainty about the future. Mega cities have problems on a scale so large that governments are at a loss as to what to do. The slums of Mumbai will reach a population equal to London and New York City in years to come, creating urban challenges never before encountered at this scale.

For some this is a frightening future, yet others see enormous possibilities to solve problems and create value. Entrepreneurs see these trends as opportunities to create value and have distribution to larger and concentrated markets that are easier to access. These mega-cities are highly interconnected, through communications, commerce, labor talent, and have mobile entrepreneurs who readily work across several cities to source and sell into these markets.

What are Entrepreneurs?

Entrepreneurs see opportunity where others see chaos in the activity of a mega-city. They exploit the uncertainty that causes others to freeze and instead create new value with action. Desire is not enough; it needs action to create opportunity where it otherwise might not exist. This is true under the worst possible conditions, where people are living in horrendous conditions or in the middle of a war, people will still figure out how to conduct commerce to survive. In the advanced economies, we have an abundance of options. Some are easier, like getting a job, but in doing so, what are we giving up?

Notions of freedom and self-determination should include the ability to pursue entrepreneurship or self-employment, and not be limited to working for a company or organization as the means of survival. The self-determination to start a business and generate value is liberating even if it fails. Modern corporations and institutions, which were formerly enormous monolithic organizations, are trying to restructure themselves into autonomous business units that are better able to compete in dynamic global free markets. Unfortunately, large and entrenched interest serves the existing power structures, making it difficult for these monoliths to transform. These ideas might sound radical to some. When one reviews a comparative study on economic development and finds that countries where it is easy for entrepreneurs to do business do substantially better than those where it is difficult to do business, causes one to wonder why this is the case. How may this inform a new model for large corporations stuck in a path of pending mammoth extinction due to its hierarchical organization?

What is an Entrepreneur?

The working definition for entrepreneurs in this book is "An entrepreneur is a person who creates new social and economic value for the benefit of themselves and others through active business innovation."

No single definition of entrepreneurship will cover all interpretations. So much is dependent on the context within the entrepreneurs' practices. It is defined by the entrepreneur and is simply a reference to the experiences they have working in environments that feel uncertain rather than the perceived comfort of being a company employee.

Entrepreneurs take measured risk, use creativity, and solve problems in the face of uncertainty while enrolling others in the effort to advance the business. It is as much a mental attitude and disposition as it is what an entrepreneur does. The active business innovation is the pursuit of continuous leaps in improvement that increase competitiveness. This is inclusive of all forms of innovation, be it new products, increases in customer satisfaction, cost efficiencies, speeding up the supply chain, improvements in workforce productivity. An invention is an intentional change that achieves a better social and economic outcome than whatever preceded it as an innovation.

Entrepreneurs start and grow companies, or they work within an existing company as a change agent to influence the adoption of an innovation. They may not have invented the innovation but they do make it useful and available.

We will focus on entrepreneurs who innovate in the market. They may replicate portions of other businesses but they create new value through innovation. For example, a retail business that uses a novel way of delivering its products to consumers by allowing them to order on-line in the store and pick up the item immediately would involve sophisticated technology coordination and would not be commonly available to the consumer at other retailers.

An example of the type of entrepreneurship that is not the subject of this book are franchises and life style family businesses, of which the owners do not intend to grow. They acquire these businesses to sustain their livelihood, but limit the risk of attempting novel business practices that might create new value for the customers. The life style business will tend to limit the risk by replicating a known business model. While all new business has substantial risk, the ones that seek to limit the risk to the degree of replicating a franchise model are not the subject of this book. Franchising and similar small business structures that replicate known models are one of many forms of entrepreneurship omitted from this book and well represented in other books on small business.

Many people start small businesses by replicating an existing business structure and products, for example the thousands of ice cream shops available in major cities. In the town of Lares, Puerto Rico, a small ice cream shop sells favors that are highly unusual, including one made from fish. A flavor novelty puts a little shop on to a tourist visit list and expands its sales well beyond its local town. The innovative entrepreneur will generate new value in the market in creative ways that has high potential for growth and does this by creatively changing aspects of their business structure or products that customers respond to positively.

The distinction between small businesses and high-impact entrepreneurship is not a judgment of the merits of either. This book is for people with aspirations beyond their personal lifestyle choices, who want to use their advanced education and competences to full potential. The challenge of forming and growing a high-impact business has a better chance at producing results of new economic value than either starting a well-prescribed business structure, as packaged by a franchise or duplicating the next gelato shop.

Entrepreneurs Create Value

Entrepreneurs create new growth in the global economy.

The Kaufman Foundation states all new net jobs in the U.S. came from entrepreneurs and not corporations. From 1980 to 2005, U.S. corporations did not produce net new jobs. Entrepreneurs created all new growth in the U.S. economy, about 40+ Million jobs created by companies less than 5 years old. These are startling realizations given the amount of media attention that large corporations have, the hope they will help the economy grow. Many of the largest corporations become acquirers of innovations from smaller companies and claim them as their own to help fuel their market growth.

Large U.S. multi-national corporations dominate commerce and make up over 50% of the U.S. economy. Many of those companies get over half their revenue from international sales and operations. They expand globally not domestically, find new markets and sources and operationalize their businesses to reduce cost and increase distribution sales volume. They commoditize their products and control the distribution but they may not be creating new value, other than for their shareholders. As these global corporations get larger, their industries consolidate into a few entities that mostly acquire their competitors or buy innovative entrepreneurial companies. The stars of the new economy, companies like Cisco, Google, Microsoft, Yahoo, Apple, have become acquisition machines and are no longer centers of innovation.

Italy, by contrast, has a dominance of small businesses with approximately 90% of all companies with less than 10 Million Euro in revenue. Many of these firms are family businesses. It has enormous global corporations and the government is a large employer. As a percentage of the population, Italy has more small business entrepreneurs than the U.S. but these entrepreneurs may not grow their businesses due to government regulations, taxation, risk aversion, and cultural preferences that constrain the aspiration.

The U.S. is associated with entrepreneurship, free markets, and the American dream. Compared to other parts of the world, this may not be as true as many Americans think. In most parts of the world, entrepreneurship is the means of survival and people may not have another choice but to be entrepreneurs daily. These survival forms of entrepreneurship -- underground economies, subversive economies, black markets -- are informal economies. An advanced economy like the U.S. would not function without an informal economy. Just walk into the kitchens of over 10,000 restaurants in New York City, or consider the approximately eight thousand bicycle delivery people who service those restaurant customers, and one will quickly understand the layers of dimensions that exist in an economy. The U.S. has an estimated twelve million undocumented workers who are doing many types of jobs, from picking fruits in the farms to construction jobs and all for wages that are less than what would be paid to a documented citizen. The U.S. economy was built on a history of labor exploitation which continues today. Those twelve million people, larger than the population of many countries, have their own informal economy and demonstrate a resilient entrepreneurial spirit to thrive.

The U.S. celebrates the myth of the self-made person who came from nothing to create much personal wealth. This may not be the norm and a modest form of entrepreneurship is common, one that makes life style choices to limit business growth and risk and therefore remain small businesses. Entrepreneurs in the U.S. may not realize they have much in common with entrepreneurs in Italy, and by extension the rest of the world. The U.S. small business community and the informal economy are co-dependent and exist as much of the rest of the world economy does.

Other myths that perpetuate in the U.S. are that of the child billionaires and the magical leader. These myths are actively promoted by the media, the publicist for the iconic figures, the corporate marketing departments, and government policy makers. Celebrating corporate personalities does not serve anyone other than as another form of entertainment. These are not representative of the vast majority of entrepreneurs that create economic vitality, are successful through hard work, innovate, and grow, either, by choice, or need. This book is about unleashing the entrepreneurial latent potential of people who are fortunate to have an advance education and can apply their talents to solving real problems and creating new economic value. These are the people with the potential to have a dramatic impact on the world by becoming entrepreneurs.

Entrepreneurs Change the World

Desire is the most important ingredient of an entrepreneur. Desire needs sustainable action. You need to be intrinsically motivated as an entrepreneur and endlessly optimistic, even in the face of a harsh reality. Ultimately, you need to *want* to make it happen to take action. Through action you find out whether the business can happen.

Having a higher calling, acting on faith, wanting to have a legacy, thinking you can change the world, having a strong need to do something of value; these are strong motivations for creating a business. With all the challenges ahead, your intrinsic motivation is essential. Otherwise, you are likely to quit at some point.

As an entrepreneur, believing the team can change the world and thinking that it is possible and worth doing are preconditions to starting. Deciding whether the team wants to make the difference together is the last driving piece needed to get to concrete action. The hundreds of leadership books published each year speak to this ambition that all entrepreneurs have, be it the modest corner store to the mega-global corporation.

Entrepreneurial Action

Do you know anyone who thinks the world is perfect? Act on this opportunity to make a difference that improves the lives of all. Entrepreneurs see a world with problems to fix, plenty of opportunities to make a difference, and get passionate about going into unpredictable markets.

The billionaires Michael Dell and Bill Gates dropped out of college. Richard Branson dropped out of secondary school at age sixteen. What is it about these people that made them chase an entrepreneurial vision? They left the certainty of finishing school for the doubts of starting a business they knew little about. They made the irrational decision to go into markets that had not formed and to leave a path of formal education, conditioning that by all consideration one would think may be enough preparation to foster entrepreneurial skills. They had an inclination to act under uncertainty but they understood the need to master and control what can be known, and figure out the rest as the opportunity that others might not try. They could see the world differently than it was and believed they could make the changes that would move it to a better world for everyone. Ego, greed, over-confidence, naiveté, smarts, power, all these must have been factors in driving them. For sure, the obstacles were daunting and early failures discouraging, but they acted with persistence when others did not. Granted, these entrepreneurs are extreme examples and several factors beyond their control helped to open opportunities they could step into. Not finishing school did not make it easier for them and random historical luck needs to be recognized. Against this backdrop, acting on desires and persistence with overconfidence surely helped propel them forward.

Finding the Entrepreneur Within

We are taught to think rationally as if that is the way to make sense of the world. Much remains unknown about how the world works and the unexplored is larger than science has uncovered. Some find artistic expression necessary to help grasp what is unknown and to use intuition to explain it. People who live creative lives and embrace the nonsensical occurrences around us as an inspiration for expression can teach entrepreneurs how to grasp the uncertainty of their efforts and how to use our intuition to express how the world might be improved.

People may mistakenly assume that artists do not solve problems. If you watch an artist at work they are solving detailed problems about how to visually represent an image so the mind can perceive what they are trying to express with an interpretation that has a shared meaning. The range of art is as varied as the range of entrepreneurs; both are acting creatively and solving problems in similar ways albeit with different mediums.

Like an Artist

For an artist to develop a craft they need to make several sketches to create a masterwork. For the entrepreneur, they need many tries before creating a product that will sell. They are both aware of the situation, the environment they are in, how they relate to it. They have a view they want to express through a medium so they master the craft; then they are free to put into action their passion.

Does an artist know what the artwork will be when they stare at the canvas? Does the entrepreneur know what the business will be like when they get started? Both start with what is at hand and the means they have to act to acquire missing resources. Then, they get started with an optimistic view they have of the situation. The artist's goal is to express something, and similarly, for the entrepreneur, it is to create value, what it is and how it happens is the process. The artist and entrepreneur are not goal oriented. As the work is revealed, eventually they catch on to a vision of what is unfolding then try to reveal that value on the canvas or in the business. Along the way, they might toss out the canvas, paint over it, white out portions, adopt a genre or style, get feedback, step away to see better, focus on one section, and inspired to innovate by changing techniques and mediums.

Starting with an artist analogy highlights a point that entrepreneurs face: high doubt in the creative process. Artists cause the viewers to ask a question, whereas designers answer the questions directly. Engineers solve problems and scientists understand the foundational basis for the problem. Entrepreneurs work on this continuum from artist to designer to engineer to scientist. To learn how to act and think like an entrepreneur it is necessary to have fluidity of thought and action from artist to scientist.

The Discovery

Entrepreneurs like to discover new markets even when they do not understand why those markets are buying the product. They may not ever figure out why the product works. If it sells then they sell more. Understanding the buyer affords important insights into the next innovations. Entrepreneurs focus on getting the business launched and growing fast. They do not have to understand why it is working; they just aggressively chase the market.

Entrepreneurs may view a large opportunity space but they cannot pursue every path to finding the best one. They pursue a path that is good enough to make money, and then improve it so it makes more money. They find a theme, try out variations, and improvise along the way, looking for cheap ways to fail fast and learn until repeated success starts to happen. This creative, yet chaotic activity can be unsettling when spending money, without achieving clear outcomes. This is how breakthrough business innovation happens. On occasion random luck might appear sooner, all too often the first success cripples further discovery or worse the discovery process takes over, and nothing settles into a business. Early success is as dangerous as prolonged failure.

Entrepreneurs are addicted to learning. They do research to get the basic understanding, then go through trial and error cycles to uncover unknowns. Along the way, the attempts start to work and those set the theme that guide the variations used to refine the product, until the desired market effect is consistent and growing. Causation might be discovered, if not, correlation is good enough, neither is necessary to make money.

Self determination

In the advanced economies, the conditioned workforce is directed within a preset objective and means provided by the employer institutions. This conditioning starts in the schools where the teachers provide the objectives and dictate the way of learning. Companies continue this pattern in their management; they want compliant employees.

It is no different for professionals who work in industries that require expertise. They solve problems and might be a little creative at work, but they are working within the fixed goals of the executive management of the company and need to conform to the standard procedures. The best examples of this are the popularity of operational quality control and the adoption of Six Sigma applied to service oriented industries. It attempts to remove all variation in service delivery at the expense of a humanized customer experience.

Entrepreneurs decide the means and the ends to achieve their goals and resist the prescribed path of conforming to a preconditioned pattern of work. They imagine several ends and find new means and resources to achieve their goals. The intrinsic motivation found in entrepreneurs comes from being self-directed, self-reflective, meta-cognitive, and the habitual learning and change.

The business school MBA programs perpetuate this preconditioning supported by the corporations who sponsor the students. This may explain why so few MBA graduates go on to start a business. Many of the best graduates work in investment banks or strategy consulting, with the rest working in the corporations that sponsored or hire them. Again, the analogy with artist is relevant since so few people who study art ever become artists; they are preconditioned by the formal institutional education that are stuck with testing measures for assurance of learning that have nothing to do with being a successful artist. Similarly, the MBA programs suffer from these issues. The measure of an MBA graduate is not on the profit they created, and neither is an artist measured by the number of viewers who found something to appreciate in the work. Entrepreneurs are compelled by self-determination and define the means and the ends to be achieved, who they want to work with, buy from and sell to, and what the product is, why it has value, when and where it is sold, and how fast they grow the business. Few of these opportunities are available to people who work for a large corporation, including the CEO of the company.

Context of Personal Assets

Your personal assets as an entrepreneur are who you are, what you know, and whom you know. These are assets that every entrepreneur understands intuitively and uses to get the business going. Who you are is your identity, your traits, preferences, and abilities. These can change over time with experiences that broaden exposure to other cultures and ways of thinking. In the U.S., people redefine themselves and may have to reinvent who they are to find opportunities to pursue. The flexibility and variety of the American identity is fertile ground for an entrepreneur to explore what works for them to build associations that help their ambitions. In many countries, the identities are less fluid and culture, language, traditions, religion, lineage, birthplace, socio-economic status, and other factors contribute to an identity determined at birth and family upbringing. The entrepreneur exploits their identity when it has benefit. They freely change and adopt their identity to expand opportunities that may not be present through circumstance, they do not let others define who they are; they declare it and redefine the terms under which they will thrive.

Your competence is what you use to create a business. It is the expertise and experience you bring to situations you create. Before starting a business venture your competence should have achieved a level of mastery that is exceptional, recognized by peers, ready to be applied, and relevant to the startup. Having achieved mastery in one area helps to build confidence that it can be useful in another area. In business, it needs to start with value the entrepreneur is bringing to the business they create. I am not referring to getting excellent grades on a standardized test. While that is important for signaling the degree to which one has worked in their studies, it is not a determinant of success outside of school. What the entrepreneur focuses on is how to apply what they have learned in ways that create value. It is in the application where they acquire mastery.

The connections in your professional networks are your resources to solve problems and provide access to help you in your business. These are not just the contacts you have but the connections you can access by providing value to get value. This is common in academia, where people collaborate on research and share knowledge. In business, there are competitive, concerns but networking within an industry among competitors is common. We will cover this aspect of entrepreneurship further in the chapter on Social by Design.

The most important connections one can set up as an entrepreneur, is to find a mentor, coach, or guide, who they can go to for advice. They need mentors and coaches who can guide them through the entrepreneurial process and point out what one cannot easily see in oneself, the trap of self-perception that cripples the entrepreneur from tackling the problems that prevent them from advancing. Forming these relationships can often expose weaknesses and vulnerabilities detected by the coach or confessed by the entrepreneur. A coach can help to foster a bias for trust that is so essential for forming working relationships with people quickly. This bias for trust varies across cultures and is one of the key attributes that has helped fuel the global technology economy. Without a bias for trust, the cost of building relationships across geographies and cultural differences can quickly stall rapid growth of a business.

Making it Happen

Entrepreneurs need to understand what their tolerance for loss is before they jump into a venture. It is like going gambling; you set aside money you can afford to play with and do not go above that amount. Your affordable loss is not just money; it includes time, reputation, opportunities not pursued, and other costs you incur. This starts with your personal finances. Once you have figured out what you can afford to lose you can calculate this for the business and each person you bring in to help. Not all costs can be determined, but you can still figure out your threshold, the amount where if you spend beyond, you hinder the capacity to recover financially. For later stage entrepreneurs, this could the equity in their home or a portion of their savings. For someone just out of college it could be forgoing a job at a corporation to start a new venture instead. Calculate the dollar cost and the intangible opportunity cost to decide whether the venture you will pursue is worth the effort. Much will be impossible to determine. The process of thinking through these issues will give you the confidence to try.

It is not possible to guess with certainty what the future will be in five years aiming for a venture. You can decide what will not happen based on your choices. If you chose not to start the business then it is certain the business will not form. If you start the business, it is not certain that it will survive for five years. Everyone on the founding team and everyone that is first hired needs to calculate their affordable loss to give the business the best chance at not ending prematurely, caused by one of the founders not having prepared adequately. Will everyone have enough money or equal risk tolerance? Understanding what that is for each person is important. Fear of poverty, for those who never experienced it, can be a strong motivator for making hasty decisions that can affect everyone on the team.

Entrepreneurs create the future and do not try to predict it. The extent to which we can control the future is what we can predict. Part of that future is coupling the affordable loss with contingencies that can be advantages if the business gets into trouble or one person miscalculated their affordable loss. Of all the preparations that an entrepreneur can make, calculating the affordable loss and the contingencies are often overlooked, yet an important starting activities. This oversight then carries forward in the business and the lack of personal financial management influences the poor early decision making of a new venture.

With all the planning for the personal disaster scenario of managing the downside risk, the entrepreneur needs to have a bias for action and refocus on the next step in creating the business. Excessively thinking about risk or ignoring it can be crippling. Finding a balance of mitigating risk and taking the next action is a constant juggling act. This daily routine must settle into a consistent and productive pattern for everyone on the team.

Built to Last

Can you imagine chasing your dream for the rest of your life? Designing the life and world you want to live in starts with figuring out how to create the most value with your talents and potential then acting on it consistently for a longtime, possibly the rest of your life. The decision to act is already a large part of the satisfaction. Whatever the outcome, that becomes secondary to the pursuit and sense of self-determination.

Managing ones ego will be one of the hardest challenges with the business. The business needs to function on its own and not be personality dependent. Early on it will take a force of skill and personality to have the will to make the business emerge from an idea. For it to last and grow it needs to survive on its own merit and value.

Along the way, you may have conflicts with employees, partners, suppliers, and customers. Working out the protocol for how to resolve conflict before they arise is critical to solving problems. When an issue happens, it will be hard to not get lost in the specifics. The protocol does not try to anticipate the problems, it eases the means by which they would get resolved. It may be voting, it may be consensus, it may be one person decides -- whatever works for the team you have assembled should be known by all.

The virtue of generosity is one that can help to resolve most conflicts quickly. This is generosity in every sense of the word, from being generous with time, with money, or simply listening. Generosity creates the space for seeing the other side. This is critical in all negotiations for determining the fairest compromise that helps to accomplish the greatest good for all constituents. Having an attitude of generosity opens the possibility for decision making that may get to better outcomes than if conflict and challenges were either avoided or closed off to discussion and consideration. Being generous is not comfortable, it takes a position of being vulnerable, and having that feeling of being taken for granted, or worse, taken advantage of. It has a benefit of revealing the character of those around you quickly. Generosity can provide great strength in building lasting working relationships when all parties take this virtue on as the theme. The situations where people are being guarded, secretive, have a win-lose attitude, or are unwilling to compromise; these create exploitative relationships that reduce the overall potential to accomplish extraordinary achievements. A simple example of this at work can be observed in the performance of companies that have employee shareholders versus those that do not. While my suggestion of generosity goes well beyond just stock option grants, the common structure for high tech companies is to institute such option grants from the beginning of the company formation.

The Founders

Entrepreneurs find an existing business context to follow their passion for creating value or they create the conditions that allow and support them to focus on the new venture. They do not aspire to be leaders and instead focus on getting the business to happen. This could mean they decide to not be the CEO of the company or one of the other executive positions if they can attract someone who can do it better and it allows them to focus on the competencies they have. The ambition to be a leader is not a precondition for being an entrepreneur. One can find self-declared leaders in every corporation that willingly take credit and responsibility for the hundreds of employees they manage. Few of those employees would testify that the executive has been of value to the work they perform daily. The entrepreneurs who figure this out earlier fare much better than the ones who do not and they will focus the company on taking market leadership and having that notion set into the entire company so it is not dependent on the personality of the CEO.

With all the credit given to Steve Jobs, a careful listening to his interviews would show that he clearly built a myth but did not believe it himself. He recognized the people at Pixar and Apple that made those companies great. He understood the myth of the hero and exploited that to great effect for the company shareholders benefit. One can find great companies where the public does not know who the CEO is nor would they ever care and those companies are not at a disadvantage for it.

To be a leader you have to learn how to nurture competence in others. To appreciate what they do, you may need to try the task enough to understand why it is important, and what value it brings to the company. This includes practicing your competencies and showing them consistently and reliably for the benefit of the company. I never understood why people are fascinated with others who are recognized as leaders instead of being interested in the people they were surrounded with who put them in that position. A founders' success is proportional to the effort and results of the team that forms the company. A winning coach is still just the coach and without the players on the field, the coach is not interesting. Hundreds of published books about leadership proclaim a formula for success. None of them have proven patterns to guarantee consistent performance in every situation. In this way, leadership is full of myths, as are those of founders. It is far easier to understand when leadership is absent and failure has occurred yet this topic may not sell books or help self-professed leaders from commanding fees in the speaker circuit, so one will not find that book published anywhere.

Do not be a solo founder; enroll peers who share the vision to change the world. You will need associates you can turn to along the journey. Entrepreneurship is a team sport, except in the game of business there are no fixed rules, so it is a challenge to pick the best team from the start. The co-founders and first few employees have to either find a working business structure or create one jointly in order to get the business going. This intensive exploration leads to a set of myths, a belief system shared across the company. This is what leadership refers to and is typically ascribed to one of the founders. It is important not to fall into the trap of hubris; therefore go ahead and create the myth that binds the company together, but do not ever believe it. This is the difference between the personal brand image and the person; one simply refers to the marketing of the other. If you focus on serving others, be it customers, suppliers, investors, and employees, it will do more for having others recognize and declare you a leader than a specific act of brilliance.

Founders Dilemma

Can we escape our distant past of our 10,000 years of ancestors? Our brains are set to work in wild nature but struggle with a world that has removed physical limitations. We can fly anywhere in a day, we can talk to anyone on the planet instantly from anywhere; food comes magically to our stores, energy to our homes, water to our rooms. We work in boxes, staring at colors on a screen. Our world is constructed, imagined, and malleable. Our brains are plastic, we can learn anything, yet its cognitive processes remain the same, which subjects us to behaviors that are inconsistent with what we believe we do.

If you were in the wild with just a twig and a rock how would you survive? If you could not get a job, the government did not send you money, and you had no social safety net, what would you do? What if you moved to another country, did not speak the language, and did not understand the culture? What if it is easy to identify you as being different, and therefore you could not fit into the mainstream of the country culture? What if your degree was not accepted in the new country? What if you were considered illegal in the country and had no recognized identity? These are not hypothetical scenarios. Yet somehow, people are able to figure out how to survive, make a living, and send money back to their home communities. Remove all these adversities and what excuses remain for not producing value by being an entrepreneur?

We take a great deal for granted in our daily lives, such as the degree to which we trust technology and the constructed physical and social environment around us. This clouds our thoughts and instincts making it easy to invent new worlds in our minds that have dissonance with the world as it is and as we wish it to be. The founders' dilemma is this gap between what the founder perceives, desires, and invents, versus the market reality and trying to make sense of the needs of customers and the irrational buying decisions they make.

What can go wrong?

Once you have taken the first actions of reviving the entrepreneur within, suddenly, uncomfortable problems you did not expect happen and those problems are within you. It is a self-reflective process where you are challenging the notions of life expectations. It will not be easy nor will it feel rewarding at first, and self-doubt sets in quickly.

Becoming an entrepreneur takes practice. It is like sports training: first you visualize the win, and then you go into training routine to push the limits of your current abilities. It will be painful and feel worse than the alternative of not competing. If you get beyond your limitation then the next problem you will find is the team is not working as well as it should be. You struggle with the human dynamic and communications and again question why you should be doing this, more goes wrong than right. It becomes an endless stream of problems as you try and figure out with others, who are just as confused, what the market wants, how to build it, get capital, and not run out of money before you can break-even.

In developed economies, people have choices, and are conditioned to pick a path that appears easy on the surface but strips the inherent creativity that entrepreneurship provides. In developing economies, entrepreneurship is out of necessity and faces the reality of the environment. To get beyond the sense of endless problems takes a strong desire to create, to discover, to want to have problems worth solving and solve them with others. Becoming an entrepreneur in an advanced economy is not a rational decision if one thinks that getting a job in a corporation means success. Once one realizes the comfort of the corporation is not satisfying at all -- the reason has to do with self-determination -- and you suddenly become driven to do purposeful work with others that create value.

Founders Symptoms

All investors know of a common happening with founders, they watch for the symptoms to show up then they will move to replace the founder. Understanding that this may happen, you can avoid the common mistakes that first time founders make. It takes honesty, self-reflection, and a team that is willing to work towards the best for the company instead of self-preservation. The clearly identifiable symptoms are cognitive biases that our brains are predisposed to and that become amplified under the pressures of entrepreneurship. The cognitive biases are variations of the same underlying problem. They reveal themselves to different degrees depending on the context of the situation.

In the visionary insight of the founders, they elevate themselves into the realm of having delusions of grandeur, and a state of mind where they forget they need to create value for others. The venture is not about appeasing a sense of the exceptional self. This can lead to making all sorts of choices that affect the founders' lifestyle. In their belief of exceptional abilities, they do not think of the consequences of choices that may affect their family and later on trigger selfish preservation decisions. Not coping with the lifestyle choices and treating them as temporary, postpones fracture points between the founders. This is one of the major causes of infighting and divisions that derail companies.

Founders syndrome is easy to recognize; perpetual self-doubt manifested in hiding behind over-confidence, hyper-mania, amplifying successes or diminishing losses, never transitioning to operational management and always restarting and never completing, forgetting it is about creating value for others and not just personal greed. Beware of cognitive biases. In the following paragraphs are short list of issues that entrepreneurs encounter throughout their journey. Cognitive bias is a subject within behavioral economics, which is worth studying, in particular choice behaviors. In becoming self-aware, it is much easier to see the market with clarity, understand customers and suppliers, and therefore use this insight to avoid biases in your decision-making and exploit consumer biases in market situations.

Irrational Decision Making

Business decision making can be alarmingly irrational and full of cognitive biases in the process. An entrepreneur will start with wishful thinking, wanting the world to be different than it is, then seek out information that leads them to confirmation bias, and stopping with the first alternative that is found good enough. Wanting to see the world in an optimistic way distorts our thinking and we gather facts that support our view and ignore others that would lead to a different conclusion. In our search, something is tried that might work, and if it gets results, the irrational decision makers will just stop there and want to continue doing the same. This may be logical to the entrepreneur until they find the one example was a rare exception and what they thought was an early adopter was in fact a novelty buyer. Start-ups and investors have fallen into the trap where they thought they had huge corporate client doing a beta trial and it was just an educational experience for the executive who agreed to give the product a try then decided they do not want to buy, and the company scrambles for what to do next.

Cloudy Thinking

Entrepreneurs can underestimate future uncertainty and have the illusion of control over market forces.. Cloudy thinking is the belief that one can minimize the consequences of decisions and disregard that every decision reveals new layers of problems to be addressed. In a close team, company amnesia sets in where rejected choices are quickly forgotten and the options selected start to appear like the best or only choice possible. Part of this is from seeking behavior that wants to find positive signs in the market that anchor support for the premise of the business. Once that information is available, all other information that does not support it is discarded. The perpetual optimism that is so important for entrepreneurs to maintain has its consequences -- it supports cloudy thinking, those cognitive biases that avoid clear problem insights in favor of the easy belief that all is fine.

Resisting Change

As a company has small successes in confirming its business, status quo starts to set in quickly; there is an unwillingness to change the market approach that showed signs of success. New information is selectively screened out as unimportant, peer pressure bounds the groups' opinions and the patterns get fixed into the mindset. People who support the status quo are credible and deemed friendly and the company starts to reject or dislike anyone who challenges the belief system. Eventually the company is surrounded by people repeating the mantra. New people start to believe what they hear often. The story of early challenges, alternative market insights, variations of the product, are put into the distant past and forgotten.

The entrepreneur starts to attribute the team's success to abilities and talents, and attribute failures to external forces and factors, and blames them on bad luck. When the competitors succeed, they are declared to have unrepeatable good luck. When they fail, it was their big mistake. The hope of the founders is that this all becomes a self-fulfilling prophecy, that employees, investors, customer, and suppliers expect success of the company. Therefore, success is bestowed with an abundance of progress, not due to random luck, and thought to be the result of talents and choices of the team who claim to have made it happen.

Perception Biases

It is hard for entrepreneurs to understand their own perception biases without trying hard to reflect on how others might see the same problems or solutions. Entrepreneurs want to filter out information that may distract them from maintaining a preferred position. Seeing the situation with clarity, in the customers view, and as the suppliers, is an essential skill for entrepreneurs to develop. Cognitive biases have a purpose and they can be used by design. It is when the entrepreneur is unaware of the cognitive biases, and it happens out of a naturally forming social interaction, that it can be problematic.

Understanding the limits of your brain will help you understand the limits of rationality. It is easy to observe the tricks one's brains can play on perception by viewing an optical illusion. Understanding that if one is aware of the perception differences it is still impossible to control how one initially perceives what one sees. The mental tricks that are easy to experience with visual illusions are present in every layer of our thinking and detecting when they are present is impossible. Ignoring this and not trying leads the entrepreneur to truly irrational and largely unpredictable decision-making.

Thinking like your customers or suppliers might necessitate you being a customer and supplier and knowing all the aspects that influence their biases based on what they are able to perceive. They may see the same product in different ways than you intended.

Entrepreneurs need to learn to see the world from several perspectives. Without clarity, the cognitive biases take over and failure starts to escalate simply due to unmet expectations. Find the shared reality in every situation and move it to an improved state for all involved. Active learning requires a meta-cognitive state, awareness with clarity, insight into the different points of view and vantage points of everyone involved. The more people on the team who can do this together, the better the aggregate result.

Oops, did not plan that!

Close your eyes for a moment and imagine a train wreck that has gone off the rails. This could be a major international company announcing a layoff of 10,000 people. A photo one would see in a newspaper, lurid, horrific. Is this what failure looks like? Is it a successful picture in a news program? Our media is good at representing failure and bad at accurately representing success. The failures, with all the pain and consequences are often catastrophic, and the successes momentous; yet both of these extremes are exceptions. The amplification of the extreme cases causes fear of action. When someone does act the impossibility of attaining this representation of success is surely to leave one discontented. The dramatic imagination is just that: representations to provoke an emotional reaction. When we are bombarded with these extremes, it perpetuates drama. These dramatizations of failure and success have little to do with the daily challenges of business. For that matter, people get fixated on these as excuses for being complacent in acting on their own behalf and making the decisive action of pursuing an entrepreneurial ambition they have. The chance of failure is just too great, and the lack of winning mythical iconic child billionaire status too remote.

Success is often built around the myth of the leader, with little inspection beyond a basic examination of the magical powers of an iconic figure. Failure is analyzed to find out the cause and left to be mysterious when not found to be a single person who is responsible. We learn little from the success of businesspeople. This does not stop publishers and magazines from writing the annual assortment of leadership books that claim to explain the secret. The failures in business are not easy to discuss since they involve the reputations of the people that were involved. Their short-term memories and storytelling of a revisionist historical account mask the underlying causes of the failure, in particular when it involved an area of incompetence, negligence, vulnerability, hubris, random market event, or other possible explanations for a company under performing.

Framing the CEO as hero or villain sets the focus on them, as if they decided without council, or that a company functions from the actions of the top executives, instead of the hundreds of daily decisions made by the people who are performing the business products and services.

What we should be doing is celebrating the learning process. When someone fails and understands why and explains this to others, and learns, that process is of real value. Business education ignores this and so do most people. They want myths, idols, to hear stories from those who succeeded.

Entrepreneurs do not engage in these views of success or failure, instead they get to the business of problem solving, discovering the market, the product, the innovations to the business structure to distribute the product, and working with a team of associates that are empowered and recognized for their decision-making and contributions to the company success. Charting new business built on innovation comes with great challenges that require a team of focused talented people working closely with the founders/CEO to get the company past its early stage and into profitable operational mode. Failure and success become secondary to placing them into a context of learning through problem solving. How decisions are made, based on adjusting quickly in response to what they find out from the market, matters when contemplating failure, or success.

Failure

What is your definition of failure? Write your own rules instead of letting others define your path to success; it starts with understanding how to work with failure scenarios so you use it as an asset instead of a terminal condition. Never starting guarantees failure. Not defining failure in your context guarantees that others will declare your efforts a failure and you might accept their sentencing of your business.

Failure can be: not anticipating an event, not understanding what happened, or a process breakdown. Failure requires a belief, an attitude that, it could be done better. In this regard, failure can be a motivator. Winston Churchill said, "success consists of going from failure to failure without loss of enthusiasm." He uses failure to define success and underlines the emotional reactions to failure as the key that bind failure to success.

Failure Defined

A definition of failure is "When fear prevents action because of experience or uncertainty, and the decision to quit is based on irrational influences." Concisely: "Fear plus irrational thought equals failure." Failure can be understood broadly as when your emotions trigger a cognitive bias which prevent you from thinking clearly enough to evaluate and predict, and you make a decision based on a reaction or unrecognized bias. Reflecting on these definitions, one can conclude that we are emotional, habitual, reactionary, and unaware for most our day; failure is a part of the human condition. The definition is circular and it is impossible to define either failure or success by its opposite. This is why acts of learning are most important; the rest of our experiences are subjected to our own cognitive biases and are not reliable.

What is your definition of failure? This settles the question and allows you to move on and stop worrying about it. The same logic applies to concerns of success. Both are not useful to contemplate; instead treat them as just internal state of learning continuously. Based on the definition offered or your own definition would it be possible to recognize failure when you are a part of it?

Irrational thought is not a failure. Each circumstance calls for action, some of which cannot be rationalized. For example: you have two equally sub-optimal, time critical alternatives that you cannot know the outcomes for until it is attempted. Do you avoid making a choice? You cannot pick both since the alternatives are mutually exclusive. If you pick one and it goes wrong, do you assume the other choice would have been better? The failure would be in not making a decision at all for fear that the one you pick might fail or be the wrong choice. The outcome of the choice not made can never be known. Therefore the decision can never be judged a failure or a success since the criteria was simply that making a decision is better than not making it. This is why perspective matters in a context of proportionality.

Fear alone is not a failure. Fear is a great motivator of action. If you fear your competitor will out sell you, and you do an analysis of the customer and find sparse information, it is a failure if you do not act to learn more. If you act and learn, and use the outcomes to uncover missing information then you have succeeded.

Failure Types

One simplistic representation of failure type would have two axis, the X being the scope of the failure from None to Total Disaster, and the Y-axis the Duration of the failure, from Temporary to Permanent. A Temporary failure of limited to no scope is harmless and at the other extreme a failure that was permanent and total in scope would be a catastrophe. Such a representation would be linear with a point on the X and Y-axis, indicating the Scope and Duration of the failure. Failure is cyclical where lots of smaller failures happen first then ever larger attempts made as confidence builds up which leads to a catastrophic failure.

When a sequence of repeated success has occurred that had no intermittent failures and the business gets overconfident, the odds of the next occurrence failing is high. The longer the sequence of success, the greater the overconfidence becomes and thus the business will take greater risk. You can observe this with many companies that grow too fast then suddenly file bankruptcy without warning.

What would a chart look like for success and would this be the opposite of failure? Would it be repeated small and short successes leading to a large success? Would it be an undetermined outcome for a longer duration that exceeds all competitive outcomes? Success is declared at the end. While the approach is to attempt small failures to learn, success is not the opposite analogy. With success, you want to build on previous success and increase the scope and permanence of the outcomes.

What does success feel like versus failure? Prospect theory has shown experimentally the emotions of a gain through success are not symmetrical with the risk of pain in failure. Much depends on the context and social pressures related to the scope and duration. The short-term risk of dying from smoking is low to none and the longer-term risk of decreasing life span and complications in health of prolonged smoking are well known. The social pressures, legislation, and trends reverse the number of smokers and this did not stop people from smoking or finding new alternatives like electronic cigarettes. Marketers of smoking products understand that our personal decision-making is flawed. As entrepreneurs, we need to be aware of this phenomenon in our own decision-making, and that of our customers and suppliers. It is much easier to remember the pain of risk gone badly than the gain of the reward of success. Entrepreneurs work hard to reverse this so that success is not left to nostalgic memories. They instead compel risk reward behavior and counteract the tendency for the pain of risk that discourages further attempts at success.

Reasons for Failure

A study by www.chubbybrain.com of the top twenty reasons startups fail based on an analysis of thirty two failures post mortem reveals: eight are attributed to people, seven are related to the product, and four to funding. The conventional myth is that companies fail due to insufficient capital. This candid survey, albeit small and based on anecdotal experience, is an accurate representation and shows the people and product being the primary causes with funding being dependent on these two.

The reasons listed in the study from most to least relevant are as follows: ignored customers, no market need identified, not the right team, poor marketing, ran out of cash, needed a business structure, product mistimed, lack of passion on the team. Other reasons include: failure to pivot the business, poor product execution, pricing issues, did not build and use a network, disharmony on team, loss focus, burn out, competition beat them, no financing, bad location, a part-time business, or bad time to start. While the list is long, this is a small sampling of what can go wrong. One of these alone is not enough to sink a company yet combinations of them are challenging to resolve. It is easy to see how each can cause or aggravate others or correlate with each other in the same circumstances. Avoidance is not the solution. Knowing how to spot and adjust then learn from each of the ills can make a difference. Awareness of the common company problems can help it survive for the duration, out last the competition, and thrive. Be a company that has gained tacit knowledge to chart a path forward so it focuses on consistent performance and continuously learning to improve its competitiveness.

The product is dependent on the people so the wrong team will risk the business. The wrong product for the market is second. All else being equal, a lack of funding contributes to failure. Yet funding is the responsibility of the CEO so this remains a people failure. This is why one may conclude that all failures stem from underperforming team dynamics and why the socially constructed company, starting with the founding members is so critical to get right.

Failure Analysis

The Japanese have analyzed failure methodically to understand its' causes and what it results in. The Japanese industry, with their emphasis on quality control, developed a culture of failure analysis to help categorize unexpected events, record and diagnose what may have caused them, and research the failures over time. The taxonomy that is used starts with placing the failure into a responsibility quadrant, the individual, the organization, neither, and nobody being responsible. The difference between nobody and neither is responsible is unknown cause of an abnormal occurrence of a phenomenon versus a poor response to a change in the environment or economic factors. These categories are used if an individual or the organizational fault cannot be identified. Diagnosis places the failure outside of human responsibility. When it is the organization at fault, it is due to organizational management or staff problems, poor value perception in the culture, or poor concept. When the individual is at fault, it is categorized as, ignorance, carelessness, disregard for procedures and communication, misjudgments, or insufficient study or research of the situation.

Failure analysis has a long history in statistical quality control in manufacturing and its organizational manifestations in Six Sigma. While large corporations have put this to good use and reinterpreted the techniques for human service processes, they are primarily useful for operational measurement, control, and improvement. The tech startup community, heavily influenced by software development practices, developed its own practices that apply to new venture creation where uncertainty exists.. Lean versions of Six Sigma, new interpretations of extreme programming and agile development each evolved in response to the intense creativity in startup tech companies that center around communication and collaboration in the pursuit of discovering and evolving market solutions. These processes have built-in failure analysis as a daily practice with a model that uses frequent testing of all assumptions and embodiments within the cycle of product development and business structure discovery.

Seeking Optimal Paths

In operations research there is a classic problem called the "traveling sales person" which tries to solve for the optimal route along many paths given certain constraints. The salesperson wants to visit as many potential customers in the shortest period of time, while reducing the cost of travel from each destination and maximizing the early sales so they can sell the inventory in their car as fast as possible. Other factors to consider include whether the customer had bought in the past, quantity of product inventory, if the customer has expressed interest in the product on the phone, when they might be available in their store, whether they have shelf space and competing products. The calculation seeks an optimal solution and operations researchers can determine what path the salesperson should take to get the results they desire.

This problem is complex and with an increase in the number of variables, computation is needed to calculate the probable solutions. These calculations could not be done manually within a timeframe that matters. With the best plans, randomness impacts the path taken and it is not possible to have perfect information, thus the plan is constantly readjusted and no longer a reliable plan. Therefore, all plans are suboptimal, a best determination with the information known, and the rest left to in situ judgment of the salesperson. It is better than a random walk but not guaranteed to be much better.

Do not make the mistake to think that your new venture can be analyzed and an optimal solution can be found. You cannot succeed without first failing many times and using that experience to learn and chart a new course for your venture. Adjusting to the situation that surfaces and refactoring the best-made plans is the reality of new venture creation. For a new venture, the number of variables that remain unknown and undetermined is far too high to attempt trying to calculate an optimal path. Where aspects are known, or self-imposed constraints are decided, the entrepreneur should use all the analysis possible to help understand that situation, recognizing that no optimal path may be found. Entrepreneurs do not engage in guesswork, they need to formulate a view on the market, document a plan isolating all the assumptions being made, control specific variables and timing, then find what was not and cannot be known until the business tries to enter the market. The faster that market engagement happens, the better the information available to adjust the plan for the next cycle.

Entrepreneurs are learning machines. They figure out how to solve the traveling salesperson problem quickly through experience, using local optimization as the situations unfold and global optimization against the plan they desire. They do not keep the lack of an optimal plan from having them walk out the door and get to the first place to sell something to then figure out how to find the next one. They might not be optimal. It is better to be out selling than not.

No Google map exists for solving problems in business. You do not have a map and no optimal solutions exist. You have to find a path through a large unknown space that is ever-changing. Entrepreneurs create new paths through the maze and create a new maze where one did not exist. As in a maze, walking down dead ends will happen, guessing what the maze structure is, redrawing it as the path is discovered is the norm. Nothing is comfortable about this but if each attempt is deemed a failure and the entrepreneur gives up, the business will not succeed.

Business Knowledge

What is business knowledge? Does it have a theoretical basis? To the physicist, the economics of business appears to be an art form, a designed function, not a science with mathematical rigor. Economists take a position on the patterns of macroeconomics and attempt to apply statistics to prove an assertion they have. For the artist and designer, the topic of commerce may be viewed as a corruption of human expression. The engineer may view business as having a function in society with its structure and modes of behavior. From each body of knowledge one can see the enormous gap that exist between applying each disciplines' competency to business such that new economic and societal value is created. It would be so much easier if a prescriptive path to business success could be studied and theoretically researched. Unfortunately, business is the ultimate interdisciplinary area that borrows from all others and puts it into its own context.

Business information and processes can be learned with diligent study. This helps you understand the language and mechanics of the business, accounting and finance, organizational behavior, marketing, product development are all areas to study business. The sum of all this knowledge still will not be enough to create a successful venture. They are pre-conditions to operating a business and the most important aspects of a new venture are in the realm of what cannot be known and require decision making with insight, intuition, and creativity. This is where the new value is created. All else can be replicated by others and will not give your venture a competitive advantage. Business knowledge is in the realm of experience, tacit knowledge, and ones' ability to self-direct a rapid, effective, and participatory socio-economic learning process.

Rational thought and predictive projection are a given for a business to succeed. These are techniques not prescriptions that guarantee success. They are a necessary pre-condition of competence that one needs to establish on the team. The team needs to act in a creative dance that brings the desired goals into action. Without a baseline foundation of business, primarily the common language and practices of operating a business, one should not start a new venture. This foundation may acquired through formal or self-directed training and experience. The management of a business team's learning process makes up the accumulated business knowledge. It will drive the company forward towards successfully achieving its goals. While no particular theory exists, the ability to understand human systems and interactions, and operating theories in many disciplines, are essential to learn.

Philosophical Position

The epistemology is a phenomenology, or experience, generalized from observation, not theory, or method. Like all truths, this philosophical position holds partially. In specific situations, certain patterns that are common, can be tested empirically, therefore perspective orients the position. For a financial investor the numbers tell the story, for the inventor the patent tells the story, and for the entrepreneur the story they are creating through experience is the truth that matters to them. Yet, the market ultimately determines what the future adopts. That experience rules -- the truth of the moment. As unsettling as it may be, revisionist and relativism best describe the state of the entrepreneurs' mindset.

In business, knowledge is the reality of common sense that is socially constructed. Tacit knowledge rules in most companies. This is one reason why people matter so much and become integral to the business operations.

Accounting systems use empirical data for rational analysis and is one area where knowledge can be quantified. Since accounting requires interpretation, it may not be a true reflection of the business. The struggle is to create standard operating procedures that codify the knowledge so that it is independent of the individuals in the company. Finance does not tell the entire story of a business; the most important decisions are the tacit knowledge within the company.

Philosophy informs a value system for your business. Asking the questions concerning ethics and moral judgments is where perspective and a point of view greatly influences the kind of business and the manner in which that business is conducted. The history of commerce leaves an ugly trail of exploitation, abusive practices, and a close association with war, politics, and religion. For all of its problems, and despite the trend of concentration of wealth and power, entrepreneurs are finding creative ways to survive and thrive. It is a human activity as old as trading beans and shells. On the scale of the small groups of entrepreneurs, the ethics of fairness and trust have existed for a long time. It has recently emerged as a high-tech phenomenon -- sharing of assets with the commons has helped to fuel the tech economy, borrowing practices of academia to maintain integrity and share knowledge as a gift to society. This is not to say the brutal capitalism and the premise of the "Art of War" are not endemic in business, it is simply to say that with hope, possibly naively, today's self-determined entrepreneur is reliant on knowledge assets in the public good.

Making Sense to Create Meaning

The following descriptive list of characteristics is from John Doerr of Sequoia Capital who makes a distinction between two different modes of conducting business. He uses the terms *Mercenaries* versus *Missionaries*.

"Mercenaries drive paranoia, are opportunistic, focus on the pitch and deal, sprint, obsess on the competition, act like aristocratic founders, think their business is only the financial statements, act like greedy wolf packs of bosses, deferred life, lust of for money and success."

"Missionaries have passion, think strategically, focus on the big idea, run the marathon, obsess on customers, operate as a meritocracy, have a mission and value statement, act as coaches of teams, find a life balance, lust to make meaning through a significant contribution."

John Doerr is a Buddhist, so the statements above reflect his value system. It is consistent with the desire for business to be ethical and the movement for corporate social responsibility in business practices. Within the context of the situation, either approach might apply. The typical venture capitalist looks for the mercenary over the missionary, especially if the venture capitalist is a former investment banker. Being a mercenary has a short term focus and is not personally sustainable, with high burn out catching up to the entrepreneur eventually. The missionary focus might be suitable for someone who has made a self-determined decision to pursue entrepreneurial ventures for their entire life and not just in reaction to a situation presented. What is important is to reflect on these values and associate with a team and investors who share the essence of what is driving your ambition. The mercenary is incompatible with the missionary, although both may co-exist in different roles within the same team and at different phases of growth. It is when the business is not going well do these values surface and challenge everyone involved to reconcile their core values of which sometimes they have to be compromised with troubling personal consequences.

Culture of the Entrepreneur

Entrepreneurs are doing something outside of the norm and breaking the status quo. This threatens the established authority and power structures. Leveling out the power structures through fast and creative innovation can change an industry. Since entrepreneurs need to compete and have no backing to fall on, they have to recast the terms the industry treats as norms. Holding in awe a dominant corporate entity and the executives within it is not of use or value to the entrepreneur. It is useful to find ways to flatten out the power structure and to start with the culture of the new venture treating each member of the team as a valuable contributor and removing a sense of hierarchy.

As an innovative entrepreneur, you will think as an individual and act with a group of like-minded peers. You will need to engage with diversity of gender, culture, opinion, age, skill, expertise, to get the best representation of all perspectives on the issues you will have to solve. Faced with uncertainty of a new venture drawing in a diverse peer group will help bring in new perspective to the many problems that will emerge. Slowly the team starts to act with predictability and that which is known converts to operational practices while what remains unknown leaves ample room for continued creative problem solving. The shared long-term vision binds the group with purpose and a direction to construct meaning through successive achievements gained by solving the latest set of problems. The rapid accumulation of company learning experiences defines the successful new venture and prepares it to compete with larger companies that cannot replicate these conditions unique to small-scale, purpose driven groups.

Given the enormous challenge of forming a business and faced with a multitude of infinite uncertainty the one characteristic that is essential for a new venture is having endless optimism. Recognizing setbacks, temporary failures, misdirection, random interference, an attitude of optimism is what forces the learning to happen through reflecting on each hurdle to extract every possible value that can be gained from the experience. The optimism comes from faith; regardless of the situation, something worthy can be learned that will advance the shared purpose of the new venture.

Summary of Entrepreneurial Spirit

Do not waste your time if you think you will just casually try business and if it does not work, you will just get a job. For that, just get a job now. To be an entrepreneur you need to gain mastery and use it, discover your path forward, be willing to change course, never quit, find meaning, and make a difference.

If you know, what motivates you and what your values are and can connect with people then you are ready to start a venture now. You do not need to start the venture; you can be entrepreneurial by adopting another venture as your own by joining a team. Entrepreneurship is a mindset. Regardless of whether you start your company, join another company, work in a company, institution, government, you can think and act creatively to solve problems that are worth solving and use your drive and passion to make a difference. Connect with others who are entrepreneurial and make the lifelong choice to act entrepreneurially in whatever you do. Focus on creating new value and not just settling for the status quo.

Ideas to Execution

"Of two equivalent theories or explanations, all other things being equal, the simpler one is to be preferred." - William of Ockham (c. 1285–1349)

The prevailing notion that entrepreneurs start with an idea, and then pursue turning it into a business, is not how most businesses get started. The entrepreneur may already be working in a business, through that experience saw an opportunity, and then started the journey without knowing the details of what they were going to do. The ideas come out of execution, not the other way around, where first the idea comes then the person decides to execute it. This refers to business concept ideas as distinct from intellectual property of the product being invented and commercialized. Business concept ideas are seldom unique in the abstract and are building on a pre-existing market activity. It starts with the need not the object. For example, people used rags to clean before paper towels. The paper towel is a convenience, and the need to clean already existed. The idea of substituting paper for the cloth of a rag comes out of using a rag then having to clean the rag. How does one eliminate the cleaning of the rag? We will use a disposalable material that acts like the rag but does not have to be cleaned and is low cost so the convenience of using the paper towel is negligible to the cost of cleaning the rag. As paper became an abundant commodity, other uses for it than for print material became possible. The idea was low cost convenient wiping; this might have come from the question "for what else can we use paper?" Ideas and execution have an interplay that is essential for the ideas to be useful.

In this chapter, we discuss the myths of ideas, the notions that people have about ideas and their formation. I have found, from my own experience, these myths do not hold up in practice. Therefore, the reality of my experience has taught me that my previous understanding of ideas was not productive as an entrepreneur.

The first notion to dispel is that ideas exist apart from the environment and processes that give them substance. An idea is simply that which one gives an expression to for which others comprehend as a shared understanding. Its manifestation may take many different forms that are all recognizable as layers of relatedness and association to the original idea. Ideas are grounded in whatever preceded them and builds on a previous understanding. Conceptual change or paradigm shifts are ideas that push the boundaries of the current understanding. The stacking, merging, and morphing of ideas is what products benefit from and businesses are able to exploit. Having an insight into these ideas to execution processes can greatly help an entrepreneur quickly discover the best products for the market. That is where creative problem solving matters most, the generation of ideas to reframe the problems and the solutions.

Topics

1. The act of generating ideas is polluted with myths that are each dispelled by highlighting the reality of developing successful concepts.

2. Converting ideas to markets is necessary for value created by the entrepreneur to emerge.

3. What to patent is reserved for inventions not innovations.

Ideas, the myths and realities

Wetware

Wetware is your brain, how it works, and how it does not. These represent different ways of viewing reality and understanding the myths that give us a sense of place. How we perceive what we see and hear, sense and feel, interpret as ugly or beauty, when we reason that something works or is broken. The various ways of perceiving and converting that perception into meaning is what allows us to enjoy the questions that art poses, the answers that design provide, the functions that engineers make, and the science that attempts to explain how it all works. Entrepreneurs create value using wetware by understanding these different modes of perceiving and acting, an artist's aesthetic, a designer's form, and engineer's function, and a scientist's exploration for the how and why.

Entrepreneurs use all of these modes at points in the journey. They see the world differently than what it is and want to change it. They ask questions of why and then say "why not." They design solutions that can be made functional through engineering and take advantage of science to push the boundaries of the possible. They understand the night sky has at once a scientific, cultural, and mythical view hidden in the night of the cities in clear view in the desert and in the light of day, the deeper meaning bathed in sunlight and clouds. Such are the markets with respect to the ambitions of entrepreneurs. They want to rocket into the cosmos overnight but have to first deal with the distance from the ground to where they want to go. They must try to make sense of myths of the sky, when it collides with the science and experience of looking at it.

Creative Action versus Prediction

As entrepreneurs, we rely on problem solving as represented by the pieces of a box puzzle and as creative actions represented by a Jackson Pollack painting. In business trying to fit every piece of the puzzle in its proper place is not enough to creative value. Neither does taking paint and pouring it on a canvas produce art that would ever sell. A successful business does both: it gets creative with new approaches that break the rules but it also has to solve the market puzzle to get to a commercial product that people buy. Scientists are trained to solve the puzzles and form new ones when we dissect the understanding and reconstruct it. Entrepreneurs dissect the markets as a means of problem solving. Artists are trained to express through abstract interpretations of experience put into mediums that others can bring their points of view to and get what they can from it. Entrepreneurs create products that consumers experience in ways that are not anticipated. Entrepreneurs work across these approaches when attempting a new venture. They control what they can, and design creatively for whatever their circumstances. This creative action uses prediction to imagine what the market will adopt and works through a process that borrows from the practices of both the artist and scientist. Eventually, entrepreneurs design and engineer the business to make money.

The Epiphany

Myth: Ideas happen by inspiration and turn into products by magic

Reality: It is just a puzzle or painting, you compose within a context, and just the last piece feels like an epiphany

Much is made of the inspiration for ideas as if the idea is an end not a means. Inspiration is simply the driving motivation to act, think, experience, and create. You have to try to shift the moment of satisfaction to be neither the start nor the end but the journey, and finding continuous motivation to restart and relearn from what happens. Do not wait for the epiphany to happen to get started and do not expect that this will feel satisfying at the end. Each idea leads to many problems to solve and as those problems are resolved, new ideas emerge, so it's best to focus on the journey, not the artifacts.

Idea Process

Myth: A method for finding good ideas exists that you need to learn.

Reality: Start somewhere, anywhere, and figure it out, do what works, stop doing what does not work.

Many techniques and strategies are available to form ideas that all do the same thing. They try to jolt one out of the stable reality of existence to reassemble the world in a new way that produces value. The methods are not prescriptive, will not be the same for each person, can be practiced, and require engagement with others to create tension and resolution of the ideas through expressing an understanding. As soon as you learn a particular method, it works for a while then goes stale again and another magic method in vogue is sought out. It does not matter what method and techniques are used, what matters is that whatever you do it stimulates the regenerating activities of creating with others and continues as the business grows.

Need one Idea

Myth: Good ideas are hard to find

Reality: If you cannot create hundreds of ideas, you are unlikely to find the one that fits the times. It is all about the action not one instance

Children at play have no difficulty inventing characters, role-playing, removing all boundaries. They live in the flow and have a stream of creative play. We go to school and unlearn this quickly. Children do not get smarter, they get predictable, as they replace the creative with the rational. The creative and the rational can coexist and are synergistic. Unlocking the ability to invoke imaginative role-play, fabricate, and simulate, reclaims the childhood talents that are useful in a businesses that are looking to produce value through innovation.

Best Ideas

Myth: It is all evolution and the best ideas win

Reality: The environment selects the ideas that survive. Fitness is of greater importance than the best idea.

This is a misunderstanding of evolution and how innovations are adopted. The social and economic environment can change faster than the business entities, and therefore those products that fit the societal environment can survive even when they may not be the technically superior solution. We have bodies and minds for a pre-technological world and we are rapidly addressing societal threats with massive technical complexity that cannot be fully comprehended. We replace horses with cars which need fuel that pollutes the planet and sets up geopolitical forces that cause suffering for some of humanity while others drive in luxury vehicles. Every solution that is contemplated to solve the last consequences of a previous technology is just the discovery of the next layer of problems. All ideas that solve problems are suboptimal, they cannot control the pre-existing environment they exist in, therefore the pursuit of the best idea is reduced to pursuing a better idea and best describes a past that had the conditions for adoption of some innovation that only historical artifacts consider best for that time.

Novelty

Myth: Ideas need to be unique

Reality: Unless hundreds of others have the same idea, it will not become a product and be viable in the market. Copy the abstract idea and change the specifics.

Since an idea is influenced by many factors, it is unique in its expression, in the same way that artwork is unique. The single physical instance of the object is unique. The content of the work is recognized as having cultural associations and therefore fits within a social context. A vase remains a vase no matter what shape and design it has so long as it can still function as a vase.

People like new ideas

Myth: It will work, make money, is a solution for a problem that people did not know they had

Reality: It is the gap between what people do today and what you are asking them to do tomorrow that defines the likelihood of adoption

We live in a commodity and disposable world of mass consumers, so when you have a new idea you will hear many people react that it will not work before you find anyone who thinks it will work. You want this to be the case so you are pushing the boundaries in the beginning. To convert the idea into a product means the product is similar to other products with an incremental improvement that is enough for people to consider switching from what they did before to doing what you are asking for. Combining and changing the business structure with the incremental improvement is what we typically think of as innovation.

It takes a genius

Myth: A sole inventor creates innovations.

Reality: Many heads are better than one. It is all a social construct, genius and leadership are myths and do not exist.

Who painted the Sistine Chapel? Most people would answer Michelangelo. It was Michelangelo plus 13 gifted artists and a crew of 200 that painted the Sistine Chapel. Through all of history, it has been a creative group, a team, a movement, and many influencers and experts who help to push the boundaries for what the next generation of masters can do. What we know as genius are people who through an artifact of historical recording is ascribed the moment of the discovery. On close inspection what is revealed are the many people around the "genius" greatly influenced and often co-created the masterwork.

Need for Expertise

Myth: There is only one correct path to the solution

Reality: Ideas have a life, need an environment, execution and persuasion is all that matters. They need many paths to pursue. Experts only have one path, the one they followed in the past.

Look at the number of different mobile phones in the market, each with distinct and overlapping features. This may be design differences and the path they each took to the final product are likely different. As the products mature, they are built on common components sourced from suppliers that sell several variations. The market matures towards commodities and components and needs differentiation and competition to sustain the business. They make breakthroughs not by being experts but by working with a diverse team that can help merge ideas from different areas into something new.

Solutions

Myth: Problems need to be solved

Reality: Problems need to framed, the solution is revealed by the execution, by letting it emerge and shift until a framing works

In a sense, reframing problems is similar to using failure to get to success. Each time a problem is reframed, it is an admission the previous framing had no obvious solution. With reframing, you change the problem to understand it until a solution is revealed that is feasible.

This refers to the context of an entrepreneur who has choice in the problems they will solve and therefore can shift to take on challenges for which the resources they have can be used to produce a solution. The solution can adjust to the market and then reshape the problem that is being solved. When you do not know what the problem is, or the solution, then where do you start? That is why creative action is required and just thinking about this will not be enough to get the venture going.

One of the consequences of fixating on the solution is that when it is not adopted by the market the business tries and applies the same solution to a different problem. This is solution chasing or trying to find a problem. The post-it is one of the best-known innovations that came out of an experimental accident where the solution was at hand and the inventor had to figure out the problem it solves.

Protecting Ideas

Myth: Ideas need protection and to be held close

Reality: The idea is not worth anything until you tell as many people as you can about it and let it expand, evolve, and take a shape.

For an entrepreneur, it is about the business and they understand that speed to market matters over all else. Ideas are not inventions or the process used to generate the embodiment of the idea. An idea needs to be sold so it is necessary to tell as many people as will listen. If the idea has merit then no reason to keep the idea a secret, assuming the competences of the entrepreneur are suitable for rapidly converting the idea to value. An exception is when chemical compounds are patented since these are scientifically absolute with one way to make the compound molecules. Pharmaceuticals and food companies, when filing chemical or plant patents, can have a strong defensible position therefore aggressive patent strategies are warranted.

Holding on to an idea and not telling others does not produce business value. A patent invention needs to be disclosed to the team that will convert it to a working product and often the product design will improve the invention and this is typically how a patent embodiment is commercialized. . In the Fashion industry protecting ideas does not work since these designs cannot be patented or copyrighted. How they deal with innovation is speed to market, variety, protecting the design process. Once it is on the fashion show runway it is open and gets copied the next day. This forces innovation and the creativity is what is sold and needs to be repeated consistently to stay in business.

If an idea is novel and unique then it may be an invention and the disclosure can be protected through the provisional patenting process until the invention can be describe in detail. This has consequences since the embodiment has to be filed and then is available to anyone to read. This does not suggest that expertise and trade secrets should not be protected, it refers to an idea, a concept, and an abstraction that is far from being realized as a commercial product. I have seen far too many aspiring entrepreneurs fall in love with an idea they have then pursue it for years in secrecy to never emerge with a business. Then they live complaining about how a company did what they were thinking and must have stolen the idea somehow, with rare exception has this ever been the case, the other company just delivered and sold the idea to everyone they could speak to.

Stability

Myth: Ideas stay the same as you make them real

Reality: What you end with will look nothing like what you started with

Look at a product that you use and see if you can make it better. What you will find is obvious design problems that did not account for how one would use the product. With all the study and observation, the product design can be improved. The idea is just a sketch, a representation, a conceptualization of an imagined object or service. Whether an idea would ever work as a business is left to the market to decide. The entrepreneur will struggle with adjusting the business structure until the realized idea can make money. What that idea is in practice is often different than was thought might be the winning product.

Ownership

Myth: Whoever thought of the idea owns it, and is the only one who can execute it

Reality: Whoever creates the product, sells it and makes the money

An idea is not going to be generated and formed without talking about it to others and then shaped by how they react. If the idea is a compilation of input from many people who would one credit all influences to, both direct and indirect? Whoever gets to market will be given credit even if they do not want it or the idea was a compilation of suggestions from many people. Owning an idea is useless if it is not put into action to convert it into a winning market product. The patenting, copyrighting and trade secrets are not enough to prevent someone from getting to market first. Intellectual property rights have a place. That is not in blocking others, it is in protection against others claiming they own the idea. Intellectual property should not be confused as being the business; business puts value in the marketplace in a form of a product for sale.

Commitment

Myth: Inventor commits to an idea early on

Reality: Inventors commit to an idea only once it works and until then will repurpose, hybridize, morph, and test, many ideas until they become products

Inventors are committed to forming many ideas, testing ones that are promising, adapting to findings from experimentation and willingly abandon ideas that do not produce useful results. Entrepreneurs are committed to putting ideas into practice and see idea generation as creative problem solving and not a self-indulgent act of entertainment or ego satisfaction. Many corporations have mistakenly thought they lack ideas that would lead to market innovations, only to find that ideas are worthless if they do not have entrepreneurs to convert them to products.

Garage Entrepreneurs

Myth: Great companies are born in garages, kitchens, basements, dorm-rooms [HP, Apple].

Reality: 90% of companies are started based on prior work situation. Organizational experience builds confidence, gains knowledge, forms social networks, and spots opportunities that are all necessary for starting a venture.

The story goes that Silicon Valley started in a garage. In a small garage in Palo Alto, California in 1938 to 1939, William Hewlett and David Packard experimented with numerous electronic devices, including a prototype for an audio oscillator. That product enabled the entrepreneurs to launch Hewlett-Packard, one of the largest high-tech companies in the world today. American business history offers many stories of successful entrepreneurs, such as Walt Disney and Steve Jobs, whose garages served as early workshops for the products and services that eventually launched prominent U.S. businesses. Is this belief accurate?

United Parcel Service was started in a basement. The dorm room is where Michael Dell founded Dell Computer. Yet 90% of companies are started based on prior work situation with 50% them founded by people who have worked together previously, people with strong prior social ties. In Silicon Valley over 50% of the technology labor force is foreign born. Similarly, the number of founders and CEOs who are first generation immigrants all shatter the notions of how companies are formed. These proportions are not new and have been true for places like New York City for a longtime, so Silicon Valley is not unique. Generally, small businesses are often family businesses and those have a start that does not happen in the garage or kitchen table, but in family dynamics and aspirations.

Organizational experience is a better prerequisite for starting a business. Organizations create opportunities for people to build confidence by exercising competencies and building up the social support they need to launch a business. They gain broad knowledge of the industry and find entrepreneurial opportunities. The companies provide a means of building a social network to facilitate mobilizing resources necessary to form a new company.

Converting ideas to markets

Entrepreneurs need to be able to answer the question "what do you do?" in less than one minute. To have a response you first form a business idea, figure out what the product means to the customers, sell that idea to as many people who will listen, make it your mantra and have others recall and repeat it by branding the idea with a few tag words. This creative process starts to convert an idea into something the market might buy.

Idea Topics to change the world

Start with one of the many global grand challenges to think of business opportunities. It is best to try to combine two or more areas into an idea. For example: water and health. How do these relate, and what needs would be worth addressing with your skills? Starting a business is difficult, so you might want to start with the largest possible market, the entire planet. Figure out which of the many problems fit your current competencies, resources, and experience. Then, work out how you would solve the challenges with viable solutions. Areas to consider are health, arts, education, media, shelter, cities, food, water, community, people, environment, waste, transport, logistics, opportunity, commerce, energy, and natural resources. Within these are many subcategories and these are a short sampling of areas of grand challenges. After picking an area, think of these in several dimensions, the political, economic, societal, and technological, to form ideas for changing the world.

While it is unlikely that any particular single company will ever solve a major global problem, for the entrepreneur, not thinking on a grand scale may lead to the trivial and mundane and just perpetuate the global problems that exist. This does not produce new value, it might make someone rich to create a new candy. If that candy causes many dental issues that cost people their health then it may do more harm than good. The new economics of the 21st century demand that social responsibility is an essential consideration for new value creation and ignoring this has effects that limit the market potential for the company. Solutions may have unintended outcomes that are both positive and negative, which one could not have anticipated. At least the intent needs to be to produce overall goodwill for personal, shareholder, and societal profit.

The grand challenge business idea framing helps in expanding the thinking beyond the provincial and can lead to possibilities that would not have occurred to the entrepreneur. The reason is the enormous global problems are on a scale that it takes much imagination to guess at understanding them and this first step opens the speculation for the future.

It helps to give meaning to the business beyond the profit motive and this purpose can help in attracting people to take part in the business formation. It becomes part of the company narrative, the story of why it was formed and the benefits to its customers within an implicit promise to not harm. The customer trust happens when this promise is fulfilled, but first it needs a context that is larger than the single store or single product.

Idea Building Blocks

The reality of idea generation is that no set process exists that guarantees an outcome. Entrepreneurs can use techniques and devices to get started. Play sets a few rules of engagement while still leaving enough room for freedom of imagination, interpretation, and expression. Observation of the interaction of the players creates meaning and understanding its significance. Improvisation creates unexpected possibilities that inject freedom on the play. Play, observation, and improvisation are all building blocks to help spur ideas. For adults this is not easy to do since they are used to having a structure as an organizing principle. It wants a social bond be present or easy to form. Corporate human resource training rediscovered the power of play and have used it in the team outings. They try to break the preexisting group dynamics. The constructive play that entrepreneurs engage in cannot be simulated when an imposing power structure is present, such as in a corporation. With entrepreneurs, they are choosing to take on risk, and so are the people they engage, those vulnerabilities allow for an open form of playfulness to produce ideas that solve market problems.

These aspects of generating ideas are not the kind of play where one wins and others lose. This is an open context form of playfulness. One is not sure what will come from the interaction. The form of play that children do, they take a role and make up the rules, and when the rules no longer work, they change them.

Idea Generation

When playing the idea generation game, anything goes; remove all constraints and let your imagination free. The impossible ideas can generate new ways of thinking about the world, the visionary ideas may not be obvious how to solve today and remain within the realm of the imaginable, and the grounded ideas are those that can be acted on today that move the effort towards the vision of the imagined future.

What was absurd thirty years ago is commonplace today and the pace of technology adoption is increasing. We cannot know what will be possible in the future. To help stimulate idea generation, use these three categories to free one from the constraints of preconceived limit:

1. Crossing the unknown ocean ideas that are crazy, whacky, magical, and absurd, against known scientific possibility. The paradoxical works at this stage, for example: a clock that does not tell time.

2. Lost in the forest ideas that are novel, unique, exciting, risky, fresh, progressive, thought provoking, and forward-looking, on the edge of science and nature.

3. Sitting in the grass ideas that are safe, incremental, obvious, plain, and predictive, in the realm of the known.

Research labs are many years ahead of the products in the marketplace, so if one can imagine a future it is likely that we are closer than one could imagine. The future is here already, we just need to bring it to market. While it is tempting to think of the outlandish ideas as coming from science fiction, they can come from anywhere. Something that sounds horrible might create a new product idea, for example, what would ice cream made from fish taste like?

Act and Learn

The design firm IDEO follows a sequence for idea generation that starts with the user and buyer and works backwards to find the solutions. They observe first in the environment, record what they see, create stories for each persona, then abstract the themes from many observations, within the themes an opportunity for innovation emerges and proposed solutions are imagined, those solutions are created in working prototypes and put into an implementation plan to cycle through the process again. They go from tangible experience, to abstract design, to concrete action, all from the users' perspective. They find the products that fit the environment of the consumer instead of expecting the user to learn how to understand the product. In this way, they are not trying to form ideas in a fictional world of their own invention that does not exist in real practice.

The IDEO teams have a varied background from doctor to anthropologist, or, musician to designer architect. They intentionally force diversity into the emergent process to create hybrid ideas that would not occur to the team without having different perspectives on the situation being observed. The technique they use is called ethnography, where they pattern a persona from observation through a story telling; they find a theme in the stories and from it comes the opportunities and possible solutions. Mocking up a prototype allows for quick simulation scenarios, then the messaging is communicated to the user subjects involved in the field-testing. IDEO has a focus on consumer and industrial products that are used by people, so this method works for them. If one was solving a transport problem involving the packaging and movement of goods the techniques may be different. Each industry and business product have their own characteristics and therefore good judgment is needed to select the coordinating processes that a diverse team would use.

Empathy Map

Designing a product and the business that will deliver it, requires having deep insight into the buyer and how they may use the product. First, create all the possible buyer segments you may want to support. Segments are groups of buyers that have similar characteristics; that may include age, geographic location, profession, social identity and other demographic or psychographic. Humanize the segment by giving prototypical buyers a name, a persona, bringing them to life. Empathize with the segment by putting them at the center. Compose an empathy map using leading questions. Inquire about the buyers' pain, what troubles them. Ask what they wish to gain and what they believe they need.

What do the buyers think and feel, how do they see the world, what do they listen to, and what do they say and do? These questions are not simple to answer. What a person will say when you ask them in a survey is often different than how they think and act. The user has to be watched in the act, unaware of anyone seeing them, so it does not influence their behavior. What drives the inner working of the mind that creates aspirations and worries? The entrepreneur has to view the buyers environment, the area they live, work, and play in. What are the buyers exposed to in the environment? How do they interact with friends and family? What are the communication channels they rely on and how does this influence what they think? What are the behaviors in public and the attitudes they display? How do they deal with conflict? Assembling all these observations allows the entrepreneur to form an empathy map of the buyer.

After creating an Empathy Map for each supporter persona or segment, make sure that your ideas on the Empathy Map represent supporters. Validate the map by interviewing a sample of trusted supporters to distill your understanding. Adjust the Empathy Map as necessary from these conversations. Just like buyer personas, use the completed Empathy Map as a foundation for content creation and communications. In turn, your messages will become relevant as they are enhanced by your understanding of your audience.

Empathy Opportunities

Much is learned from simple observation. The ideas for products need you to "see" clearly what is going on by removing the biases and notions that constrain your understanding. Intentional empathy can help jolt one out of the internal perception and into the minds and feelings of others.

To understand the buyer one needs to have a clear sense of the pain points that would get the customer motivated to make a change and the perceived gain they expect from buying a product. The pains are usually shown by frustrations and obstacles the buyer feels. The gains are related to the wishes, the passions and impact the buyer is aiming for in seeking a product or service. When the gain to pain ratio exceeds a threshold, the buyer feels they have enough information to make a decision. That is the time when the sale can be made. Buyers may not have complete information and act on impulse based on what they see others do. Perceiving pain and gain may not be absolute, therefore these are fluid notions. Buyers are not rational in their buying decisions and can be influenced by marketing and design.

If you understand the human dynamic relative to the pain and gain and the cognitive biases at work in the buying decision, your chances of creating a winning business increase. This is also true for scientific products that have independent measures of performance. Competition will create several performing products that may not be distinguishable on soft reasons in the buying decisions and therefore marketing to the buyer's ideals and cognitive biases is equally important. It is easy to find products in the market that have captured a large market segment with a product that was not as good as the competitor's product features. Review the product marketing and you will see that it spoke to the customers' perceptions and invoked a loyal following. This typically happens when the product has an aspect of its design or delivery service that accounted for empathy; the buyer likes the products form and presentation and its fitness for use.

Convert Ideas to Markets

To convert ideas to markets one would move through a cycle of stages, from the idea, to building with the early adopter customers by co-generating the solution, to creating the product and service, then prototyping, demonstrating, and testing using measurements. Using the data, refine the business structure and learn from the results, and improve the ideas and go through the cycle again. This cycle of market development needs to race to create the product and develop the customers to learn and discover until it has a product the market segment of buyers are willing to pay for.

When the problem and the solution are not known and the entrepreneur is trying to create in a space of high uncertainty, the way to learn is to build something first. Build a prototype from an early guess at a concept that is just good enough to show a customer and get reaction. Then observe whether it fits a problem or wish they have and recognize the starting guess may be wrong. These early product versions are prototypes, but they need to be engaging enough so the buyers seriously consider how it may have value to them. For the new venture entrepreneur, getting the feedback cycle going is the hardest stage since it takes a leap of faith that the starting point is in the right direction.

Engagement with the customer at the idea stage is critical to set on a course that will create new value. Just creating something without understanding the customer will not work and is an expensive way to start. Using the Empathy Maps, one can create low fidelity prototypes to understand the user and reduce the cost of iterating through the cycles of co-generation. In other words, sell first the concept then build if you are getting buyer interest. The most frequent mistake that an entrepreneur makes is to build the business first thinking the buyers will come. For example, if you lived in an area without a grocery store, first try to sell fruits and vegetables out of a cart. If you get a line of people, then try a truck and different corners. If the line continues to grow then go and open a grocery store before someone waiting on one of the lines does it. If the grocery store works maybe you sell prepared foods and if many people are buying then you open a restaurant next the grocery store. The customers will lead you to the business if you listen and empathize with their needs and wishes.

What to patent?

Most inventions probably should not be patented since they would never be converted to commercial products. The patent process has become a land grab for corporations to lock out competitors and therefore may hinder innovation. Some areas should allow patents, like pharmaceuticals where billions of dollars are invested to support the research and the company needs to secure its position so it will get a return. Some argue that these inventions should be a common good, but that is a question of politics and morality. Building high potential businesses on a patentable invention is not a prerequisite to innovation. The innovation can come from all aspects of the business, from employee management, efficient inventory control, product packaging, customer service; the entire business structure is candidate for innovation.

Even with the questionable rational for patenting, anecdotal experience demonstrates that many new ventures wish to secure a place in the patent record. This is partially driven by the belief that patents can secure a market and therefore be attractive to investors. The experienced entrepreneurs may view the patents as a necessary process to protect against litigation and focus on patenting the embodiment. The most experienced entrepreneurs think of patents as strategic and understand that it is the rigorous process of drafting the patent that has the most value and broadly creating intellectual property assets as know-how and trade secrets, and patents may be one of several components of the overall value of the company.

Ideas Classification

Innovative products are both novel and useful and can be delivered into the market as an innovative business. Low novelty and value simply is an irrelevant reproduction of an existing business. The scientist will start with high novelty through a lab invention, and when taken to market for it to have high usefulness its novelty may be applied to an existing solution that creates an incremental improvement.

Only the innovative business has high novelty and usefulness. They are the ideas that make new ventures grow. The innovation may be in the business structure that delivers the product. When an innovative product combines with an innovative business structure, the potential for accelerated growth increases. While an incremental improvement might be enough to create a business, it is unlikely to remain competitive over time. Products that copy or imitate other products become a commodity and have downward price pressure.

Inventions are not products. They can be patented sometimes and the intellectual property sold if the patent is well written and granted. This alone does not create new value. The invention would still need to be converted into a functioning product and that process will need an innovation.

Entrepreneurs might imitate or copy an existing product or service to start then improve over time and within that activity invent something new they believe is suitable for patenting. The idea classification is meant to highlight the type of breakthrough innovative businesses that grow rapidly have a feature of being both unique and useful. One could make money simply copying an existing business; that is known to work. However, it is not the subject of this book, which instead focuses on new venture creation where new value is being introduced into the market.

Patent the Invention

An invention is candidate for patenting when: it is new, novel, has not been made public, is original and non-obvious, and lastly it needs to be useful. Several kinds of patents may be filed, utility, business process, design, plants, and chemical. Each of these require special attention and consideration and they may vary by jurisdiction. For example, the European Union does not allow software patents although it may be possible to file it as a hardware device.

One cannot patent abstract ideas, laws of nature, physical phenomenon, literacy works. Literature and media of all kinds are copyrighted and brand or signifiers are trademarked. The United States has a one-year grace period. In the rest of the world, once an invention is disclosed it cannot be patented. The U.S. changed its patent ownership rules to first to file whereas previously the inventor could claim to be the original inventor even if they had not filed a patent first. The patent has to describe the invention so anyone schooled in the art can reproduce it to prove that it works. The patent is not the product or the business, so do not confuse these.

Patent are used by companies to defend the intellectual property they invested in developing. They may be used offensively to block another company from entering a market by developing a competing product. There are many ways to work around a patent so there are no guarantees of protection. An entrepreneur patents the invention when they commercialize the innovation . They must understand that an invention is not an innovation and neither are necessary for creating a moneymaking business.

Technology Transfer

The typical technology transfer procedure would have the following stages; research and development, invention, assessment, IP protection, marketing, licensing, products services, and royalty income. The technology transfer process is used if you had an invention that came out of university research. Unfortunately, while many research universities have a tech transfer office, the reality is that, they have been ineffective and one would be challenged to find examples of royalty income going to the university from this process. Exceptions can be found and a few universities have reaped returns from the investment in technology transfer when it licensed a patent to a company that used it and grew. Stanford is one of the best known examples because of Google paying large sums of money back to the University over ten year period but with thousands of colleges and universities this is not the norm.

Other exceptions do exist such as MIT, CMU, and UCSD. In those cases, review the number of patents filed relative to the investment in the research, then analyze the degree to which those patents are granted, and then licensed to corporations and converted to products. If you find that a corporation licensed a patent, then search to find how it was manifested in actual products. Technology transfer from universities has a place but it is to give the researchers a way to step into the commercialization process without risking much and therefore it is an extension of the learning environment and not a means for the university to gain added funding sources.

Part of the reason this process breaks down so often is that researchers have little incentive to leave the university setting, and then create the market value in a new venture. While this is risky, the rewards for research that is valuable can be large. Tenured faculty is party to this insider affair, not explicitly but implicitly through the processes that prevents business value from entering the academic community. The resistance in many disciplines is substantial, concerns over academic integrity and corruption of theoretical research in favor of practical and pragmatic applied research also prevents the technology transfer process from being realized to its fullest potential.

Research universities become publishing houses, where "publish or perish" is the status quo. The research may be locked into copyrighted work. The published work is owned by the university. It becomes part of the University's revenue stream. Schools that do this well can make great revenue, such as the Harvard Business School. Once the knowledge it published it is used by the business community to make money and therefore no royalty is ever paid other than the buying of books. This happens in the sciences and in the arts. In the Harvard case, this has several benefits; it promotes the school's brand while funding that promotion through publishing in both scholarly journals and business magazines. Harvard is a rare exception and is able to fund this through its large endowment. This is not available to other Universities that lack the funding resources to invest in continuous brand building.

It is possible to use the technology transfer process as a commercial path, one needs to understand how it works and how best to manage the process so it does not hinder the commercialization. Corporations are weary of academia and patents that are filed within the tech transfer process; they understand the incentives in academia are biased away from commercialization and they could likely just hire the researchers or fund directed research if they needed a particular problem solved.

Keep it simple

"Make everything as simple as possible, but not simpler." - Albert Einstein

Keeping things simple happens to be one of the hardest tasks of the entrepreneur. It is easy to make the problems and solutions complex and build an imagined world that has the illusion of a controlled market, but reality sets in quickly. Without simplicity, it is difficult to scale the business to support fast growth. Lasting value comes when something that is inherently complex appears simple to the consumer. What we take for granted each day in a technology dependent world involves an enormous amount of complexity that cannot be grasped. You want to mask the complexity of your business so your products are understood by your buyers.

Summary of Ideas to Execution

To quicken the idea to execution process, an entrepreneur might produce many ideas through observation and mock-up each. Then tell the story and test the reactions. See if they can sell the idea concisely, then abstract, associate, and iterate on variations of the theme, partner with diverse points of view and talent along the way, and hybrid, morph, discard, add, adjust, iterate until a moneymaking business idea emerges. How long this takes and sequence it happens varies tremendously; do not let the guesses prevent you from getting started.

Business Structure Formation

So far, we have learned what an entrepreneur is and decided that you are one already. You have come up with a big idea that will change the world, and learned that ideas are fluid and ever changing. Next, you are looking to place that idea into a context to help convert it into a business. With the idea as a business concept, we give structure to it in a representational model. The model will help sort through the issues and discover the unknown.

Topics

1. Business structure, what is it and how to innovate it.

2. Winning strategies to understand and put in motion for your business.

3. Business planning as a means of discovering what remains unknown about the structure.

4. Negotiation, since it is always occurring within your team.

5. Business pitch, how to explain what your business is.

6. Sales strategy. It is not just talking to people to get them to buy your product; there are methods and techniques to sell well.

Business Concept Structure

You have started the company!

You have already started the company if you have the desire, an idea, and can figure out a business structure to help give it shape. The business structure will guide the process to help establish the company as a functioning business.

The business will need resources to develop a product that is sold to customers. Those customers will define a market with competitors and choices. The market makes up an industry or ecosystem of companies and customer groupings that are associated or complementary to the value and cost chain. Once an industry is mature it forms a cluster, typically in a region and eventually those clusters will become transnational. To grow a big company that will change the world is a long journey, hopefully you are on your way now.

Idea for a Business Concept

To structure an idea for a business concept it is best to start with a concise statement with as few words as needed to get to clarity early. This is one of several exercises at the end of the book, it is inserted it here as an example. This exercise is deceptively simplistic, in many years of building companies, consulting with entrepreneurs and investors, and teaching, I found few who can do this exercise easily. They want to elaborate, explain what they mean, give context or worse, try and explain how it works or why they are the best. It is easy to understand this challenging struggle since the business world is so messy and vague therefore any over simplification will remain deficient in capturing the business. Simplicity is hard to achieve but it's the reason why if one cannot explain the business this concisely in one minute, then they should reconsider starting it.

FOR target customer

WHO HAS customer need or desire

THE product name

IS A market category

THAT one key benefit

UNLIKE competition

THE PRODUCT unique differentiation

Your ideas are expressed with a concise statement that helps communicate to others what you are thinking of and where it fits within the existing environment. This helps you get feedback and enroll people to the cause. You can produce as many of these concepts as you can think of and then change aspects of it until you find a concept that is speaking to people and getting them interested. If you cannot enroll others then you probably should not aim for the concept since you are either not communicating it properly, it is too far reaching, or it is not well formed.

Samsung teams with Google to compete in the globally

We will evaluate the Samsung Smartphone business as an example to help understand each component of how the business structure has made large profits for that company.

Executing on each aspect of a business structure is essential since they are all interdependent. Samsung does all aspects well to create an experience for the brand and a loyal following. The product, is not just what they are selling, since they have many products. It is identifying the brand, the ease of use of the products, the design appeal, the form. Samsung may charge a premium for this experience, and price it more than an equivalent product from a competitor, and they have a product for every price point. They did not invent the technology or the product or the markets, what they did is innovate the product into a vertical offer that is well designed and delivered.

As we review this business structure, think of which aspects Microsoft is missing and why they are not as competitive globally, even with the recent acquisition of Nokia. Many other smartphone and cell phones are on the market that include digital music and app stores, so how did Samsung grab the lead in a market it did not start?

Samsung Business Concept example

FOR the mass market consumer

WHO HAS digital music, photos, and apps

the Samsung Galaxy 5

IS A Smartphone

THAT stores, and plays digital music, photos, video, games, and apps

UNLIKE Microsoft smart phone

THE PRODUCT uses the android operating system and the google play store

Using Samsung as an example, we can guess at what the business concept may have been when they started. Whether this is the correct statement is not as relevant as being one of many possible ways of expressing what they put forth to the market. The statement expresses one concept and the reality of the business concept is they have many dimensions. We are opting for simplicity at this stage to allow for clarity and variations on a theme. Try to come up with your variation.

The competing Microsoft products have nearly the same claims but the difference is nuanced. The Android operating system is freely licensed to many cell phone companies giving it a much larger market share and its play store is available for developers to access that large market. Samsung had its own operating system for cell phones but decided to leverage the adoption of Android on other competing devices and focused on making a very good smartphone device. It knows what business it is in and how to segment that market of customers and partners.

Business Structure Formation

Generating the business structure is the representational form of how the various aspects of the enterprise relate. It consists of a value offer, a means of distributing the product to a customer group of similar desire, the use of resources from suppliers, what the cost structure is, and the revenue stream drivers.

Find an existing business, evaluate and dissect each structural component, then try to reproduce the characteristics to get started, figure out one aspect that can benefit from innovation, design how that innovation might work, market the innovative business structure, record the feedback from all the constituents, then iterate through the cycle again to produce improvement through innovation.

The value offer is the most important aspect of the business structure and the hardest one to get right. As an entrepreneur, you will find many appealing customer groupings and many resources available but until you can find the value you are creating, it is not possible to create a product and sell it. The value does not have to be unique, it just has to be competitive.

Typical value offer questions are: what value are we delivering to the customer, which one of our customer's problems are we helping to solve, which customer desires are we satisfying, what bundles of products and services are we offering to each customer grouping. The value offer can vary from anything as superficial as brand recognition and design to price and convenience or usability. As the Samsung case has shown, these can matter a great deal to customers.

Customer Groupings

Which customers is Samsung serving and what do they want to do with the products?

The customer groupings can be many but for our purposes, we will be trying to find at least one segment for the new business concept.

For Samsung Galaxy it was the mass market. This is the mass market in advanced economies, since many people in the world cannot afford and would not need such a smartphone device. Therefore, the term mass market is a bit meaningless in that it just says anyone who would buy it. Specifically, it refers to consumers and no other companies. This is referred to as B to C or business to consumer as opposed to business-to-business.

Samsung has market segmentation based on price point. Consider how many models of the Samsung phones are sold and review the price breaks and features of each. They each appeal to different customer needs that may overlap. Sometimes a customer may have several devices, one for running, another for business, and one for the home.

You want to try to define your target customer grouping with specifics and particulars so you can use it to help discover the value offer. It is fine to start with a narrow customer group and broaden it later.

Value offer

What value does Samsung deliver to the customer that satisfies a need or desire they have? It is a seamless digital experience for all recorded media available all the time from anywhere.

Focus on addressing what the customers will gain from your product and business structure. Start with your tag line then figure out what it means in the minds of the consumers or how you will get them to associate value characteristics to the product.

With the Samsung Galaxy, it was convenience of finding it in all the consumer electronic stores. Once found it was the usability of the interface, newness of the design, and brand status. They created a business structure that was seamless and trouble free. Before the Samsung phones, people could play digital music with an MP3 player that Samsung made and could buy digital music on-line and go through a multi-step process of getting the music loaded on their devices. What changed was the ubiquity of combining the phone capability with the Google store. Samsung exploited to great potential, and synergistically the strength of Google with the strength of its own capabilities to make an excellent phone to use with the Google Play store.

Distribution and Logistics Channel

How does the customer want to be reached? Retail Store, Google Play Store, Amazon, all the cell phone carriers' stores, and the gray market of corners stores.

Get the product to the customer in all the points of contact that are possible. The product needs to be where the customers are. Samsung made it available online and in the stores and established a relationship with huge retail outlets like Best Buy in the U.S. to provide superior service to customers. The retail stores and on-line presence have a consistent availability of a brand that is considering every aspect of what customers see.

Connecting to Customers

What is the nature of the relationship being set up with the customer? Integrated entertainment with Samsung providing a Smart TV's, laptops, connection from the phone to all the consumer products they sell.

What the customer sees and feels matters in a commodity market of many choices. They will seek out those products and services that are most appealing for their sensibilities. Tapping into the cultural stream requires insight into the market's preferences and guiding those preferences through branding and identification help to reinforce a sense of belonging to the population of Samsung users who chose to buy into the integrated home entertainment systems. Whether this adage has truth to it, or the buyers are simply a victims of excellent consumer marketing, has to do with understanding buying decisions than an objective measure of performance of fitness for use of the product.

Revenue Flows

What are customers willing to pay? Large hardware revenue and cross-over sales of other integrated consumer products.

Getting the pricing right is a difficult challenge. It needs to make a profit and if you charge too much or too little the consumers will not buy. The ideal price point is determined by a complex and shifting market. Products can be priced on perceived value and others are based on a margin against cost. Take most designer eyeglasses, the cost of the plastic, and lens are minimal while the margin for the branded design is substantial. For commodity products with much competition, the pricing needs to be aggressive and be slightly above the cost of the manufactured product.

To mitigate pricing risk, it is necessary to come up with strategies that create multiple revenue streams that are complementary and not so coupled that one revenue stream damages the other. The Google Play store works with Android Operating System, the devices are profitable and the sale of digital music and apps is of marginal profit. It was necessary to couple these two products to create an experience, and the pricing for one helps the sale of the other.

Access to Resources

What assets are essential to the business structure? People, Brand, Agreements, Samsung Hardware and chips, Software expertise, Patents.

Having resources are a prerequisite for developing the product. Without the resources, the company cannot get into the market. Not all the resources need to be owned by the company, such as Samsung synergistic association with Google, yet they need to be sourced and managed to achieve the outcomes of the business. The business needs early determination of the core competency that would allow it to distinguish from the competitors. No single resource type will be enough to make a company, so it is the collection of the resources and how they work together that matter most. They need to be complementary and compatible.

With the Samsung Galaxy Phones, they need great hardware and product designers with great software engineers. These need legal agreements to secure patents that let them innovate. In addition, the global brand marketing is a resource that combines with competitive teams that produce market-leading solutions.

Core Activities

What does Samsung need to perform well in the business to be competitive? Hardware design, patents for freedom to operate and marketing

In every business, one assumes that everything needs to be done well to succeed. This is unlikely, so focusing on the most important critical activities lets the company perform and the supporting activities will rise to the challenge.

With the Samsung Galaxy phone, the hardware design cycles and the marketing need to be coordinated. Announcing a product too early may stall the market for the existing products, leaving inventory on the store shelves. Waiting too long may not build up demand for the product when released. The hardware design cycles need to be coordinated with the market adoption and obsolescence cycles so the hardware is innovating ahead of the competition.

Suppliers and Partners

What partners and suppliers does Samsung rely on to provide their business critical capabilities to create the product? OEM, chip fabrication, Google licensing of Android Operating System.

All products and service are dependent on a supply chain in some form. The partners in that chain need to perform reliably for the company to produce winning products. The partners are where components are sourced in the manufacturing of the finished good. Many companies outsource noncritical aspects of the business that no longer give them a competitive edge. One example is payroll processing, a function that every company has but is best to outsource to a provider who can do this economically at scale.

The components of the Samsung Galaxy are sourced from many providers and assembled in a plant. The parts are provided by manufacturers who may sell the same components to other companies. It is in the assembly and packaging where the finished product is made. The Samsung Galaxy needs a continual stream of new Apps to fuel buyers desire to keep up with the trends; thus, the App developers are a key partner with Google and Samsung in the distribution of digital entertainment products.

Cost Breakdown

What are the largest fixed and variable costs for the Samsung Galaxy business? People, manufacturing, global marketing, sales, and global distribution. Given that Samsung is the largest patent holder in the world, they invest a lot in Intellectual Property.

A company with high fixed cost would need to have large capital infusion to get started so they can sustain the operations until they are profitable. Start-ups focus on reducing the fixed cost and keeping it to a minimum and shifting the cost to be a variable unit cost that is associated with each product sale. When you are starting a business, the highest initial cost is likely labor.

In Samsung's case, they have manufacturing costs that need investment before they can have a product to sell. The fixed costs are high for hardware and low of digital distribution of entertainment media. The digital products like

Apps can scale without requiring additional cost for servers and hosting which have reached pervasive commodity pricing.

Samsung Galaxy Business Structure

After bringing all the elements of the business structure together, one can start to see how they relate to each other. A change in one area affects the others. Adding new resources creates capabilities to expand or add to the value offer. Expanding the customer groups might add new revenue streams.

When starting, the shifts in the business will happen often, as you discover a business structure that works in the market. As an entrepreneur, you are trying to match resources to needs and develop a process to produce new value.

For Samsung, this is one of several business structures that are operating simultaneously. Each aspect of one business is leveraged for another. Much of the structure used for the Galaxy Phone business requires additional key partners. These partners provide the components of cellular radio and software added to the media player device to make it a smart phone. Prior to the current generation of smart phones the cellular phone was a separate device from the media player. Through good partnership, Samsung, has been able to source the components and combined them into a new device.

Business Structures are Messy

Our treatment of the business structure has been simplistic. It is useful to understand at a high level the structure of how a business works. The details of a business structure and the interactions of each aspect is a complex dynamic system with many considerations. How are these aspects related, managed, and configured in infinite ways, makes for a competitive structure. No universal single structure applies to all businesses. The business structure framework is a useful pattern to use in evaluating an existing business and generating new variations.

Business structures have core drivers that govern how they operate. If one is in a commodity business then driving down cost matters and other aspects, like finding, and securing the right low cost partners are essential. The way to compete is to find cost reduction in the business structure. This allows for aggressive pricing of the products. Other drivers can be the customer groups, the revenue streams, or the distribution channels. Each of these requires specific talents and resources to execute.

The business innovation comes from finding the drivers that provide the opportunity to create new value in the business structure that is competitive. The high potential companies find an X-Factor multiple that leads to dramatic improvements, not just incremental advances, in the business.

Winning Strategy

The business structure is important to understand so you have a means to communicate what the drivers of the company are. The structure is not the business. It is necessary to execute on the structure before knowing whether it is going to work. The business structure has a dynamic context that requires constant evaluation to refine the execution strategy. We will cover the techniques for finding and acting on a winning strategy.

Understanding Trends

Having a good sense of what is happening in the world -- nationally, regionally, and locally -- is essential to understanding the environment that your customers and suppliers are operating within. Political and regulatory changes can open opportunities or present challenges. Macro and socio-economic forces affect trends and speed at which they are adopted. Societal and cultural experiences set expectations for people. This influences how they view the world and the products they consume. Technological advances reset what is possible in the minds of the buyers. Having a big picture view helps one understand the challenges of a start-up by placing it into a context.

It is important to have a view of what you are operating on and continually test whether that view is shared by others and is based on observational evidence in the way people behave. A big idea needs a big canvas so stepping away to see things clearly as you are painting helps with maintaining the vision of the work, and see the big picture.

Porters Five Industry Forces

The five forces that shape industry competition are: rivalry among existing competitors, the bargaining power of the buyers, the negotiating power of the suppliers, threat of substitute products and threats for new entrants into the competition. The business of the entrepreneur is to find how to balance these forces in ways that gains an advantage over the competitors while locking out new entrants and substitute products, gaining advantage over the suppliers and fueling demand and scarcity with the buyers to drive the price up. To understand your market you need to put it into the larger context of the industry the market works in. Each industry has particular characteristics that are important to understand and analyze. One of the strategies is to review the interactions within an industry. Look for the industry forces that affect changes and shifts, these will present new opportunities and challenges for the new venture business finding its place in the market.

Situation Analysis

Once the key trends and industry forces are understood, you have the context for doing an analysis of the situation within the market you are targeting. The analysis will lead to a strategy for change. A simple means of understanding this is a force field analysis where one considers the forces that are driving change versus those that are resisting change.

To create an action plan to implement change, identify all forces related to the change goal, remove obstacles with solutions, strengthen supporting forces, add new forces to reframe the target. The forces may be either driving or restraining change. To figure this out, list all the attitudes, practices, norms, vested interest, traditions, resources, relationships, trends, values, desires, costs, people, events, and power structures. One would list all the forces as pro or con, and weight them to determine if the forces are likely to result in changes or maintain the status quo. Then determine what new forces to add or existing one to reinforce or mitigate to get the results for change.

SWOT Analysis

A SWOT analysis reviews the strengths, weaknesses, opportunities, threats. It considers these from internal versus external to the company what is helpful versus harmful. You may do this for competitors to understand their relative positions compared to your company, and use the conclusions to devise strategies and tactics to mitigate risk and accentuate the gains in the marketplace.

Amazon successfully used its internal strength in IT infrastructure to create new opportunities by providing value to a customer group of software developers it was not addressing before. They addressed a threat that those developers would continue to create e-commerce websites that would compete with Amazon. They addressed a weakness in the fulfillment area to create new opportunities and address a need by an underserved segment of small retailers who do not want to hold inventory.

Review the types of SWOT questions to consider.

Strengths - Competitive advantages? Experience, knowledge, data? Location?

Weaknesses - Reputation, presence, and reach? Financials?

Opportunities - Market developments? Competitors' vulnerabilities?

Threats - Competitor intentions? Market demand? Obstacles faced?

Value Innovation

All businesses need to create and raise value while eliminating or reducing cost. When this spread is dramatically better than what currently exist in the market, it is a business structure innovation demonstrated to have achieved its high impact goals.

To establish breakthrough value one needs to deploy a Blue Ocean strategy where you have a wide-open expanse of operations that is charting new waters. The basis for a Blue Ocean strategy is to find the X-Factor multipliers that dramatically reduce the cost while simultaneously increase the value of the products. Large companies strive for continuous improvement. A start-up has the opportunity to recast the way business is done. For the industry sector it is in, startups can reset the expectations. This type of strategy often requires an invention that is converted into a business structure innovation with dramatic performance results. These are what high-potential companies do before they are funded by Venture Capitalist.

Eliminate – which factors can be eliminated that the industry has long competed on?

Reduce – Which factors should be reduced well below the industry standard?

Raise – which factors should be raised well above the industry standard?

Create – Which factors should be created that the industry has never offered?

Business Planning

Business planning is taught in most MBA programs but for new venture start-ups, it has been criticized as being irrelevant. One cannot plan what one does not have control over and therefore for the innovative startup, well-crafted business plans become obsolete immediately once they are put into action. The primary reason is new ventures are inherently highly uncertain and are trying innovations in unstable or emerging markets. The market patterns may not have formed, and therefore, are highly unpredictable, making planning inaccurate.

This is an unfair criticism. The main issue is that business planning is often misused and the plan becomes the goal instead of the business it represents and in this manner, it is problematic. When properly used it is a valuable tool. One can take the candidate business structure and plan the financial aspects and articulate the current understanding of each. In this regard, the business plan is an analysis and communications tool. It helps articulate what is known, and expose what remains to be discovered. The business plan may be emergent with most aspects being a guess in the early stages. It serves as a desired future state of the business to strive for. If one cannot make up a plan that works when half the numbers are made up, then one needs to question whether they should start the business.

A recasting of the business plan is one that uses it as the means to record the "as is" state of the business against the future desired state to help expose what essential aspects of the business structure need to be addressed to make the future desired state possible. For high potential start-ups, the convention is to provide a business plan presentation highlighting the major areas of the business.

What are Business Plans for?

No entrepreneur has an accurate business plan, it is at best an approximation. The business is a dynamic living system. It is in the minds of buyers, the staff, the investors, and changes constantly in response to market needs. Just like in a movie, the script is not the movie and the movie is not the act of watching it, the feeling of the audience is remembered individually. Your audience is the customers and the success of the business is solely dependent on how the customer lives the experience.

When planning and acting on the business, become a storyteller. Set the scene, record what you know and expose what you cannot know. Give your characters a voice, situation, props, then act it out. Afterwards, record your story. Being an entrepreneur is like being a director or producer of a movie. It has high risk; the rewards of telling the story when it connects with the audience is beyond the money the business makes.

Business Case

When drafting a business case it is helpful to understand how lawyers create their cases. They use a technique of JIRAC, jurisdiction, issue/facts, rules/regulations, analysis/argument, and finally conclusions. An analogy of this framework for business might be the market, situation, patterns, opportunity, and tactics. Lawyers are evaluating their cases, whereas entrepreneurs are interpreting their markets when they are creating a business structure innovation. Find the leading competitor in the industry and draft a business case to learn enough to copy them, do an analysis of what they are missing, then innovate to beat them.

To understand business, try to interpret the situation: what patterns are present, where opportunities are, and why the tactics are used. This interpretation is valuable and builds on an analysis of the business. A clinical view helps the analysis and compiles the facts, determines the rules applied, what argument support the decisions, and what are the concluding results. A nuanced understanding will extract the value, when reviews of the financials are supporting information and not the only data used.

It is fine to start with a clinical evaluation. The point is that it is often not enough and an interpretation is required to have a deeper understanding of what makes the business successful. Do you think one could understand what makes Samsung successful by reviewing the financial performance? What about adding the engineering diagrams for the product? The financials do not predict future performance and are not sufficient as a diagnostic on what is not working, it is only a static view at a point in time.

Business Plan Outline

A concise business plan outline would include: company purpose, problem description, solution demonstration, trends and why now, market size and research, competitive landscape, product and technology IP, business structure, team, financial projections, and next steps.

Writing a business plan at the initiation stage is like a sketch not a finished drawing. Make it concise and packed with information. Do this in a visual form using as few words as possible. Start with ten slides using a large font that prevents using many words. Use the notes section to capture your thoughts and facts if necessary. With the company purpose, define the business in a single declarative sentence stating why this matters. The problem describes the pain or desire of the customer. Outline how the customer addresses the issue today. The solution demonstrates the company's value offer to make the customer's life better. Why now defines recent trends that make your solution possible. Market size profiles the customer. The competition list slide includes competitors and list competitive advantages; this can be a matrix comparison chart. Show the product line-up (form factor, functionality, features, architecture, intellectual property). Explain the business structure drivers that create value. List the team founders and management, and the board of directors or advisors. Be specific with the financials Profit and Loss, Balance sheet, Cash flow, Capitalization table, lastly, what is the deal. Once you have a sketch of the outline, you can iterate many times to refine the concept until it shapes up as a viable business on paper.

Winning Attributes

An appealing investor business plan would have the following attributes: clarity of purpose, a large market, rich customers, focus, pain killers, think differently, team DNA, agility, frugality, an explosive market. Start-ups with certain characteristics have the best chance of becoming lasting companies when they can describe the business on the back of a business card. They go after a large or growing market that allows room for many companies and mistakes which gives enough time to find where the margins come from. They find customers who will move fast and pay a premium for a unique offering. They focused the customers on buying a simple product with a singular value offer. They address clear painkillers, pick the one thing that is of burning importance to the customer, and then delight them with a compelling solution. They think differently by constantly challenging conventional wisdom, taking the contrarian route, creating novel solutions, and outwitting the competition. They set the team DNA in the first 90 days, all team members are the smartest or cleverest in their domain. Agility, stealth, and speed, will help beat-out large companies. The team will have a focus on frugal spending and spend on the priorities that maximize profitability. A huge market with customers yearning for a product developed by great entrepreneurs requires little firepower.

Business Structure co-Creation

Create the minimum viable product and get it to the early adopter customers as fast as possible. The problem and the solution are unknown or not understood when starting a new venture that includes a business structure innovation. The way to discover what business might work is to create something and test it, to progress from uncertainty to predictability.

The process of co-creation is attempting to create a new company and a new market niche when the venture is innovative. This is challenging, to construct two operating environments. The market niche are early adopters from a similar market. The start-up needs to develop both the product and the customers since the customer would be unfamiliar with the innovation and the product is doing something new; they both have to work together to develop a business structure solution that is viable.

The product development process includes: user stories, scenarios, requirements, release process, and acceptance testing. Prospective customers are engaged by setting expectations, allowing them to discover the value, validating the premise of the innovation, incorporating customer feedback through co-creating the product, and finally getting them to commit to buying the product. As the business structure is generated, it starts with a hypothesis, progresses to experimentation, insights are gathered, a manifestation of the concepts produced, and then it is tested and refined through iteration. Notice the product, business structure development, and customer, are managed in parallel and executed concurrently so they inform each other and allow for both the market and the business structure to emerge. This takes an intentional and methodical effort to do well, which is why the team dynamic is so important to a new venture.

Make the Structure Real

To organize a plan that is useful for tracking progress, it is best to start with the overarching milestones, the assumptions and qualifications are those milestones are based on, and a list of specific task that need to be accomplished. The plans indicate the resource, when it needs to be completed, and the dependency sequence of the work. Sequence the dependencies and track what needs to be done. You need to work on the business and in it concurrently. Plan just enough, act on the plans, then adjust based on the new information.

Do not get lost in just building the product; it needs to be packaged within a company for customers to buy it. That packaging needs to have the working business structure.

If you are clear on the milestones then the task emerge as the team attempts to work towards the goal. The assumptions help to clarify what was understood at the time the milestone was set. This helps with a reflective process of learning where the business performance can be evaluated against its own expectations.

The milestones need to include those goals that are known and the focus should be on exposing what remains unknown to help the business move from high uncertainty to predictability. In the early stages, the need to establish the milestones for what needs to be found out is often missed. It is so much easier to deal with what is known or routine administrative tasks and avoid charting into the unknown. Often those things that are set up as assumptions turn out to be false or not clearly understood. Building a business on mistaken assumptions can lead to insurmountable challenges.

Grow the Business

To grow a business is an iterative process; seek resources, sort the options, set in place, simplify, standardize, support, and sustain growth, then cycle through again to scaffold the scaling of the business. Create new value then operationalize it by integrating the new product and service into the business.

As an entrepreneur, you will be perpetually seeking new resources to expand your capabilities. As those resources are acquired, you have to evaluate them by sorting through the promising resource options. Once you have secured a resource you need to set it in place with your existing business workflow to integrate the new capability. The adoption of new resources can be a challenge so simplifying then standardizing increases the capacity to make use of the resources. Once activated, each resource will need support to maintain its condition and allow the company to accumulate capacity to have sustained growth. Growing the business is not like running it operationally; growth activities are beyond the day-to-day management. In my view, mastering growth-oriented activities while balancing the operational needs is what new value creation is all about. The core competency of a successful entrepreneur is the ability to grow a venture and knowing what pace of growth is appropriate at every stage. In addition, this same activity is needed to sustain a lasting enterprise since being able to grow a business means it can be reinvented to survive market changes and product obsolescence.

The skills to grow a business is what is missing in most MBA programs and this is not learned by entrepreneurs who settle for nominal profits in a lifestyle business that is enough to earn a living but is not enough to ever compete globally.

Experiencing Business, what does it feel like?

Imagine playing dice, poker, and chess, and recall how each has a distinct feel and engagement in your decision-making abilities. Dice is a random game of chance where every toss is unrelated to previous tosses. Chess is a game of perfect information in that both players know all positions of the pieces and each tries to anticipate the decisions the other player might make. Chess is a two-player, non-random, perfect knowledge game. As a result, it should have an ideal strategy that will result in either a win or a draw every time. So, far this strategy has proven elusive, with the computers no closer to finding it than the humans. Poker has aspects of both dice and chess, some cards are known, and others are unknown and randomly distributed. The players bet against odds and preference strategies of each. In poker, they try to anticipate what the other players are doing. Therefore every move is a negotiation of revealing risk and advancing the strategy without ever being certain of the odds, skills, incentives, or intentions of the other players.

As an entrepreneur, you will want the business to feel like you are playing chess, where you can see the entire board, have a strategy, anticipate the next moves, block and attack, control the center and advance to your goal. Often business will feel like you are playing dice with each roll being random, yet you feel as if fate has intervened when a good or bad number comes up. The cognitive biases will try and find patterns in the dice roll and consider the chess move made by a rational decision, yet neither of these are an accurate depiction of the game of business. The business structure you create will be like a poker game rather than chess or dice. For what is known and under control, it may feel like chess, and for what is unknown feel like dice, with each situation being a surprise. For the poker game of business, you will secure the financial resources and make selections as to whom you want to play with, then with partial information after random assignment of cards you enter the game. Watching the other players and their choice patterns, their bluffing and risk temperament will help you navigate through the game. Some rounds you will lose and others you win, with each, you start to understand the other players and sort through the negotiations with each move.

The analogy applies to how entrepreneurship feels since you can overcome obstacles and barriers with determination, perseverance, knowledge and a good attitude toward how you manage and negotiate risk. The game of business is a team sport that requires a lot of communication and coordination with practice being the daily routine and the wins the reward. With the team sports analogy not even the most dominant teams win all games, the odds are increased with a well-prepared team but never guaranteed.

Negotiations

Great groups start with superb people who have a coach that focuses on performance and effectiveness. The great groups recognize talent and know where to find it and self-organize to work together. The group is on a mission that transcends the individuals; it forms a team identity. They will have their own culture and know that connecting to people outside of the group will introduce new ideas and talent. The great group likes to compete with other groups and see themselves as disadvantaged and therefore needing to try harder. They are optimistic and focused and do not linger on losses for long and instead look to the next challenge. They have the right people working on the most important issues and stay lean. The coaches provide them with what they need to perform then get out of the way. Great groups deliver and they treat work as its own reward.

Creating the Team

Do not confuse big company experience with effectiveness. Larger companies have many functional silos that allow for building highly specialized skills. In a start-up, multiple skills are needed and the silos can be an obstacle if the support is not provided. Have high expectations of your team so they achieve full potential.

The sales person is the most important hire. Without a salesperson, the product cannot get to market. The customers make great products. The winning products fit into the market needs. The engineering process is secondary and is assumed to be of high quality just to be in the game. This is particularly true for startups founded by sharp engineers, scientist, or technologies, or are based in founder's competencies. Entrepreneurs are driven and can be brilliant. They easily mistake that competence for an "I can do it all" attitude. While this belief can remove obstacles, it can blind the entrepreneur with not recognizing that sales is not just having a people-oriented personality. It is hard work and good salespeople are exceptionally intelligent; it may be an emotional and social intelligence that dominates over scientific knowledge.

Find co-founders, and make everyone an owner so they are enrolled in the challenge. Look for people in your network and check references even if you think you know them well. It is easy to hire someone you like and have no idea whether they will perform under pressure. If you worked with someone before, given a new context and new people involved, be aware that what worked in the past may not work again.

Hire talent not education; Steve Job and Bill Gates never finished college, and Richard Branson never finished high school. I have had the great fortune to have worked with a few highly competent people who never completed their formal education and were exceptional self-directed learners. On the other side of the spectrum, I have hired people with doctorates that were impossible to manage. Evaluate each person on what they can bring to the situation. Put the emphasis on demonstrated competence relevant to the business needs. This should increase the chance of forming productive alliances.

Size the staff appropriately for the stage of the business. It is easy to over-hire for skills and experience you do not need, or too many people after being funded. The desire to grow leads to mistakes in hiring before the need, instead of hiring for growth. Hire people who can grow the company while pushing the limits of performance. To grow, the people need energy and talent over experience; of course experience matters but that should not be the sole criteria. New ventures require people who act and put function over form, they get results when and where needed instead of the best results when it no longer matters. Avoid the perfectionist that never completes things, they might be talented but they will not get results.

To hire the best people takes sales skills. If you cannot get the person to believe in the business and be an evangelist, do not hire them. Many startups mistake the job market as having an abundance of talent and think they need to interview the candidates as the first step. First, try to sell the candidate on the company and if you cannot do this, do not hire them no matter how good they are. For example, I once made a bid to consult with a high tech company with a team of investors. The CEO rejected the investment and the consulting offer but in the process, he made sure we knew enough about the company so we would tell others about it; in effect he turned us all into his sales force.

Hire as a last alternative, not the first, and consider outsourcing as much as possible. While outsourcing might appear to be an expensive option, it often can be far cheaper if managed properly. Labor can be a fixed cost and the single highest cost to the business while outsourcing can be a variable cost, which can be managed as needed in case of a downturn and to support growth. In the U.S., a try and buy option exists where someone is first hired as a subcontractor and if they perform they are hired. Labor laws vary tremendously by jurisdiction, so understanding the regulations is critical to managing growth and human resources.

Talent Management

When managing team talent it is important to set the expectations for what and how they perform. Goals that are set too low may result in the team exceeding expectations and being complacent, while setting them too high will produce under-performers.

The team should be able to operate in a self-organized way. It is important for each person to take on a primary role. The expectations on each person help to define the capacity and performance of the business. It is important that each person be aware that just meeting the milestones is not enough and the manner in which they do so makes a difference. You do not want people who are exceeding expectations on the goals and destroying the relationships along the way. You do not want people who everyone likes but cannot get anything done.

The goal setting starts with the company's strategic goals; these need to be stated clearly so everyone across the entire company knows what they are and how their work relates to those goals. The goals need to be long, near, and short term so that each has a context for what is to come and how the effort build up to an accomplishment for the company. Each team then has goals that match the company goals. The team goals are partitioned across an organizational structure where the roles that each person has match the competencies they exercise and fill the roles that are needed to run the company.

Each company will establish its organizational structure and many variations can work. For a startup the choice is often a lean matrix and multifaceted organization. These flexible organizations have people working in multiple roles but when someone is making a decision and performing a task they need to be clear under which role are they making those decisions. Caution needs to be taken not to have roles with conflicting interests that skew the decision-making. For example, someone with strong accounting and modeling skills making decisions on engineering technology that is skewed towards cost savings and disregarding the consequences of short term accounting for pennies. Similarly, avoid engineering folks who should be supporting sales, telling the sales people how they should be working or sales people directing the engineering plans; both are a bad practice.

Each individual contributor needs a clear statement of what they are accountable and responsible for and the goals that are set within the role(s) they take. An early stage company has insufficient talent to satisfy all the roles and tasks it needs to accomplish. The team members need to take on roles that may be peripheral to the core competency they have to contribute. The team needs to be prepared to release some of their responsibilities when new is hires are made that can do the job better. To grow the company fast it takes people who are willing to work towards making themselves obsolete in the jobs they have at the start and move on to take on greater challenges. A young engineer who is a top coder may grow into managing a small team and no longer is coding. Possibly the top coder should continue to code and not manage people since they have not demonstrated an ability or willingness to learn the people management skills needed to perform well in delegating and managing team goals. The variety of challenges with growing a company around talented people is enormous, and those who are willing to grow personally will do best if they are self-aware and put the interest of the company before their own.

While it is easy to think that having the next generation of leaders would be the best, these often create challenges and contention between the team members. Some will need to become the core fabric of the company and put the company before their own career ambitions. It may be necessary to let go of someone who is talented but either cannot grow with the team or has outgrown the team. While this is counterintuitive, getting rid of talent may speed things up occasionally.

In a new venture, there are limited resources and the early stage team may need to be multi-talented and exercise many competencies. The team may need to take on new roles. They may not have much interest in these roles but the team needs to be willing to fill in while the company grows. Talented people are capable of taking on many different challenges, learning fast, and getting something done. It is easy to miscast someone into a role where they under perform. It is easy to rely on a trusted professional who can perform well and the way they do their task creates a high dependency on them and alienates others. Coaching a team to perform with high impact and setting the company up for growth is not easy. It is an entrepreneur's task, to get others to produce the value collectively by setting up a team that works towards a common goal collaboratively and not solely in their own self-interest.

Sales Focus

The typical sales cycle has four simple phases: prospect by identifying the customers' problem and getting them to respond to an appeal, engage the decision maker with a demonstration and trial, acquire the customer with pricing negotiation so they make a buy decision, keep the customer with a positive experience so they give a referral.

Sales need a process with tracking metrics, just like the engineers would need to test and complete the product. While engineers may view salespeople as engaging personalities, the effective salesperson does a bit of social engineering. This happens using emotional intelligence instead the mathematics of the sciences. Everyone needs to learn how to sell in the company even if it is just to sell others during the hiring process or remind colleagues what the value is when the company is not doing well. Every point of contact can enroll new resources early on and identify opportunities. While not everyone will become a salesperson as their primary function, appreciation for the sale process is necessary to facilitate the communications feedback needed to help discover the market and customers view.

Sales can benefit from having intimate knowledge of the product and industry. With this background, they would be better prepared to address all the objections and challenges the customer may raise. Salespeople who are engaged in gathering, analyzing and communicating competitive intelligence can be an enormous asset for the product managers, designers, and engineers. They help the company to serve the exact need of the customers and exceed what the competition may be offering.

One common observation with inexperienced salespeople is they forget to ask for the order and payment for the work. Sales people are so caught up in building the relationship. They forget the objective is to be paid for delivering value. In the sales process, achieve enough customer satisfaction that they buy again and recommend the product to others. Early adopter customers will resist paying for products and treat their involvement as payment in-kind. This may be necessary sometimes but it is better to have a customer paying for the product, so you find out the products value, which can be defined by the customers' willingness to pay. Far too often, the early adopters are being entertained by novelty and that wears off once they have to pay for the value.

Young entrepreneurs in high-potential growth industries are reluctant to do sales and instead focus on building the product or the team. The product they can control; in sales, you are dealing with the irrational decision-making process of people and trying to understand this creates confusion and uncertainty. It is essential that the founders are out selling, listening, and getting customers to buy what you have built or helping you define what it should be.

Influence Maps

Use an influence map to reveal what goes on in a company. It is necessary to create an influence map that captures hidden factors that contribute to a buyers' decision-making process. Find the people and entities that communicate with one another, have influence and the degree to which that influence impacts the decisions. Mark the direction of the influence, the net ratio and the frequency of interaction. For example, for a pharmaceutical company, the influencer might include community leaders, government regulators, nongovernmental organizations, doctors, experts, employees, media, and suppliers. Understand the constituents in a network who influence the opinion of the factors that contribute to a buying decision.

To sell you will have to understand the network of influences that factor into the buying decisions. In poker, this is reading the table. By reviewing the cards shown, your hand, and what they have done in past rounds, one can assess the players' risk profiles. In the real world, the influences are many and some you will not see or know about. As you uncover the network of influences, the better chance you have at appealing to the entire network to gain support for your product. This is especially necessary when selling to large companies and government organizations where consensus decisions might be the norm.

Organizations that have consensus decision are very challenging to sell to. It is not clear what the decision process is even when they have a process. The influences are never disclosed and the consensus is meant to protect against biases and corruption. These organizations will be highly political and no one wants to be responsible or accountable for anything. Groupthink takes hold and either they have a lot of infighting or a few people would set the time for the rest and establish power through influence while not having any responsibility when something goes wrong. The worst situation for a startup is to be selling to an organization like this. Equally challenging is when selling to a user who cannot make a decision, such is the case with engineers who decide on the solution but then the finance executive approves spending the money. The sale is to both constituents, but one will not make a decision without the other.

Within your company you will have influencers that affect how the company performs that are outside the official roles and titles. It is the hidden mesh in your company. You need to know what this is and understand it so you have a chance at guiding it to productive activities and attitudes. You may call this playing politics and find it distasteful. Others see it as the social fabric. Regardless, recognize that it exists, and use it to your advantage. It gets uncomfortable when it is obvious the influence map is being manipulated by a few at the expense of the many. This is what people refer to as playing politics since some win and others lose. This form of social exploitation is not what is being advocated; instead use the influence map to move towards a winning situation for all by providing a clear benefit to a clear problem.

In frontier markets, the influence map might include bribery, corruption, collusion, and other factors that are of questionable ethics. Yet it is the reality of doing business in those countries. Not knowing this can lead your business into wasteful sales efforts and situations that your values will not permit. One can think of the influence map as the political network that needs to be serviced to get a sale. Playing politics and manipulating a network of relationships can be uncomfortable and personally challenging but ignoring this will not help your business. You can decide on a case-by-case basis which customers have business practices and influence maps that match your values once you know what that map is and whether you can improve it to be inclusive.

Negotiation Model

Negotiations can be modeled as two parties that have a degree of concern for their own versus the other's outcome. When the concern is low from either party, they are likely to avoid the negotiation. If they have high concern then they will be collaborating to find a solution. Most negotiation will have tension and each party at various moments in the negotiation will be in one of three states, yielding, competing, or compromising. Understanding these states and being able to recognize them during the negotiations can greatly facilitate getting to a conclusion. This is essentially the model that a mediator uses, but in their case, they can maintain an objective position making it easier to identify the states and move the dialogue forward.

Many factors go into negotiation: cultural, language, financial, authority, decision-making styles, communications styles, listening abilities, problem solving, urgency and timing, power structures. To resolve conflicts quickly, it is worthwhile to understand the other's concern in your negotiation to help frame the issues under consideration. Having research on the history and culture of the other party, the context of the concerns, and the patterns of previous negotiations will help.

It is important to set a target, understand the limits, do research on the issues, find points of advantage, identify items available for bargaining, and issues that are easy to agree on. You will have to influence the other person's points of resistance.

Know the other parties "BATNA" – their best alternative to a negotiated agreement. Without a clear alternative, they are forced to bargain, if they have many alternatives they may be less willing to compromise. A disconnection between values can fracture a negotiation quickly, especially when both parties do not have the same interpretation of what is fair or have an inflated sense of worth. It quickly turns into a personal attack on the other parties worth when a position is taken that is not matched with what they think they are worth. Entrepreneurs need to learn these skills fast to deal with all the stakeholders in the sale or to work with suppliers or raise money from investors. Having a sustainable partnership with other co-founders requires negotiation skills.

Persuasion

Leadership, teamwork, negotiation, and sales all require influence. Influence is the central competence that all soft skills have in common. To have influence, one must be persuasive. To be credible you will need to have competence and present in a convincing manner. The influence allows you to be a coach to the team, and negotiate sales with customers.

Being persuasive is the first skill a founder needs to acquire. Without it, the business concept will not get support from others no matter how good it is. The most important sale you make will be to your internal team, the second to your partner resources. The sales to your customers are the last stage and the most important in the sequence. If you have not sold your team and your partners, you will not be able to deliver to your customers.

I have coached hundreds of entrepreneurs in my teaching, consulting, and in my own ventures, and one of the early sign of failure is an unwillingness to persuade the other person and persist in a belief that what they are doing has merit solely on applying the competency they have to build the product. I know a few brilliant people who have fallen into this trap. When faced with objections, rejection, and challenges, they resign themselves to the other person not understanding how great they are. Instead, they should have continued to figure out what is needed to convince the person to the point where they are willing to buy or provide support for the business. The ones who master this turn others into their surrogate sales force quickly or incorporate the feedback and try again until they get more acceptance than rejections. It is a learning process. What is learned is how to persuade the other person of your view, in a way they absorb it as their own.

Summary of Business Structure Formation

The co-creation of the business structure is with your team and partner resources and your customers. The value offer is made among all these participants. To engage your resources you will need to have a credible story and evidence of traction. Most of your resources will be established businesses and therefore they are taking a risk by selling and engaging with you. It is important that you position the company to be able to sell 360 degrees in every direction and in every way.

Build the minimally viable product, iterate, and learn as you deliver to customers. This is the best way to discover what should be the business. Often what you build and what the customer thinks they are paying for are not the same. Adjust to the customers view.

Be aware of the network of relationships that influence one another. The influence map will help to establish support and garner sales to help the business structure emerge. Use the few diagnostic strategy techniques to understand the market and competition.

Social by Design

How do innovation intensive, high-growth industries use global resources to sell to international markets? They design the social constructs they need to rely on, an extended trust network of buyers and sellers. The trust network is a fairness economy where common interests are pursued with engaged, winning relationships. Businesses use legal contracts and commercial banking services to protect each party's interest. These are not enough to set up a global network quickly. Issues of money flow timing and differences in laws and enforcement make doing international business particularly challenging. All startup businesses need to be born global to have a chance at competing in a rapidly changing international market. This requires an understanding of social design.

I live and work in NYC, when a new restaurant opens in my neighborhood it needs to be on yelp.com and all the other social media websites that make it easy for people to find. The restaurants want to get a good rating and they need to be able to appeal to the millions of tourist that visit NYC throughout the year. This is just as true for a small medieval town in Tuscany, Italy as it is for NYC. Santa Fe, New Mexico has an annual festival of cultural arts each year that is visited by craft people and consumers in large numbers. There you can find an artist who can sell 200,000 USD in craft folk art from his homeland where the material is hubcaps and the medium is sculpture. The economy of his village depends on his annual visit. A mango packaging company in Ghana sends containers of packaged food on the daily British Airways flight to London for sale in the department stores. Without the UK market, the business could not survive just with the local market. A major Tech company in Italy sells 90% of its products outside Italy and would never survive with selling to the local Italian government buyers; this business expanded by acquiring other companies in the U.S. and Japan. Tapping into the world market is no longer an option; it is a necessity for all modern business.

Social by Design is what Samsung practices. They create a transcendent brand and global business structure that is greater than the sum of its part. It becomes a love brand and people ascribe meaning to machines with consumer design appealing to a universal aesthetic sense. They are connecting to people, the social fabric, the interactions that people imitate; this amplifies their brand and increases sales.

Samsung uses innovation from global industry clusters to reduce cost and increase expertise to produce winning products. This is done using Information and Communications Technologies (ICT) and global logistics to network the communications and coordinate the business structure from supplier through to the customers. As a Korean company, Samsung has offices in all the regions they sell products and the marketing is targeted to local cultural preferences. Tech start-ups use these strategies. They learn the social fabric of an industry and design strategies for leveraging the capabilities available in the global market. This capability is not exclusive to big companies; it is available to all businesses regardless of size or location.

Innovation clusters are social networks formed as purposeful communities of practice engaged in international collaboration, particularly in innovation intensive industries. These same strategies are available to all businesses and are at the center of the tech ventures and large multi-national corporations. To have the largest market possible using the most effective resources requires that entrepreneurs develop business structures that can expand to leverage the entire global market and resources available.

Start-ups are born global; they are micro-multi-national, or transnational companies. With the use of the Internet to communicate and coordinate, and that access being inexpensive, it has opened business possibilities for new ventures that would have been impractical to consider in the past. I co-founded a company from NYC with the team in Helsinki, Finland to target the South Asian market with a channel partner in Indonesia and the first customer being an Australian company; we coordinated all activities virtually across several time zones. We had ten people on staff and access to twice as many who were engaged as suppliers and affiliates. Our small company was acting like a much bigger global enterprise, it was a mindset of being born global.

High potential ventures start the company as a transnational business and see a global market of customers. They may test in local markets first and they understand that a billion dollar business needs a large market. They find and use the best value resources globally and design the social interactions that are needed to tap into the existing networks of relationships of the industry sector. While the first market may be local, the resources can be transnational from the start.

Topics:

1. Design the factors that build social relationship

2. Clusters and why they work

3. Network Economy where everything and everyone is interconnected

4. Barriers to social design

Designing the Social Factors

To create productive interactions with partners and customers, you will have to design the social factors that help set up and keep the relationships. To get the venture started, these resources are ones you can draw on. Expanding on your business structure, think of where you might find partners that would lower your cost and customer groupings that would give you a larger market to serve and design products that give the highest profit margin. Then evaluate your value offer to extend it to the global market and figure out how you would get the product to those customers. Through this analysis you will find what new resources you need to fill the gaps.

By expanding the business globally, it will cause rethinking the best structure and this allows for narrowing the focus. If you find that you have such a broad business that it is indistinguishable from others in the same industry, then reevaluate each aspect of the structure again until you are innovating in one area that allows you to compete with the existing competitors in the industry.

Peopleware

In the advanced economies, the ability to find and invite people to help your business is speeding up and making it easier to get started. It is possible to get advice from top experts if you know how to find them, enroll them in the mission, and engage them. You have to provide value to the experts in some form so the exchanges are mutual. The social networks have implicit rules and behaviors that are necessary to learn quickly to tap into that value.

Using Peopleware requires a credible personal brand that can be verified by the social network. Establish a reputation and willingness for free and open exchange of information, ideas, and value. The ability to post a question on a forum or group discussion and get many answers quickly is a form of rapid crowdsourcing that was not possible twenty years ago. Today this can be done from anywhere on a broad range of topics and in different languages. This comes as a benefit to those who are willing to spend the time to give value to others through these forums by first answering their questions. The traditional business plans often had labor as the first or second highest expense. Given the expert capability is easily available, it may not be necessary to hire every competency your business may need.

Social Resource Management

Use Social Design as resource management to help engage customers and partners in co-creating the product and its business structure. Without their engaged and active participation, it will be challenging to sort through the many problems the business will face. The social interactions that govern the engagements need to be carefully designed by intention and consideration.

Being able to tap into the tacit industry knowledge of others will help avoid costly mistakes, and open opportunities for solving difficult problems. All industries have implicit social contracts that one needs to understand to become a trusted member of the network. These extend to how you think of and treat your competitors, if you do not know and follow the protocols, your business might be ostracized. The market is created through these social interactions. Thinking of how to design them so they are productive helps enlarge the capabilities of the business.

What is Social by Design?

It is the design of human systems for social interaction in the broadest sense and specifically for a business, it is designing the organizational cultural value system, understanding and contributing to the norms and progress of the industry sectors, and tapping into the resources of the trusted social networks of the industry. This may be referred to by various terms: business development, customer and supplier relationship management, marketing communications, training and development of the workforce, talent acquisition, and all other business activities where the interaction between people form the essence of whether the activity will produce a desired outcome.

Serious social networks such as LinkedIn, Viadeo, and Xing are self-organized reputation networks that are emerging as important sources of resource sharing, job seeking, recruiting of talent, marketing of services, and personal branding. The curriculum vitae has gone online and can be vetted through the connected reputation network. Parallel to the youth-oriented, self-absorbed entertainment of Facebook and its related image and link sharing sites, a business-focused reputation system emerged that is distinct in its purpose and use. What is different between Facebook and LinkedIn is the new business networks are loosely associated collection of contacts that form the trusted reputation network, a hyper-connected contact book that affords the user the possibility to analyze the reach and composition of the network.

Within three degrees of separation, a sparsely associated profile may have access to hundreds of thousands of people who are in some way related to the work and people the entrepreneur has met over a short career. The strength of weak ties, the seminal research paper describing these network formations is showing to be true in practice. Yet, with all the potential capabilities of these new networks, the skill of media literacy including social media's appropriate use for business is lacking for many young aspiring entrepreneurs. Those that gain the skills exploit them for excessive self-promotion and others remain invisible to the network potential. Understanding this capability, and the skills needed to exploit it are important for the entrepreneurs to compete on the global stage.

The social network is not new. Membership organizations, clubs, professional societies, academies, alumni associations, attending a house of worship; these are well-established means of connecting to resources and taking part in sharing knowledge and bartering capabilities. These are referred to as communities of practice. They need an identifying brand mark, a credential or certification for admission, maintenance and support fees or donations, and loyalty to the mission and code of ethics. They might have a rite of passage or qualification test, and often a conforming behavior or belief system.

The communities of practice have a governing process and power structure that binds the membership together and expects loyalty and active participation. In the best instance, they may capture a body of knowledge, encode it in publication, and spread the knowledge. The most useful forms have the capability for shared problem solving across an industry. The best practices are presented in the many conferences and symposiums that industry and academia organize. In the strictest form, one will find this in the medical, legal, engineering, and financial sectors where laws and regulations require the existence of governing bodies to enforce standards of practice. Many self-governing communities of practice exist which are not officially regulated. Each industry, to varying degrees, will expect the professional talent to engage in one or more of these communities of practice.

The community of practice extensively uses on-line communications to uphold its membership participation. This complements the local, in-person meetings. It has allowed these communities to have massive federation of local, regional, national, and international scope. Competing and overlapping associations have formed. With free on-line capability, it is easy to form ad-hoc project specific communities using a group forum or simple content management website.

Once an exclusive trading activity, finding sources and distribution channels and selling access through layers of intermediaries, has collapsed into a supplier direct-to-customer relationship. The ready availability of global sourcing and channel distribution is forcing companies to collaborate and benefit from aggregation of supply or sharing the cost of distribution. Cooperative competition is the new mode for entrepreneurs to break open the possibility for them to compete with the giants of globalization. A Chinese manufacturer can provide its components to the entire market through alibaba.com where the companies can source the same components at a price that would never have been possible with the layers of aggregated distribution that predates the Internet. A new venture can easily co-generate the product and service with the component manufacturers and the early adopters and create low volume prototypes that keep cost low and use capital efficiently.

Why Social by Design

Entrepreneurs seek to expand the resources they have to get the venture started and on to a rapid growth path. These resources tend be concentrated in innovation clusters where industries are in close proximity to each other. Entrepreneurs will want access to the relationships within an industry and therefore will go to the regional innovation cluster.

As the business becomes global, clusters for each industry form in regions. They become interconnected and interdependent as the supply chain expands to use resources where the best value is provided. Designing a social strategy for accessing the resources in a cluster can unlock potential for talent, suppliers, and customers. Investor, law, and accounting firms are clustered geographically where the industries they service are located. These are intersecting networks that make for a vibrant ecosystem.

Clusters

Cluster Resources

We covered one of the social design techniques using influence maps in the previous chapter. It is an analysis of the network of relationships that form an industry and how to enter the network to access the value. The reputations in those networks are what the customers use to qualify a new venture.

When hiring a salesperson, they will often promote their contact list in the industry as their value. You need to determine that person's reputation and whether they had access because of their association with a large corporation or if the people in the industry respect them for the knowledge they have about how the industry works and how to access the customers and suppliers.

Customers go to the regional innovation clusters to source and buy components and services. This is true for huge industries like financial services that are concentrated in the cities of New York, London, Zurich, and Singapore. It applies to other highly closed networks like the diamond industry in Antwerp and 47th street in New York City. The suppliers gather where the customers go, and the mutually reinforcing cycle then expands the cluster, further attracting suppliers and customers. The talent then gravitates to the cluster for jobs that further strengthen the industry concentration. The schools in the clusters then adjust to the growing demands. They establish programs that support the job market attracting students to the industrial sector, and they engage in research relevant to the industrial cluster. All this activity creates a commercial tornado that swallows up the ecosystem. These innovation clusters form as ecosystems and take years to emerge and have complex contributing factors that trigger the growth. The reason why Silicon Valley gets so much attention for its technology ecosystem is the spectacular speed at which it formed over 40 years. Preceding it by many years prior were forces on the East Coast from Washington D.C. to Boston that included the U.S. Military industrial complex and NYC financial investors fueling the emergence of venture capital and its funding of the early stages of Silicon Valley.

Cluster Automotive Industry example

Looking within the U.S. automobile industry, one can see the companies are concentrated within an area of Detroit-Warren-Flint Michigan and the adjacent economic areas are full of component suppliers. The automobile industry is not just the large car companies; they are supported by hundreds of suppliers of parts that employ thousands of people. Entire towns are dependent on that economic activity for survival. Each of the suppliers rely on other suppliers for materials, machinery, tool and die, training, facilities, and an assortment of services that is required to sustain a business. The entire value and cost chain are interdependent.

If you have an invention for a type of puncture resistant wheel, you have a much better chance of getting it adopted if you live and work within the cluster area of Detroit. Starting a company outside the cluster introduces major challenges. Where would you find the expertise and experienced talent if you started the business in an area that was unrelated to the industry you wanted to sell to or buy?

Clusters Footwear Industry example

For industry clusters in the footwear industry, one can easily see the interconnections. China is focused on the low cost and OEM segments and makes shoes for U.S., Vietnam and Indonesia OEM provide the low cost segment for Europe. Italy designs, markets and produces fine shoes for the world market and uses resources in Romania for low to medium cost shoes. Brazil is also making shoes; most likely, Italian immigrants started the industry and used their connections back to Italy. They focus on leather tanning and medium to higher priced shoes in response to Chinese competition. Portugal makes short run production, medium priced shoes. U.S. designs and markets sports shoes. Each of these regional clusters is interrelated, uses one another as sources, and sells into the segmented markets. Starting a global shoe company outside one of these clusters would be costly and would need to draw on the resources of these clusters to get started.

Thriving Tech Clusters

In the tech community, the clusters form a global value chain where providers service layers of the product development cycle. It is usual for a three-way to exist. For example, Nokia engineers in Finland, manufactures in China, and sells cell phones in Africa. In the U.S., this three-way cluster might be a business coordinated from the U.S., with engineering of software in India, targeted for sale in Europe. You find Israeli companies who are headquartered in the NYC to access the market of consumers and investors with the company operated from Israel.

These networks are highly fluid. Approximately 50% of all Silicon Valley CEOs are foreign born and they use the resources of their native country as part of their resource capabilities. Many of the tech companies executives in Taiwan went to university in the U.S., worked for larger tech companies, and then went to China to start a business to supply the U.S. tech industry with components.

For example, I co-founded with a venture-backed company that sourced chips from Southern France to put into products that we sold to South Africa and used software developers in India, contract hardware designers in California and contract assembly in China. The tech industries from San Jose to San Francisco, New York to Boston are globally interdependent on Hsinchu-

Taipei, Bangalore, Tel Aviv, and Singapore. Smaller local tech communities are concentrated around large companies like Nokia in Helsinki or Ericsson in Stockholm, both having regional impact and doing business globally. Other characteristics can drive forming a cluster like the telecom technology companies in Côte d'Azur in Southern France or San Diego, or the growth in Berlin and Amsterdam where cost of living and life style factors can attract youthful talent willing to take on entrepreneurial challenges. Each has its origin, in a large company's success, or proximity to a major research university, combined with many other qualitative factors.

Tech Cluster Attributes

The clusters are not just one massive network; they are several intersecting networks that reinforce one another. The attributes of a thriving successful tech ecosystems can be observed where start-up activity is frequent, they have an abundance of talent often coming from the universities or research institutes that have attracted the best global talent. They set up global links that allow students to come and study at the schools and have immigration policies that allow the talent to find its way into the economy. The ease of doing business is a contributing factor as are low taxes and regulations that make venture capital attractive to invest. These common attributes of tech innovation clusters are the intersecting social networks that span global reach. This creates resource opportunities to acquire the best value talent and components.

Network Economy

The new economy is a networked economy. The internet allows for rapid global communications to interconnect people across many regions of the world. Both the speed and scale of the communications has increased with the cost of these interactions dropping dramatically. At the center of this communication is the free transfer of knowledge between people and the production of new information made instantly available through the Internet. All new ventures need to tap into this stream of resources to fuel their early start up phase with important access to people resources.

The networked new economy has an expert level workforce that can produce useful knowledge from research and development efforts. The knowledge is freely transferred between individual participants in a fairness culture that helps foster entrepreneurial action. The cities where this occurs have a fairly high quality of life that includes lifelong learning, cultural artifacts and appreciation, tourism and business conferences, safety, economic stability, and a concentration of capital that allows for a portion of it to be invested in higher risk ventures. The social networks are active and engaging in ways that establish social capital that is built on merit of accomplishment and reputation for reliable contribution. These are factors that government can play a factor in. It has to do with the attitude and perspective of the people who establish the social contracts of fair bartering and notions of "passing it forward". A willingness and bias for knowledge-sharing creates the environment needed for solving problems quickly and at lower cost.

Impact of Social by Design

Serious social networks can produce value for the start-up by providing access to expertise and competencies they could not afford. The challenge is that the value is produced by the group and therefore is available to everyone. This is the basis for open innovation and needs to be used properly to realize the advantages.

The comparative advantages of designing a social network are to lower the cost of available expertise that can raise productivity and speed up performance of the team. The extended network can create access to core competencies and creativity that would be difficult to engage and hire. The challenges are that with the open sharing, everyone benefits and therefore differentiation becomes harder to sustain, especially when producing intellectual property. Securing ownership of intellectual property is central to the business ability to compete in the marketplace, so balancing the appeal of open innovation with asset protection is not easy.

The open source licensing of software components is a good example for how free exchange can fuel rapid innovation. They can leave a quagmire of mismatched intellectual property that is challenging to sort through and establish the separate company value without potentially violating conflicting licensing. Open source does not mean free and free does not mean without conditions. The open source movement was a grassroots and ad hoc community of like-minded engineers and was not designed from any pre-existing constructs. While it has created tremendous value, it demonstrates why understanding how commercial networks develop and guiding that formation is important for a new venture to consider.

What are Social Networks?

In the serious social network, communication produces value that can be acted on. The catalyst for the formation is, shared goals, problems, intention, anticipation, common interest, or expertise. The value comes from a voluntary group willing to communicate and form relationships. The ideas, knowledge, and relationship contacts are treated as a commodity. Through these useful exchanges, social capital is accumulated and made convertible. Without this free exchange, the network cannot fully form to freely scale to an entire ecosystem.

This is hard for policy-makers to grasp. These networks form through trusted fair relationships that are easily formed. Governments try to promote the formations of ecosystem clusters through tax incentive and investment programs. These take many years to emerge and much capital is used and may return a benefit if the ecosystem can take hold, grow, and reach a critical threshold in its saturation. If a closed network is the cultural norm, then these types of free commerce networks cannot take hold no matter how much money the government spends.

Social Network Design

Serious social networks are designed with the facility for organic interactions that build relationships. This includes: one on one discussion, civil group discourse, argumentation, and working towards shared goals and outcomes. This leads the kind of knowledge sharing that solves practical commercial problems. Formal structures and processes typical of corporations do not create communities. This is a serious challenge for larger companies and results in a workforce that is detached from the business beyond the daily job they are ask to do. Start-ups have an advantage because they have a smaller team and it is much easier to create excitement for a new business with a vision. Start-ups have opportunities to communicate in a manner that is flexible and responsive to the community both internal to the business, external partners, and customers.

Successful Social Design

Successful social networks balance enthusiasm with the familiar by inviting open dialogue between insiders and outsiders. They have private communications and develop a public voice to solicit new ideas and participation. When you use Social Design, it is necessary to have a value outcome and set a pace or frequency of the interaction to foster the relationship. This is what good sales people do. They build a network of relationships that span across an entire industry. Business development people are like sales people with a focus on expanding the capabilities of the company by targeting key partners, finding strategic alliances, and expanding the business structure with an expanded value offer.

The successful social design will define and focus on value, allow for varying levels of participation, create a pulse for the community, and evolve in response to changing needs of the community that was formed. It allows for intersecting networks of related complementary activity.

Implications of Social Networks

The internet has made it cheaper and easier to communicate frequently to anyone in the world. It is no longer the exclusive capability of larger global corporations or academia. Every new venture can have access to expertise and resources anywhere in the world. The social network which forms around a community of practice willingly share knowledge. This enables entrepreneurs access to global opportunities, tacit local knowledge of foreign market being disseminated, and allows local domestic businesses to think and act globally and global businesses to service local needs.

Social Capital

Social Capital is based on trust and reputation where people have a free exchange of information. Those relationships then build economic value that helps facilitate business transactions. To work internationally requires a high degree of trust. International contracts are hard to enforce, cultural difference creates confusion, so doing business globally requires that one has a reputation that can be easily assessed and design interactions that work for all parties. The network of relationships must facilitate economic vitality by providing opportunities for knowledge transfer within the network.

Modes of Social Capital

Status - Familial, Social, Religious, Proximal, maintains closed communities and exclude competition and places cultural constraints as limiting access. The NYC Diamond Market on 47th street is one example of a tightly closed community that operates on a high degree of trust and requires a common cultural identity to participate. Many family businesses within a region, that has a particular industry they historically service, would have these characteristics.

Reputation - Recognition of a reliable and consistent behavior and competency that can be trusted and measured as productive in achieving economic utility. New York and the global tech community, which is a partial extension of academia, have this characteristic where one must demonstrate clear competency, be evaluated by peers, contribute value consistency, and this is rewarded with credibility and expert status that is convertible social capital.

Authority - Hierarchy of position in a formal organization, which affords the presumption of access. The military, governmental agencies, and large companies have this structure where position and title dominant the mode over all other factors. The hierarchy tries to protect against collusion with checks and balances and oversight and the hierarchy is sustained by the rule system of authority not by merit, reputation, or trust.

These modes of social capital may exist to varying degrees in many organizations and are not mutually exclusive. They will have one of these recognizable patterns. Understanding which is present can help one navigate the social fabric to get a goal accomplished.

Building Trusted Social Capital

Building trust requires a consistency of behavior through repeated interactions of direct interpersonal contact. By association you can establish trust through reputation that will give you access to others in the network. A common point of introduction may be needed to access someone in the network. That common point will calculate the reputation through associations and known prior accomplishments that can be validated through the network. The network may have a set of predictable norms.

Social Capital in New York

In New York City, people value the professional relationships over the companies they work. They carry the relationship into new business ventures and companies spawn the next generation of entrepreneurs. Being able to access expertise and enroll talent is an important resource for a new venture. The difference between someone who starts a company, and someone who does not, may be the ability to enroll others into the business. New York is fortunate to have access to a large global top talent pool across many professions. That labor pool is highly mobile and can travel or move to where the work is needed which favors relationship building internationally. The social connections transcend location, cultures and companies and this makes for a tremendous asset for an entrepreneur starting a business in New York.

Information Flow in New York

In New York, your performance builds the reputation and gives you access, not the social, familial or authority connections. You have to demonstrate competence and an ability to make things happen in the face of obstacles. This is what people will value and it builds faith that a risky venture has a higher probability of surviving than one that does not have quality people behind it. Investors care about your past insofar as it demonstrates an ability to overcome obstacles by applying talent and an insight into how to work with people.

The quality of the information source is highly valued with the trust based on reputation and merit. The public markets depend on these exchanges of information since bad information can lead to bad investment decisions. The tech community, with the strong influence from academia, fosters free exchanges without expectation of short-term return or subject to rational calculation within the network. While proprietary information is highly valued, the recognition that a portion of information is better as a public good helps to keep the ecosystem vibrant and competitive. Simply controlling information or relationships is no longer adequate or acceptable. To compete, what matters is what is done with that information and demonstrated through competence to convert it to useful knowledge and a competitive advantage.

Entrepreneurs use Social Design

Entrepreneurs will find the largest markets and create innovations for them. They will generate intellectual property and speed to market with a product by sourcing from the lowest cost and creating value chains to the market. As they grow, entrepreneurs attract venture capital through local offices and eventually get to the U.S. market to attract public capital. Many processes are at work to go through this. The factors that make the difference is how the social interactions are designed for success.

Tapping into the innovation clusters is central to how entrepreneurs use social design. They enroll the peer experts early into the business structure, engage the key partners who have resources to contribute, and design the interactions with the customers that will ultimately make up the market they sell. Entrepreneurs will do this repeatedly regardless of whether they succeed or fail at each attempt. The social design is created often without conscious thought. It might be taken for granted but it is always present.

New York Ecosystem Innovation

With social design, three intersecting networks facilitate an entrepreneurial ecosystem, which one can easily observe in New York City and it exist in the several other cities. The convergence of the firms, research and development labs, universities with venture capitalist, investment bankers, and law firms, in a place where suppliers and customers do business. These three networks all rely on reputation and trust within a horizontal and vertical network to make decisions. These networks are highly purposeful and dynamic and are supported by ad-hoc communities of practices. The networks intersect in many ways. They can be accessed by social design. One needs to study the influence map, and spend the time providing value and building relationships. These networks are highly diverse and global and the history of New York has led to a density of activity that has it influencing other ecosystems. Historically, New York funded the early activity in Silicon Valley with Arthur Rock investments in the traitorous eight, the founding members of Fairchild semiconductor in the late 1950s.

Continuous Innovation

Innovation is put into the market by entrepreneurs. When it comes from a corporation, it is by a few people who took the career risk to set the company on a different path. In a way, innovation is not continuous. It will break the old established order and this happens from uncontrolled networks with self-organizing behavior. Performance is the criteria that matters in these networks, and having a "do first, ask later" attitude lets people willing to take risk exceed past the competition. The diverse ecosystem of New York, with its large population of global talent, is not concerned with whether they are different, since they are by circumstance and choice of coming to the great city. NYC will push people to create opportunities and have a vision for making a better life for themselves and others. There is no other way to survive in this hyper-competitive market.

Taking responsibility and risk is normal for the entrepreneurs, as is sharing the rewards, spreading the work to wherever it is best done, and executing with speed and determination. It is worth reflecting on this and asking how do these characteristics fair against your cultural assumptions? While many of these characteristics are ascribed to the new tech economy, it is easy to observe much of this is at work in many businesses in New York. Realize that this is not a new phenomenon; it is one that comes with a disruptive economic dynamism that is present in entrepreneurial ecosystems

A few regions are able to regenerate this many times for different sectors, like the variety of industries in New York. In other regions, the dynamism is narrowly scoped to a core industry making the ecosystem less resilient to externalities that influence cyclical swings in industry demand and supply and the productivity that is required to sustain a competitive global position. Continuous innovation is about the regeneration capacity of the entrepreneurs that figure things out quickly, under conditions that are never stable, and are ready to open up opportunities for those who grasp the mode of striving to live with self-determination.

Social Capital to Innovation

The connection between social capital and innovation is direct. The innovation activity takes place in the networks of trusted coordination of knowledge and do not go through hierarchies or markets. It is between people who have established reputations that are distinct from the corporation power structures. The absence of an explicit *quid pro quo* in the network enhances the transmission of knowledge that is considered a commodity. This extends to making recommendations to connect people within the networks. For many generations, business was done this way within closed networks. What is new is the meritocracy of knowledge, performance, and reputation, combined with a notion of a fairness economy between people who can connect easily using internet communications. This has allowed for networks to form and spread fast. That speed of mixing knowledge, solving problems, and having access to experts has fueled rapid innovation in those sectors that have adopted this new mode. The traditional corporate structures of controlled closed networks have struggled to adapt to the expectations of the most talented entrepreneurs who are active participants in the open networks.

Barriers to Social Design

If the innovation cluster is immature and shifting, it may be hard to establish grounding in the industry to anchor the new venture social design. It may require that stronger ties be created with fewer people to help propel the product into the market. If the area of expertise either is one that is not easily disseminated because it requires physical presence, or is proprietary and exclusive, then this limits the design of the social interactions.

A lack of physical proximity that allows for in person interactions may not foster the degree of familiarity that is needed to break through the early barriers of establishing a valuable network. A lack of a sense of belonging due to cross-national, cultural, and language differences can pose a challenge to social affinity, in particular when the cultural differences are in opposition or the implicit value systems are not known. If the relationships are task-focused and not practice based, then that reduces the interactions to transactions that are momentary.

Companies that have these barriers may require more capital to get started since they cannot tap into the flow of information or social capital that may exist within an innovation cluster. It makes it difficult to attract the talent and expertise that is needed if the scarcity of the resource will make it expensive to acquire. The tech community has somehow transcended these barriers through mediated communications. Within the software community, a global sharing fairness has prevailed balancing common efforts for public good with commercial interest.

Challenging Cultural Perceptions

Note that this book is culturally biased using the U.S. tech industry as an example. It needs to be interpreted for each culture that one is doing business. I use the U.S. tech industry example since it is my own experience and because it is one of most vibrant global business growth sectors that is rapidly changing the expectations for how business is conducted. Of the top 500 U.S. corporations, over 50% of the revenue and business activity is done globally. Tech companies are born global. They cannot survive without operating as global entities.

During one my classes, I showed an image of the former U.S. President George W. Bush next to the actor Marlon Brando playing the part of the Godfather in the movie of the same title. The picture grouping may have offended some but for others it was satirical. I show an imagine of Beppe Grillo, the Italian comedian turned political movement icon, his hand raise with his fingers making a V sign. To an American, this looks like a peace sign but to an Italian -- I will not reveal what this means in this book. The layers of association speak to the degree to which communications of all forms can get confused. The cultural biases and prejudices are layered and easy to mistake. Keeping an open mind and not judging prematurely is a challenge. If we maintain the view that most of what we may think is heavily biased and therefore wrong if projected onto to other cultures, it may allow us to see clearly where the differences are and challenge our own notions.

Overcoming Barriers to Global Relationships

Use Information and Communications Technologies (ICT) to bridge the global divide by connecting to people within your industry in other countries. Using ICT makes it possible to outsource to other locations, where the expertise or best value might be available that bridges the entrepreneurial effort. Before being able to seize this opportunity, the entrepreneur must establish an identity and purpose that is transparent and have a trail of evidence for building a reputation that is credible and demonstrates competency, trustworthiness, and accomplishments. Open and frequent exchanges makes for building a relationship that can produce results. Speaking to a local partner representative about opportunities, contacts and developments will get attention and action. This may take many country visits to understand the cultural factors in the market you are pursuing or at a minimum learn enough to realize that local knowledge is invaluable to a global business and this can be accelerated by using global ICT effectively.

I do business in Italy from New York and before I was able to do so I visited as a tourist. Then I was fortunate to find an Italian business partner living in New York. Together, we went to Italy as buyers of services, and eventually that transitioned to being a seller of services. This took many years to develop. Without the local contacts, it would never have been productive. Low cost international travel, cheap Internet communications, and ease of logistics made this possible. Without each of these, the cost of doing business between New York and Italy for start-up ventures would be prohibitive and require greater capital than it does today.

Global ICT Mitigates Cultural Differences

The assumption that ICT can mitigate cultural differences is a belief that has a U.S. tech bias. It can be debated whether the adoption of technology and the usage patterns will be the same across cultures. Much remains to be understood about how best to use Internet technology for self-directed learning and to perform research on-line. Most people who use computers can get through the basics of a web browser. The advance usage is still rather low and Internet and media literacy is not high even in populations that use it daily. Knowing how to use the Internet effectively for business research can give your company a significant advantage in competing. It is possible to appear to be a larger company while being small and compete with companies that have many more resources.

What has emerged in the global tech community is a value system, which is available to anyone to adopt. They can participate by contributing and then benefit from the social capital that was formed. The tech community has a belief in ICT as an agent of change; it provides the freedoms to participate as a way of empowerment, with equal access to information regardless of role. These assumed capabilities establish an expectation with the tech entrepreneurs that technology can contribute to social change. The social design eliminates the power distance by triggering self-organizing networks of purpose, the force of competence wins over personality or authority, making the young entrepreneur lean and flexible to adapt to future uncertainty that is treated as a norm. The entrepreneurs manage risk as a rational choice decision and push individualism into absorbing the collective.

The culture of the global tech entrepreneur treats time and space as virtual, continuous, and shifting. They move the communications skills to one that is computer mediated, yet trusted relationships can be built through network connections. The open networks that are communities of practice have high diversity of roles and cultures who work towards shared outcomes.

Summary of Social by Design

The aspiring entrepreneur starting a new venture needs to be born global. It is never too soon to start connecting to resources everywhere, treat the world as the market, and think globally while starting locally. To gain an advantage, the entrepreneur needs to think of the social fabric as an intentional design process that gathers up resources and contributes first before asking for benefits. It is essential to understand the particulars of the industry's network that you plan to disrupt. Then innovate on the entire social design, not just portions of the product, service, or business.

Funding and Bootstrapping

How do entrepreneurs find sources of capital to fund a company? Everyone wants to know how to fund the business but until you can fund it, you are unlikely to get far with attracting funding from others. Self-funding a business does not mean that you have cash that you put up to get started. It does mean that you get creative with how things get done with little to no money. So funding in this sense includes all the investment of time, resources, and cash. The way you start a business with limited resources forces a prudent management approach that creates an efficient business.

What may be a great idea for a magic circle wheel might look like a square wheel to everyone else. With business start-ups, real customers can tell you if the business has merit. Naive young entrepreneurs want to start the business only if they get funding, and think they can do this with just an idea and good presentation. The test for investors is whether you have invested in your own business. You do not need money; you need to have put in the effort to figure out how to get enough of a product built that it can be delivered to real customers. See the previous chapter on what the value of an idea is. With only a good presentation, it equals zero, possibly less than zero if one accounts for the time wasted in fixating on just the one idea, thinking the idea is enough to be funded.

The expectation for how much money the business needs to operate and grow is often skewed. For experienced businesspeople, funding expectations may be out of line relative to what an investor would fund. Be practical and funding prospects will increase. You need to show efficient cash management, and understanding how to best use resources. This is something that has to be learned quickly and by acting out the business idea. Without getting practical, the business cannot get off the ground. Continuing to be pragmatic helps with learning from failure and gaining the resilience that is needed to gain investor confidence. The entrepreneur may have unrealistic expectations and be unreasonably irrational in their belief they can make it happen, it is just when this exuberant enthusiasm interferes with decision making does a problem occur.

Topics

1. Funding the business

2. Understanding money

3. Funding sources

4. Bootstrapping

Funding the Business

If you are like most people, who will read this book, or attending a course, you are reading this section first. You have an idea you think will make a billion fast and if you could know the secret of getting someone to give you money for your PowerPoint presentation you can get going. Stop now, and go back to the first chapter and read the rest of the book. If that is too much of a commitment then put this book down or give it to someone else now. I will start by telling you the big secret path: self-fund, build a product, get many customers, break-even fast, then get capital, grow big fast, and exit the business as soon as you can, then do it again. The reaction I usually get is one of confusion. They think: "raise money when I do not need it, then sell the company when it is going well"—that sounds like the exact opposite of what someone would do. They are right, and that is exactly what I am saying.

If your goal is to make money as an entrepreneur then you will need to figure out how to detach yourself from creating the venture. You will need to reach the point where the business you are in is creating other entrepreneurs who multiply the return potential. This fractal of a social construction gets lost on many entrepreneurs; those that have made money for themselves but have not created the greatest overall value for society may not see this either. They may not have figured out what is enough and pursue making money for money sake. Understanding this nuance helps to identify who are investors from whom are just people with a lot of money that do not add value with their capital.

With the business structure, how many areas can you change at once and still survive as a new business? Not many, so limits to innovating a business plan do exist. All businesses have a business structure and plan, it might change often, the structure might not work, or they may need to discover the structure. Do not fall into the trap of thinking that you can just build a product and then afterwards figure out how it makes money or gets funded. Real innovation has a high degree of uncertainty and therefore often the business structure cannot be known, it does not mean you ignore it, you just take a guess knowing that it might be wrong and you adjust once you find out. Quality investors know this, they are aware that breakthrough businesses are going through a learning curve, and in the early stages they are funding, the market discovery.

In the business structure, you want to figure out what you are investing in and what you will hold constant and control versus remove or reduce, and what you can predict versus what you need to be creative. The best investment of funds creates new value and produces revenue. The funding needs to have a target use that makes a difference. The funding is not to be used just to support people on the staff. So raising funds is about dramatic changes that improve the prospects of the company scaling to the entire potential market, it is not about having a lifeline that protects the founders against personal risk of financial disaster.

Understanding Money

Personal Net Worth

Taking a tally of what has been invested in your education and lifestyle can be a challenge, and most people will be astonished how much this cost your parents and the government. Going through this mental accounting is useful to understanding your personal assets. What value do you need to return to society in your lifetime? When you think in these terms, you may start to shift how you think about the money you spend and whether it is being invested in activities that will bring a return.

Unfortunately, many people in the advanced economies of the G20 countries do not realize they won the lucky genes lottery. They were born in places where the chance that an investment in them by society will be made, through access to a safe environment, drinking water, food, and free education. Since they live in societies where this is the norm, they feel entitled to the investments that make for a civic society. Gross inequalities in these societies makes for a sense of entitlement and makes it hard to see that by further investing in yourself that you can then leverage that for a return. My opinion is that people are obligated to be entrepreneurs to pay a debt to society as a return on investment in educating the population and asking for a civic duty to create new value for themselves and the economy.

Think of what it takes to compete in the global market of buyers and sellers. Anyone in a G20 country who had the privilege of an education and lives within an open economy needs to leverage these assets as much as possible. Create a whole life plan by calculating what was invested in you, what life you expect to have, and how much value you need to create, what that will cost, then how would you get there. Doing this, one will conclude that working in a job is not enough. Unless you can figure out how to produce greater value, you will not meet your lifestyle goals and you will never repay your debt to society. After you get married and have many children, this calculation becomes large. It is easy to understand why entrepreneurs matter so much since without them the calculations do not add up and one can see how society goes backwards quickly with people consuming more than what they are producing in value.

Life Style Choices

Preserving your lifestyle to the level of your parents is not a given in society. Each generation has its own struggles and many of the advance economy countries have gone through 60 years of entitlements with mounting government debt. It is not certain that in the future one will be granted a lifestyle of entitlements the previous generation had.

An expectation of material wealth, which is assumed to come as a reward for working in a "good," secure job, is an illusion. Perceiving future global risk that will rebalance economies to a new level is unsettling for people in advanced economies, in particular the youth who are still trying to find their way into the economy. Family, housing, and leisure are being redefined to the new realities of economies that are no longer sustainable and are forcing people to reassess how they make a living. They are asking If better ways exist than getting an institutional job in a government agency or its global surrogates of large corporations. These "choice" jobs have always been scarce with most people not being able to break into that comfort zone. It has defined what was called the middle class, people with a living wage, in a few countries making up most the economy. The people who made the economies work were the small to medium size enterprises run by family businesses or professional management, the entrepreneurs.

The freelance economy, made up of independent artists, consultants, and part-time laborers, has grown at estimates exceeding 30% of the U.S. workforce. These people are not counted in the government figures for unemployed. No accounting is done for underemployed, people who are doing task-oriented work that does not require the level of skill and training they have. In the U.S., corporate downsizing and forced retirement are part of how corporations do business; it is normal for people to have five careers, and many jobs throughout their economic life. Increasingly this workforce is going freelance and reclaiming their entrepreneurial survival skills. Once this realization is made, they can thrive as entrepreneurs and no longer tolerate the institutional forces that once governed their life expectations. Making this life style choice as soon as possible, is an imperative so that it is made under terms that you define instead of one of circumstances. It all starts with household financial management and the better one is at dealing with new harsh reality the sooner they can avoid being pushed into a situation of economic discomfort.

Entrepreneurship is a choice that comes with lower expectation of material wealth in the beginning, not higher. People assume they want to be entrepreneurs to make money; serial entrepreneurs do it for its own rewards regardless of whether they fail or succeed. It is about living with meaning and impact and when it works, it brings rewards. Money will come and learning how to run a business helps with learning how to run your life but nothing is guaranteed. Make it a lifestyle choice before you are forced to. It is not so much adjusting to lower expectations as it is shifting the value system of excess material accumulation that consumes your personal resources and pushes your family into situation of dependency on the institutional economy's forces that you may have little to no control over. Starting a business or acting entrepreneurially is not easy. One thing is guaranteed, your life skills for creating economic value will be strengthened and the ability to withstand disruptions in your economic life will be resilient.

Entrepreneurial Finance

Most people have a disconnected relationship to money. As money become electronic and disappears into the systems, we become less aware of the value of what we are spending. If it is someone else's money that you are the steward of, you may be distant from how to use it. Understanding value and money are essential to succeeding in business. This understanding is not just numerical. You need to develop a sense of the flow of money. Master how to assess whether each situation warranted spending.

Can you figure out what your relationship is to money? Is it careful accounting against a home budget or spending without much thought about whether that present is worth buying? How are you with your family's money? Have you needed to live with your family's support well into your twenties? Did you try to achieve financial means as a teenager? I was always cautious with my pennies as a child; it comes from living below the poverty line and appreciating every cent. I married a woman who has the same consideration for money and without such a match, I do not think I would have been able to go through the entrepreneurial journey and achieve a degree of financial success. Being an entrepreneur is something you start doing immediately, not later, when you get funding from someone else's money. It starts with how you think of what is in your pocket now. Do you spend that Euro or figure out how to use it to make two Euros?

Money is the language of business. It is a unit of measure, the accounting for money flows. It has a time value that can discount the money into the future, or increase its value if stored in an investment instrument. Money costs money. The most important lesson is to understand that money is not the same as value; it is the currency accounting of value and many aspects of value are not reduced to an accounting unit. Money can be invested against a level of risk with an expected return and money held, as cash is a tender with floating value against other currencies throughout the day. In a modern advanced economy that has money in an electronic form much of these basic understanding of money are lost as an experience, swipe a plastic card and magic happens, you are allowed to take the goods, whether it was a stick of gum or a Rolex watch it was the same process. Walk in a store with a thousand single bills to buy that Rolex and you will have second thoughts as you count that money.

Personal Investing

If you want to understand how an investor thinks, then do investing yourself. What some people find when doing personal investing in the public markets, is if they can manage money well enough with a balanced portfolio approach, they can get a return that is equal or better than if they start certain types of businesses. They focus on the business of the household and work for a company while saving and investing their money. This is a rational path to take and thinking entrepreneurially will help. You need to understand how businesses act and think to be a well-informed investor. Regardless of whether you become an entrepreneur yourself, this exercise will have much value for you to understand how investors think and act. You can apply these skills to your personal investment strategy.

Putting your money to work for you gets you thinking about how to make money using money and this is an essential first step in understanding how an entrepreneur thinks about every facet of getting a return on their effort. The investment mind-set trains the decision maker to consider not just how money can be invested but how effort, time, talent, resources all are invested in a business to get a return. Slowly the risk of investing is understood as you observe the stock market rising and falling in ways that are unrelated to the information you have, forcing you to think in patterns instead of transactions, from hourly stock price shifts to global market trends. You eventually graduate to understanding dollar cost averaging and diversifying the portfolio risk to take advantage of cyclical patterns. As you become an experienced investor, you start to understand managing risk for the short and long-term and that investing is not a quick win game, it takes a long-term view, 20 years to get the best returns.

Once you start to put your money to work, you ask how you can do better than the stock market over time. You may have calculated your savings and investment rate over 25 years. Concluded that in the best-case both the investing rate and the returns would never be enough to support your modest lifestyle and family goals. Will the career path and job be satisfying? Will it pay enough to buy a house, get married, have children, go on vacations, and save for retirement? This does not include a sense of obligation to contribute to the society that invested in your skills through providing an education. I often find people in New York who bought an apartment with an interest only mortgage, leased a luxury car, have student loans and credit card debt, and if they were to calculate their net worth it would be zero or all debt. On the surface, they are doing well, the fundamental financial situation is dire and an unexpected job loss can unravel this life quickly in a distressed market creating a crisis. These people have not managed their personal business well, or worse, the business of the household. This is not a situation leading to becoming an entrepreneur with self-determination.

The question is: how does one avoid these personal financial issues? How does one get to positive net worth and have it grow? If you concluded the job you can get, and in the best-case advance to the top of your profession, still would not get you to a positive net worth that can secure your lifestyle, then maybe an alternative needs to be considered. As risky as starting a business might be when compared with the alternatives of working in a volatile job market and never being able to get to positive net worth that supports your desired lifestyle, a business that can get a much higher return starts to look appealing. Investing in yourself, starting with an education and continuing this learning for your entire life is the first step. The second step is controlling your personal finances. The third is figuring out how to create value the market is willing to reward you for rather than just getting a job. This is often the mental calculation that entrepreneurs make. They decided the best path to take that will give results and a life they are seeking is to be an entrepreneur.

Funding Sources

Funding in school

This is an overlooked source of funding in the broadest sense. Courses, classmates, alumni, and faculty, are all sources of invested effort that should be leveraged. Scholarships, stipends, and sponsorships, each of these sources of indirect and direct funding can create value if you know how to use them wisely. University research is funded by government grants and the tech transfer offices are motivated to license to commercial entities under negotiable terms. If you are a researcher, you can get the technology transfer office to invest in filing a patent for an invention. Grant writing is a useful skill to pick up and a source of funding for research that is available for patenting and commercial licensing.

Securing each type of funding listed above is a competitive process that tests whether you can construct a value offer that others believe and want to fund. Selling skills and business structure formation are important to learn and apply in these preliminary pre-business funding stages. If you read the details of a grant application, it will request a spreadsheet for how you plan to spend the money and track the use of the funding. They will ask for a description of the new value to be created. To get the grant you have to show how others will be involved and what the relationship will be to each contributor. These are all useful skills to pick up and practice while in school.

Funding through Corporate Sponsors

Corporate directed research would be challenge for a student to get and they would likely be working on a research team lead by faculty. The corporation sponsors the faculty so they qualify for this source of funding. Directed research is problematic for ownership of the work, so it is a way to get experience with the problem and unlikely to be the means of getting a business idea funded indirectly.

While business plan competitions are a valuable learning experience, few companies are launched through this process. The Rice business plan competition is the largest. Many others exist and each school has goals for having their own version of a competition. MIT has a long history with the 100k contest run by students for 20 years. Akamai, a Billion dollar company being the most successful example from the MIT 100k contest and other smaller companies have launched from this competition. The competitions all have criteria that have to be met. The Rice University contest is open to all. The winners from other competitions are the ones invited to participate in the Rice competition. At MIT, it is a closed contest for MIT student teams.

The benefit in trying some or all the funding alternatives is to test ideas and to learn from the process. Acting on the concepts in multiple ways helps to understand and solidify what works. Having a format, a process, a deadline, and getting feedback are all good ways to get going, so entering contests can be helpful. I have coached a number of teams who went on to win competitions, the ones that have done the best are those who enter and keep trying. My criticism of these contests is they all have slightly different strategies and often the winner is a bizarre choice depending on the experience and method of judging. It is not worth putting too much value on whether you win or lose the contest. It may have skewed judging. Yet it is good they exist as motivational incentives for people to try.

Funding while working

If you do not invest in yourself and your own company, then you will be working for the investors. Investors are aggressive about owning successful companies. As you succeed, they will want to own a greater percentage, so keeping ownership early on is important but faced with a fat check from an investor you may be at a disadvantage.

You need to create a personal financial plan before understanding whether you can go into business. You do not want to go bankrupt by starting a business; this is just foolish and unnecessary. You need to understand your affordable loss tolerance and that requires a personal financial plan. That plan has to set aside enough money so you can partially fund the business yourself and you can sustain your own needs for at least 18 months. Reduce your cost of living and create discretionary income to increase your savings rates. You cannot start this early enough. Saving money is not a reason to get married yet having a two-income household surely helps a great deal. I did a talk on startups recently to a group of young engineers and they asked me what is the one thing they should do first before starting a business. My answer was get married and live on one income and make sure that marriage is a healthy partnership. With such a high divorce rate that appears risky, when I explained that partnerships all fall apart at a point in the company growth they understood. If you do not have your house in order, it will likely interfere with the business and conversely. Families run most of businesses in the world, find out why and start with your own.

If you are trying to start the business, while you are still working then all your time off will go into creating the product and getting the first customer. This bootstrapping is typical, the entrepreneur would use every holiday and vacation day as investing time in the business. Using credit card, cash, home loans, and revolving credit are common ways that business bootstrap in the beginning. Just be careful to do this within a budget and stay within your plan. It is far too easy to get into the mind-set that if you just take out loans you will crack the business open. Set your thresholds and time frame and stick to it.

Funding through consulting

If you have mastered your craft and are at the top of your profession or possess skills and experience that are not readily available, then you may consider doing consulting work as an alternative to a traditional job. This is the business of one, the freelancer warrior, the mercenary hired to get the job done. This is not the same as being a subcontractor to companies not hiring and those companies using this practice as a means of managing variable labor. I am referring to consulting that comes from experience that is not present in the company. The reason for this distinction is that top consultants can command large fees for their expertise; this gives cash that if saved, can be used to start a business.

In the software technology business, contract work has always been a means of making cash to use to build a product. This works if the legal documents are clear and allow the consultant to hold a portion of the intellectual property. The contract should not simply be a work for hire. If this is a situation you can create it may be worth aiming for. It may be possible to get recurring customers with similar problems and as you develop the solutions these convert into a commercial product that is sold to those customers. This co-creation is rare but when the conditions for this opportunity are available, it is well worth doing.

Funding the Seed Round

Asking people for money is hard unless you can explain why it makes sense for them to invest. Family and friends may be obliging, you want them to be professional investors so they have sensible expectations and understand the risk. Founders, family, and friends are usually the first round of investment with the highest risk; within this group, the founders take the risk first. Then the founders can go to friends and family who they know can afford the risk -- they do not simply go and ask everyone. Some will fund your business out of dedication and loyalty or overconfidence in your abilities. These kinds of seed investment can be problematic. If the business does not grow and get a return, or needs additional money from professional investors, they will come in to fix the under performing company and push the valuation down which negatively impacts the first investment round from founder, family, and friends. If you have to educate your friends and family about the risk then do it and avoid them investing blindly.

Fortunately, in many parts of the world family businesses dominate the economies. Therefore, pooling risk capital is typical. What is different, is the style of growth and financial engineering that is the subject of this book. This is not common in many countries. Growing on a global scale requires professional capital and investors who understand what they are investing in, why, and what to expect for future rounds of capital. Jump-start the process of your family learning how to invest by helping them to understand your investment.

Do not risk the family farm on a risky venture – there are many other ways of going into business, that would make money. Family businesses are not high-potential growth firms and are formed to service the needs of the family life style. That is not to say that family firms are small -- some of the largest companies in the world are owned and managed by generations of family members. This starts with modest ambition and copying an existing business first before innovating the business structure for growth. Family businesses can grow but they usually do so at a much slower pace.

When seeking funding from friends it is better to create an environment where they can help in several ways. It can be in-kind work, using their expertise. Ask them for the help you need and let them decide if funding is the way they want to take part or maybe they want to work on a part of the business first so they fully understand it before investing money.

It is best to avoid fools investing in your business. These fools are strangers who you meet and who are not professional investors, but for some reason they believe the business concept will be worth a great deal of money. These investors will likely bring problems later in following rounds of funding.

Funding Social Ventures

You can try the nonprofit route, but it is not easier. You may find that nonprofit companies are harder to run and the money from investors have requirements and conditions on how it is allocated so the internal cost of this money is high. This is true for government grants where the accounting requirements will be extensive to address the use of public money.

All funding has an internal and inherent cost of capital that is beyond an interest on debt or discounting on the equity. The cost to carry out a funding transaction and the accounting for the money has higher burdens than if the money was invested through self-funding. For social ventures the disclosures and transparency requirements impose a much higher burden on the organization than in a private business.

Several types of social venture funding are available and each one will have particular conditions and expectations on the social return on capital. Foundations like Asoka, Skull, Draper Richards, are early stage grants of 100k each year for 3 years. Program related investing are zero interest loans by foundations to social ventures. Regional target funds include the Acumen fund for India, Pakistan, and East Africa. Pooled Funds are available from the Nonprofit Finance Fund. Corporate grants are given by Shore Bank, Google, and the Gates Foundation. They focus on large-scale themes with significant amounts of money granted. Impact Investors are Investors' Circle or the Good Capital. These are just a short sampling of funding sources for social impact. This does not mean the enterprise is a not for profit, it just means the funds look for large-scale impact with sustainable solutions and expect the return will be in the social good it creates not just in the profit it may produce. These funds are interested in consistency of purpose in providing solutions that do well and do it in a way that does not have negative consequences.

Funding through tech programs

The U.S. technology community is fortunate to have many choices for seed funding; government programs from the U.S. National Science Foundation, NSF Small Business Innovation Research grants, Small Business Association Loans, Tech Incubators, y-combinator, betaworks, Founders Institute. Each of these varies in requirements, usage, and relationship, to the entrepreneur business. For example, a Small Business Association loan is for an existing business, while admission to a tech incubator or accelerator is for a business in the early stage of formation. Equivalent programs exist in Europe through E.U. Horizon 2020 SME Instruments or the startupbootcamp.org based in Amsterdam. Each global tech cluster has some form of these which are a combination of government and private investor support.

The competition is high for these tech seed programs. You may not get enough funding to get the business started and you may have just enough to learn and make mistakes early. Several of these programs will take a percentage of the company. For example the Founders Institute will charge for an educational training in the form of a boot camp and ask for 6 percent of the company. Entrepreneurs beware: caution against getting involved in pay to play schemes like Founders Institute and others like it. They prey on false promises and on inspection, you will not find many success cases from these programs. I have coached many young entrepreneurs, a few who went through these Startup programs. They can be a waste of time and do the exact opposite of what they claim, by setting up expectations that have little chance at being realized. If you need training, go to school, take some courses, go to meet-ups in your area, read books, get online, get a mentor, and try and get far enough that can get into an incubator or accelerator.

Funding through Angel Investors

Angel funding can exceed that of Venture Capital in the U.S. and most of this funding goes from people who know one another or to companies that are highly referenced. Many Angel investors do not ever invest or they do so occasionally and therefore are in the charity business even if they do not think so. The early rounds of funding from Angels can take many years to bring a return, on average greater than eight years, and along the way, the company has been revalued so many times the original funding Angel's equity would be significantly less valued than what they started with. This is a lesson for the founders to be aware of since their ownership will likely be diluted with each round of funding if they survive long enough with the company to share in the growth and return.

Angel investors vary widely from individuals to groups to syndicates. The individual investors you have to find in your network of high net worth individuals. These investor types may have a family offices, or just enough excess money that they are willing to lose by betting on a risky venture. The risky venture applies to all new businesses since the odds of failure are much greater than success. If a business succeeds, there is no guarantee that it will ever be sold at a valuation that brings a return for the investors. At times, these individual investors may have had past success where they feel secure and think they know the secret formula and look to invest in what they know. They assume the next business will follow a success pattern they did and will look to their knowledge of the industry or contacts they have or another unique circumstance they believe. These can be good sources of investment when the person has a few failures to temper their overconfidence. Be wary of these types of investors if you sense they would like to be running the business. This type of investor could be a disaster for the entrepreneur; over time the investor will not let the entrepreneur run the business and slowly take over through future rounds of investment. The mental calculation they make is to invest 100k in ten things they know, watch them closely, kill off the ones that do not make it and take over the ones that do.

The tricky funding schemes that individual investors come up with will surprise the first time entrepreneurs. They can be at the borderline of integrity and ethics. I saw an investor put up money, then in following rounds convince the new investors that he could manage the money, so he was placed as the CFO, then paid himself in salary all the cash they put up, plus got extra shares as an employee. Later, he quit at the opportune time, walking away with the original cash he invested, his shares and a bit more. In another scenario, I knew an investor who listened to pitches all the time, then offered to invest at 80 percent ownership and cover the salaries of the founders who were just out of school and were happy to be making money and teaming up with an investor. If they refused, the investor would take the concept and hire his own team to create the company and own 100 percent. These are issues of integrity. It does not happen often, but it does happen. Remember that people who invest make money with money. They might have suspect morals or views on their value that are not in the entrepreneur's best interest.

Angel groups like NY Angels are the second kind of angel funding that is related to individual investor and have a group evaluation process. This extends to the latest form of Angel groups like syndicates on angel.co (http://angel.co/). They evaluate deals collectively; they may co-invest with one another. They act like Venture Capitalist and are willing to invest pre-revenue, and they might want to mentor or coach the entrepreneurs. The Angel Groups all have criteria to be a member. Simply they must be an accredited investor, and commit to investing a certain amount over a specific period. With the syndicates, this could be as low as 10,000 dollars. In the U.S. to be an accredited investor simply means one can certify they have either an annual income of $250,000 or net assets of over one million dollars. Many people in the U.S. satisfy these criteria, as in Europe, but simply satisfying this does not make them an investor. It is good that capital can flow for nominal amounts under $100,000 from individuals. It makes the U.S. a place of abundance and signals a willingness to take the excessive risk that comes with early stage seed investment. These investments happen in the E.U. through groups like the European Business Angel Network, although to a lesser extent and not as public showcase.

Look for investors who have start, run, and sold several businesses. They will have a deeper understanding of what entrepreneurship means. The investors who only worked in corporations and saved money can add value but they can be problematic if they think they know how to run a startup business. The individual investor who was born into money will likely add no value, if they are willing to stay away and let the entrepreneur build a business then it can work. Investors who were formerly investment bankers tend to be the most professional and financially sophisticated. They also tend to be the most challenging ones to work with because they will be overconfident and are used to people chasing them for money. Investors may not be all that tolerant of niceties and civil conduct so do not expect them to respectful of your time or say encouraging things.

Funding Stages

If you get this far, pass the seed round, make sure you understand the term sheets. At this stage, the financing gets complex and becomes a financial engineering and legal exercise to structure deals so they work for all parties involved. A successful company will find and hire partners who are experienced at addressing these complexities. Serial entrepreneurs will learn quickly and if they have survived the first experience, they will try again and be much better prepared for this stage in the company financing.

Venture Capitalist vary in what they consider interesting deals to invest. Look for first round early stage investors if you got seed investment and have built enough of an asset to warrant continuing the business. Many investors do not take part in early stages and wait for the companies to grow a bit and prove the market before they jump in. You need to have a real business for this class of investor. To get investment from them you need to understand what a term sheet is and how to negotiate the deal. They do not waste time with inexperience and want to invest with entrepreneurs who know what they are doing. This is one of the reasons why getting the right seed round investors matters so much. They can help if they are professional investors. If they are friends and family or an individual who took a bet, it can be a huge obstacle to getting the next round of professional investors.

Later stage investor funding is only available for growth of companies that are viable and have proven results that are trending towards a huge market. These later stage investors can be a mixture of types: corporate strategic co-investors, hedge funds wanting to take a position in a growing market, or private equity funds.. How to deal at a higher level is omitted from this book since this subject needs an entire book to cover. Suffice to advise, if you get this far make sure you have a great deal of experience on your team. This is where the inexperienced founding team gets pushed out of the company or take on new roles to let experienced people grow the company.

Funding Odds

The odds of getting early stage funding are very low but this is not a reason to get discouraged, most people do not try and those who do often quit. If you continue trying and give it time, and adjust to what you find, your chances increase quickly. If you can bootstrap a company and remain within your affordable loss, you have a much higher chance of survival.

Get started on your personal finances so you increase the odds that you can fund your startup phase. The odds of funding through bootstrapping are excellent since it depends on what you do to build a product and get the first customers. Early stage funding from an angel investor or venture capitalist has little chance no matter how good you are or how good the product is. In working with venture capital firms, they evaluate hundreds of plans a year and invest in less than one percent of those they look at with most plans submitted not read. One VC I consulted for, has a target of five hundred qualified plans to evaluate a year with one percent getting an investment. They have a small team of recent MBA graduate in the first round review, afterwards they get to the general partners of the fund who will make the investment decision.

Once an entrepreneur realizes this they understand why it is necessary to bootstrap the company and fund it themselves and with customer engagements. What is ironic is that when the company is bootstrapped, does not need investment, and is growing fast, that is when it is most likely that investors will want to fund the company. Therefore, similar to getting a loan from a bank, it is much easier to be approved if you do not need the money. This is just human nature: if you have a job it is easier to get a better one, if you are out of work for a longtime it gets harder to get a job. Knowing this I have intentionally tried not to fall into this thinking and I prefer hiring people who are not working. When I have served as a judge for business plan competitions, I vote for the team I think can make best use of the money to make progress. Unfortunately, this method of funding allocation is not the way the world works.

Increasing the Odds

To increase the odds of getting funding you will need to first fund the business yourself, build an extensive network, get a solid team, deliver a viable product to market, show increasing adoption, and not wait for external funding. Then you can fund for growth, not survival, and the additional funding is used to scale the company. That puts you in a position to negotiate the terms of the funding since you can survive as a business without it.

If you were to fund a company this is what you would want to see, so this is just good business. If you can learn how to run a company then you become attractive to investors. They want to find deals that will succeed. They are naturally skeptical and look for a few things: a demonstration of focus, business talent, measurable progress. These are not difficult to learn. Mastering the strategies and techniques requires years of being in business. Investors understand when you are doing something breakthrough such as a new venture that will change the world, that no one has done it before so you are charting new territory with lots of risk, so they expect the business to manage the uncertainty and emerge as a success.

Another way of increasing the odds is to have already started a previous company that made money for investors. They like to fund serial entrepreneurs who make money even when the second company has less chance of success than the previous one. This is true if you started a company and it failed. You could take the experience and assets and start a second company and this time make progress. Resilience is an attractive trait to investors - it shows that you are not going to give up no matter what the setbacks. They want to see that you are in it for life and you will not quit. This is a view on your economic life and self-determination and how you see your ability to thrive versus the alternative of working in an institutional setting.

Bootstrapping

The sensible way start-ups grow with limited resources is bootstrapping. It is the secret to business success, but is not popular since it is so hard to do. Without being able to do this, your chances of survival are low. It is basic business to work with the means and not to exceed your capacity. Managing to your means and mitigating the risk of running out of cash are critical to a business. It is just a determined way of using scarce resources in the most efficient way that you can devise. Learning how to bootstrap a company will make you attractive to an investor when you do need to raise capital.

Why Bootstrap

Bootstrapping lets you preserve ownership and control of the company. Being a good steward and acting prudently are qualities that you can use in all business. You may need to bootstrap if you do not have access to external funding or the funds you can get are limited. The desire to keep ownership control and increase income and wealth is a strong motivator for entrepreneurs to bootstrap. Why start a business to work for the investors? With bootstrapping, it teaches how to create an effective business that reduces exposure to risk. The team that follows your passion and believes they can create value for customers is required to think prudently and take stewardship of the mission and values of the company. This degree of commitment will not be present with an investor; an investor who wants to quantify the social return on investment will consider the metrics of performance and be dispassionate about the business. As hard as it is to start a business, an entrepreneur needs to sustain the drive and continue beyond all obstacles, so a feeling of stewardship is important. The sense of stewardship is easy to observe in family businesses where the business name is the same as the family name. A sense of pride of ownership takes hold and no one wants to see its reputation diminished, the drive to survive dominates the culture of these businesses.

Founder Activities

Founders need to show the path forward and chart the course. They are always selling, enrolling resources, and controlling how they use the scarce resources. They are focused on finding ways to achieve the business goals and investing in the creation of a winning product. They want to lessen the need for outside financing, maximize the funding capital they receive, and find creative methods for optimizing cash flow. The daily mantra is perpetually selling the vision to enroll the help needed to get all this done. We covered the topic of founders in the chapter on Entrepreneurial Spirit so this puts in context the activities and focus of the founder, in particular the one designated as the CEO. The rest of the founding team may engage in this, from within the respective roles they have taken.

Burn Rate

Learning basic accounting will go a long way toward helping you track how the money is being spent and whether you will deplete your resources. The burn rate is a term that refers to the rate at which you deplete your funding as you invest in building aspects of the business against the return on that investment. The issue is the timing of the money flows. It is seldom the case where the customers will pay before the business has spent the money to create the product. You may be able to get committed orders for the product then against that future cash flow convince an investor to fund the product distribution. Managing the cash, risk to return, and timing is critical for the business and every Euro spent counts. Being prudent, diligent with tracking, and frugal with money can ease pains later in the business. It is easy to be foolish and not have a sense of proportionality. For example, being tight on spending small amounts and not diligent about deciding on large amounts that are assumed necessary cost.

The fixed recurring costs are the easiest to mistake and slowly deplete cash without a clear result, so turn as many of your costs into variable cost that do not exceed a budgeted allocation. Then convert to fix cost those that are clearly essential. In New York City, many options exist for temporary office space where the cost is based on the number of people and most of the facilities are shared resources. You do not need a conference room for 8 hours of the day or the cost of an office-copying machine. Working globally, you may be on the phone most of the time and not meeting with people in person. Things have changed drastically in the last ten years and alternatives are available for managing what were once fixed costs. In one of my previous ventures, we got an office at a prestigious location with enough space to grow. We thought an office on Madison and 42nd Street would matter to customers. The office was mostly empty for the life of the company, sales and business development was on the road, we had no customers in New York City. I was in Europe each month for a week and with the development in India, customers in as far away as South Africa. That office rent was wasted; no customers cared and we could have used the money to add developers or marketing. Unfortunately, we were stuck with an expensive multi-year rental lease.

Matching cost to revenue is hard to do in the early stages of the company but it is necessary. Figuring what are the unit costs to manufacture, sell and deliver product to the customers will put the emphasis where it is needed. The margin can be determined based on the price the market is willing to pay less the total unit cost. If the margin is not what is typical for the industry then you will have to determine how to create more value so the product can sell at a higher price and the manufacturing needs to get the cost down to get more margin. I did consulting work for a venture-backed company that had two large corporations as customers and strategic investors. The cost of servicing them as customers was enormous, greater than the investment and the projected revenue. While it is attractive to get large customers and get them to invest, if the profitability of the deal has little hope, then there is no point in doing the business. The reluctance to fire the customers or to say no to an investment is high for the entrepreneur and this unwillingness compromises the company's negotiating position to get to a profitable business structure.

The earlier example of fixed cost of real estate falls into the category of General and Administrative and Furniture, Fixtures, and Equipment. This is business language for how accountants classify certain costs. This is usually termed overhead -- the costs that are incurred that are not part of the cost of producing and selling the product. Add to this travel cost that salespeople will incur and the funding can disappear fast. Much of this has to be controlled and the best way to learn this is to use you own money first, that will highlight this importance well. If you were to start the company with other people's money, you may not build up an appreciation for how an uncontrolled burn rate can sink the business and increase the need for capital.

Next is the largest cost: staff labor for core skills. If you are in the high tech business then this cost can be much higher than the average for a business. Make sure to isolate what is core and what is not and outsource as much of the noncore work to skilled labor in other countries where you can get better value. What might seem to be cheap outsourcing resources relative to the same skills in your country may be expensive when compared to the salaries paid in the other country. Outsourcing, carries its own risk and cost beyond the obvious cost of labor. With the founding team and early first employees, paying a portion in equity is necessary as both an alignment of interest and as a cash conservation tactic. The in-demand skills fetch higher salaries, therefore the higher the overall cost which is the reason to solve problems in the simplest way possible. The tendency of over engineering that is common among high tech firms inflicts a hefty cost burden, so avoid this and keep things simple.

Once you have the product and think that sales either cannot happen or will grow without marketing you then hit the next big cost item. Sales will complain the customer never heard of the company or the product and investors will send emails on every company they read about and the pressure is on to spend money on marketing and press releases. Unfortunately, marketing is not performance-based and the level of marketing spent may not correlate to sales. What many ventures do not figure out is to know how the customers decide. Until this is known, the effective marketing program cannot be determined.

Accounting

Turn accounting from a chore to an asset. If you can figure out how to gain insight from the accounting information then it may become a useful tool to discover where the business is relative to where you thought it would be. It can serve as a diagnostic in the best-case. To do this, you must establish the metrics for success and develop a way of gathering that information without interfering with the business or adding cost. You should research the industry benchmarks so you can measure your performance against your direct competitors and an idealized best practice. The metrics are then presented as a scorecard or dashboard over a period of time that is useful for making decisions. This is why the chart of accounts can be invaluable. When done well it can help record and account for activity at the right level of granularity to be useful for tracking the business.

The issues are reporting the metrics honestly when they are qualitative. This might be conducting a survey of customer satisfaction and not by means of biasing the survey design to get the desired results. With the accounting reports, the scorecard, and qualitative metrics, you get a picture of the business, but this might not be enough. You may need to isolate what decisions matter and figure out what just cannot be determined no matter how rigorous the tracking is and instead use intuitive judgment. Knowing what this is lets you test your intuition gradually instead of just giving in and resigning yourself to ad-hoc daily crisis management in the belief that nothing can be controlled and trying to do so is useless. The company needs to have operational control to be the foundation for managing for growth. You want your sales to grow, not your costs.

Cash Flow and Break-even

Early stage ventures need to track their cash flow carefully and race to break-even. Cash flow is simple to understand: money in minus money out, taking into consideration a safety threshold where the business does not run out of cash before it can get money in. For pre-revenue venture backed firms, the cash in came from the invested capital used to form the business, so it is easy to lose perspective and focus on revenue when the product does not exist yet. Apart from cash management, racing to break-even is the second most important focus. This is the recurring sales plus new sales minus fixed and variable cost,. When the sales are greater than the cost, the company has reached break-even. Sustainable profit is not trivial to achieve while growing. Cost and sales are not linear and have timing effects, so influencing the cash position, and learning how to track and manage this is critical to the early survival of a new venture.

Accounting will be too simplistic when you start to understand the internal dynamics of the market and the customers, it is the best that business can do now. The accounting systems are governed by standard practices that establish a common language that can be evaluated by auditors who can certify the accounting conforms to the generally accepted account practices.

Compound Annual Growth Rate

To calculate the compound annual growth rate CAGR =

(end value/beginning value)^(1/number of years)–1

27% = (150.1 Billion / 56.3 Billion) ^ (1 / 4) - 1

Investors want exponential growth and are impatient. They will settle for cubic growth and when they do not see linear growth early, they get nervous. This can be frustrating for the founders. Once professional investors have funded the company the entrepreneur must understand that the business needs to produce results in the short term while allocating resources in the potential for exponential grow in the future. The longer you invest in creating the product and the longer the market takes to adopt it, the higher the risk. This applies to all businesses, not just those with network economics that are scale-free like many of the Internet and mobile startups that get venture capital funding.

Even with a retail store it takes time before people know that it opened, what it sells and at what price and quality. You get ten customers and three come back, then they bring one friend and things start to grow fast if it works. The race and focus on growth is not just in the early stages, it is constant. Billion dollar multinational companies need to show CAGR to shareholders to sustain the stock price. Early growth is hard to start but easy to sustain since going from zero to anything is a huge jump and as time goes by the business hits a steady state and the growth is not as dramatic so new growth strategies are needed to push to the next level. This perpetual regeneration is what fast growing ventures do; they are building on previous success by continuing to innovate the business structure to push the CAGR to be as high as possible. The trajectory sets the future valuation of the company. It is this process, the entrepreneur needs to have a sense of when to exit, and get an optimal return. They then move on to the next business.

There are many ways to get a top line growth on gross sales other than selling additional products. One company I had the fortune to help grow did it through acquisitions, buying up four competitor companies to aggregate the market with each acquisition increasing the top line sales figures. This is called a roll up strategy and it is reserved for experienced entrepreneurs who can manage under this rapid change. The first time entrepreneur has to prove they can get a company going, grow it organically, and use the various strategies previously described, then they might get investment, matched with experience to go on an aggressive market consolidation, and sustained CAGR. Focus on how to do this with one company and product first before getting too far with the possibilities.

Financial Markets

Pick up a financial newspaper, look at the stock charts, then research financial technical analysis, and find the graphic visualization charts that investors use to analyze public market performance. You will not find the picture of the CEO or the products in these charts; they are strictly financial without qualitative information. A venture capitalist with a small fund of 50 million dollars is putting that money to work while they find the suitable start-up companies to invest. This is what they are looking at everyday, so when you come walking in the door asking for an investment and have no numbers to show them what do you think they will say?

Investors are managing money so their views of the world are the numbers; this is true for venture capital and private equity firms that have ex-investment bankers as general partners. They do not know about the details of your business issues nor do they care. They want financial performance and growth that is better than the public markets. Therefore, the entrepreneur has to convince them that the new company, without a record of accomplishment to show, has potentially higher returns for the risk than they are doing now. Venture capitalist are predisposed to having this belief already, they still want the entrepreneur to convince them. They will reject all assumptions and speculation and want to hear the arguments for why you believe so strongly in the market potential beyond the gut feel or overconfidence or blind faith. Your belief in the business is like a religion and you need to convert them into a follower.

Investors want to believe their startup investments are the next billion-dollar company to go IPO and they are tracking the competitors to compare how you are doing against their expectations. They want to think they can smell the next big winner and can pick the horse, jockey, race track, race event and know the track conditions they are running on, predicting the weather and winner. They expect to see the basics of business evident on your team. Beyond that, they want an extra mysterious ingredient that makes it special. They want you to convince them but they want to think you cannot. They will believe they are making an objective decision. Yet this is not possible with a new venture, since there is no historical performance available; their decision is reduced to speculation on the future markets and the people making them happen. Therefore investors make the final decision based on speculation, although they would never admit this.

As an entrepreneur, you need to be well aware of the financial markets, how they work, why they break, and the signals for daily sentiment on the market confidence perception. They are premised on the efficient market hypothesis and assume transparency of information and protections against market manipulation and unfair trading. With the vast array of financial instruments to learn about this can be daunting to the novice. Without being able to get in the heads of the investors in every way, you are unlikely to fully understand all the influences in their thinking and willingness to do risky investments. This holds true for a class of buyers, high net worth individuals, corporate executives at public corporations, people with pensions, and anyone who has a direct interest in whether their future, as predicted by the public market, on a given day is good or bad. It is the financial weather report that sways sentiment in positive or negative direction, and this can influence your risk tolerance. If you want investor money, think like an investor first and invest your money in the public markets and in your business.

Funding from Founders, Family, Friends

Communication with these stakeholders must be open, honest, direct and frequent, to uphold trust and support. It requires professional and formal agreements for all investment and involvement without exception. Bad news needs to be communicated with good news and while it is always necessary to be selling, you must be transparent enough so people can make their own decisions. Short of news of bankruptcy bad news can be communicated with a plan to remedy the situation or mitigate the risk or looking to improve in the future. When you make a mistake just own it and admit that you did not know whether the decision would work. You may not know enough to ask. Taking responsibility and having a plan and positive outlook goes a long way toward maintaining support. Beware of the sideline critic who never has anything good to say, or offers value to the situation; these people can easily disrupt the confidence of others so they need to be handled separately.

Startups have an intrinsic family dynamic because of the typical sources of investment and the founding team requiring a high degree of trust. While they may not be blood relatives, a closely held company will often have its own dynamics and dysfunctions. This is where a high degree of professionalism matters, to temper the tendency of the familiar, which can invoke contempt when things go bad and too much trust when they are going good. As much as people will say business is impersonal I have never found that to be the case -- it is personal and intimate. The main point is to strive to be as objective as possible while recognizing the impossibility of that happening yet insisting that everyone at least try. If everyone operated on objective fact, no business would ever be started or funded, so blind faith is needed at the start of a business.

Approximately 85% of all ventures are funded by family, friends, and fools, with the fools being the least of the money. Much of this money is coming from people who are not professional investors who have not run a business themselves, do not know anything about the industry you are targeting, and have little to go on to base an investment decision other than confidence in the founding team and a sense the business concept might be marginally interesting. They would have read about the ridiculous valuations that other young companies have gotten and the fast exits and that many of them were started by people no smarter or talented than their cousin, or nephew or friend. You have an obligation to these people to not just sell them on your business. You have to make the personal sacrifice and to disclose all the known risk while maintaining your enthusiasm for the possible return they may get in the future. In your excitement if you oversell and convince them knowing that what you are doing is highly risky you may have consequences in the future that will not be pleasant. The same goes for the return potential. Once professional investors get involved they do not care one bit about your relationship to your family and friends and will revalue the company to their advantage. If you have a family or friend who has a large percentage of the company, they can block the next investment, putting you into a difficult situation.

Make sure the capital structure is clear and documented with signed agreements. Too many times I have seen cash and credit cards used to fund the company with little accounting so people are sure what they own and what others own of the company. Spoken and handshake agreements and how they are remembered always create a problem once real money is involved. Do not make promises verbally that you do not keep. I was advising a young entrepreneur who had raised over 300K from friends and family and along the way was making many promises to people that he never documented and those people did work with the expectation the promises would be kept. How he remembered what he said and how the other people recalled it were different. When it came time to raise money, a few of the people who had been working without agreements blocked the next round of funding by taking the founder to court. A lawsuit by the staff is the fastest way to kill the company and that is what happened. Make sure the capital structure is clear and everyone has a shareholder agreement.

I had a European client, which had been in startup mode for over seven years, never closed a sale, and did not have a product ready for the market. They were a high tech business and had received E.U. funding from grants for R&D and innovation. They raised money from friends and family with fifteen people as owners. None of founders or investors were engineers or scientists. All of them had valuation expectations that were so inflated that it was hard to get them to realize that a company that had raised public money and private investment from friends and family, and had no sales and no product, would be valued at zero by professional investors. To make matters worse, as is typical in family businesses, the decisions were all by consensus and the founder would not make a decision without including everyone. Add to this tracking who loaned money to the company versus invested in equity and what each expected to get as a return and by what timeframe was so varied that to help this company meant I had to tell them things that none of them wanted to hear. Fundraising is important, but creating a product and selling is the most important. Do not be a professional fundraiser with a company that has not sold products that brought in total revenue that is valued less than the investment.

Bootstrap Culture

If you want to be a successful entrepreneur, learn the culture and practices that have been in place for as long as humans have been trading shells. Be frugal, treat cash as king, and find the cheapest creative solution possible, make "good enough" your friend and save the quality for where it matters most. It is desirable to achieve the same outcome with the fewest resources possible. Take stewardship of the business and responsibility for failure and use it to learn and make sure to share the success with others. Stewardship is a sense of obligation to make the best possible use of the resources made available to the business from its stakeholders. Cash in the business is the most valuable resource, treat cash as if it was your money and especially precious when it has come from others who put faith in your team. The bootstrap culture focuses on sales and having a product that people want to buy and pay a premium for so you can get cash flowing and get to break-even fast, then continue to push to get to a growth momentum that takes the company into the possible realm of bringing a return on the investment.

The topic of this book has been on fast growth ventures using the strategies of high tech startups. The assumption that many might have is that tech startups get venture funding. This is not true for most companies that get started; only a tiny percentage qualify for venture capital. The ones that learn to bootstrap will have a much higher survival rate as entrepreneurs even if the particular business they started collapses. If they learned how to bootstrap they are likely to start another company or do consulting or create a break-through innovation within an existing company. The resilience and focus it takes to build a business without investors is one that sharpens the attention and priorities.

Bootstrapping is not something that the startup programs ever talk about. They are set up to help venture capitalist find deals, and this is the main criticism of the incubator and accelerator. If they told the entrepreneurs, forget investors until you are ready to scale the company and instead figure out how to bootstrap, most the entrepreneurs would do far better. Then you create a sales presentation instead of an investor pitch, they would figure out how to elicit support from partners to get the product sourced, and in so doing, they would be much better prepared to raise friends and family money instead of wasting precious time chasing investors. In effect, the investors find the deals they want; it is not the entrepreneur finding the investors. If you have a great company started, the investors will be asking to invest. If the company is weak, you will be begging for money. If you are looking to fund your life style then do no start the company and expect an investor to fund it. If this is disturbing news then go work for a company. It is probably a mistake for you to start one up now. The life style sacrifices that an entrepreneur needs to make is a harsh reality but given the potential future rewards, this should not prevent you from trying to start a business.

Funding Negotiations

Before going into negotiations you should be clear on what your values are, what is important to you, why are you in business and why with the team and the product. Recognize that your value system and that of the investors might not match; they are not entrepreneurs -- they want to make money from money and from your effort, period. No matter what they tell you, they are committed to getting a return. If this troubles you, then do not raise money from an investor. Maybe taking on debt instead of equity is better but you may have the same conflict of values. Get over it fast; this world of finance is not going to change to fit your view. To get through the process, you have to go into the negotiations as dispassionately as the investors do. The position you want to be in is to have bootstrapped the company so you own it and can negotiate. While you may want money to grow the company, you do not need it and are not forced to do a deal that is not in your interest.

Enroll help from your network, from people who have raised money, have invested in the company, or anyone who has experience. If they do not have experience then do not get them involved; that will confuse the decision process and the investor will stop immediately and not waste time. Make sure you are dealing with professional investors and not charlatans who want to use your company to list on an unregulated exchange and raise money for you that way. I was called to help a company that got involved with investors who used money that was untraceable. They got involved in securities fraud and it almost sank the company. Outside the U.S., securities laws may not be so exact and all schemes are possible and in the U.S. securities fraud has a long history so watch out for this.

While I always advise to negotiate the business terms first, before getting a lawyer or accountant involved, when it comes to funding or mergers and acquisitions I advise the opposite. You need a lawyer and accountant as part of your team so you fully understand all the implications of what the investment terms means. Learn how the investors are protecting their interest and what exposed risk you are taking, including consequences for the future. Understanding the terms of a financing deal is complex and uses specialized language that lawyers draft for other lawyers. Many investment bankers are lawyers even if they are non-practicing so you may be at a significant disadvantage.

In the U.S. tech start-up community, the deal terms at various stages are routine and well known to many. Outside the U.S. this may not be common knowledge and therefore simple structural mistakes may happen. I am not a lawyer, but in the last year I had to advise a company and their lawyer on the components of the shareholders agreement for the founders to anticipate what may happen in the future once investors get involved. It took many rounds of back and forth to get the document accurate. The founders, left with just the lawyer would not have figured this out. This is one area where experience matters. While other areas of business you want to learn by doing, this is not one of those areas. You want to avoid making a mistake that is irreversible and costs you money or worse -- ownership of the company.

Knowing how the funding process works helps to smooth out the problems since you will not be surprised or learning the process as you are doing it. It can be an expensive lesson to negotiate a deal for the first time. Investors are not your friends, they are investing to make money. They might need you to do well, but they are most interested in the results and want to own as much of it for the risk they are taking, and you will allow. Needing cash to support the company puts you in a compromised situation where you cannot afford to walk away from an interested investor. This is one reason to bootstrap the company, so you do not need the investment to survive and you want the funding to grow at a rate that you desire.

Summary of Funding

Investors fund experience, not trainees, so start the business and show that you learned enough that an investor should take a chance on your team and business. You have to self-fund your business before anyone else will. If you cannot, then work for ten years, save your money, then when the company fires you, you will have a severance and start a business out of necessity. Not everyone can start a business, but everyone is able to join a startup business or small to medium enterprise. It helps to think and act like an entrepreneur, so no excuses. You can be an entrepreneur by acting like one in your current situation, just create new value for the company and watch how that creates rewards.

Learning how to bootstrap a business is just good business and there is no shortcut for doing this. Investors are not funding your training to make mistakes with their money; they want you to make mistakes with your money first. Invest in understanding the customer and building the product. Then sell,

sell, sell, lower your fixed costs and make them mostly variable, and make sure to manage cash and speed to break-even. If you want to raise investor money, this is how to do it so you set the terms of the investment for growth and also retain a good portion of the company.

Do not waste your time if you think you will just casually try to get funding to start a business and if it does not work, you will just get a job. For that, just get a job now. If you can afford an expensive education get an MBA and go work for a company. If you want to make a difference then invest in starting a business since that is the best way to learn business, is to do it. Trying to run a business will make you valuable for a company that hires you in the future. This skill is useful for many kinds of work including within a government administration or university.

Business Lore

Up to this point, the book has been filled with my own observation, notes, opinions, patterns, and critique on entrepreneurship and how it can be applied to creating value. When I first started working in industry I had no clue about this. I thought I would just go work for a bank, make money, then retire someday with a pension. Yet I noticed that in the corporate business setting, certain patterns reoccur. I could not uncover what these were or where they came from. I absorbed as much as I could and after working in industry for ten years I took the leap to becoming an entrepreneur and abandoned my previous mistaken understanding of my own economic life: that a corporation was the path to riches and a fulfilling life.

I made a good deal of money working for corporations, for which I am thankful. The savings allowed me to move on and become an entrepreneur as a means of reclaiming my self-determination and humanity. This allowed me to discover a deeper understanding of the forces at work that influenced my own life and those of many entrepreneurs who thrive every day throughout the world but are not celebrated. The layers of patterns I learned as an entrepreneur continued to unfold as I discovered that patterns in our brains and patterns of a designed environment influence our understanding of the world and how to work within its structures. With this in mind, I embarked on teaching and coaching entrepreneurs these patterns. Again, I encountered that much of what I thought was new already pre-existed in other forms, I was just unable to recognize it. The book reflects my current understanding and my best effort at trying to explain how to think and act as an entrepreneur and this last section shows how much has been borrowed from design patterns that have been around for possibly thousands of years.

Business has an implied understanding that has a lot in common with universal design principles, which I refer to collectively as Business Lore. These are notions that are often taken for granted or turned into management clichés under various names and stories. While not based in reason they are understood by convention, historical occurrence, mandate, or just comforting familiarity.

These are culturally biased, and appreciated in form, to varying degrees, in the East or the West. This is by no means an exhaustive list; it simply highlights for the readers' appreciation a sampling and business interpretation for further study and observation. The emphasis is on acquiring a taste, a sense for form and pattern of structure, what people call vision or intuition or common sense. These are not a means test for good practice, they can be helpful when observed in communication with others.

One can call attention to a recurring pattern or that a known approximation is present and whether that is what others understand or if in the particular situation that tendency is by design, artifact, circumstance or natural random occurrence. I refer to these as business lore, as in folklore, part of the beliefs and myths of structures and patterns that may feel like natural law. They may be part of an artificial human social construction that was observed as present in the psychic memes of business. Use them to compose your business structure and recognize that you are not alone. The journey of entrepreneurship has been traveled by many throughout millennium and the patterns persist. In our modern world they are lost in the encoding of the power structures of control we are subjected to and overcome with our entrepreneurial spirit when we can spot the pattern

The _80/20 Rule_ is a high percentage of effects in a large system are caused by a low percentage of variables. This is known as Pareto's Law and is a cliché of business productivity. The point is to focus on the most important things first, not the trivial tasks that can consume the entire day. The contrary view is the 80% does not go away and often that 80% is assumed to have been done so that is taken as a given. This design pattern is mentioned as a cliché when the 80% was done at the exclusion of the 20% that could have a dramatic impact.

The _Advance Organizer_ is a technique that helps people understand new information by what they already know. This relates to the absorption of the familiar at ever faster rates until one believes they have expertise in an area without realizing the accumulation of familiar information prevents absorbing information that does not match the prior knowledge and that new information may be immediately filtered as either unreliable or just cannot be seen. This is how businesses are blinded by their own success if it persists too long without disruption.

The _Cathedral Effect_ is a relationship between the perceived height of a ceiling and cognition. High ceilings promote abstract thinking and creativity. Low ceilings promote concrete and detail-oriented thinking. This is similar to the vision versus execution balance in entrepreneurship. Being consumed with detail can cripple the imagination but not attending to the details within the expansive space of the vision will not make it real. Building the cathedral starts with the first stone. The other analogy is the cathedral versus the bazaar; the cathedrals are monuments to authority while the bazaar is where the merchants and customers live. Entrepreneurs visit the cathedrals once a week but do not stay in them for long and instead spend most of the week making money in the bazaar.

Cognitive Dissonance is a tendency to seek consistency among attitudes, thoughts, and beliefs. This is closely related to other design patterns and one that is critically important for designing a business. If the business is asking its customers to do something that is not consistent with the current behaviors and beliefs, the business and product will struggle to get adoption. It has to be familiar and different at the same time but not introduce dissonance in what the customers already understand.

Desire Line is traces of use or wear that indicate preferred methods or interaction with an object or the environment. This phenomenon is so often missed in designing the business. Observe where people walk instead of where the architects decided the pavements should be. Crack up the old pavement and put the new pavement where people walk. Architects often create monuments to the benefactors or worse themselves and these structures have little to do with the people who will use them. Avoid the tendency to do what you want, or worse what the investors want, and instead do what your customers want. I have seen far too many funded ventures that where monuments to the founders and investors that could never survive as a business yet may have raised tens of millions of dollars -- what a waste of capital.

Forgiveness patterns are notion that designs should help people avoid errors and minimize the negative consequences of errors when they do occur. This recognizes that humans have flawed perceptions and the best designs will not always be used in the way they were intended. I recall the first time I put a computer mouse on a PC, the CFO came by, saw the new device, ask what is it, then picked it up and moved it in the air, then put it against his ear, then tried it as a microphone, then saw the little rolling ball and understood what it did. Was he out of touch? Alternatively, did he anticipate gestural interfaces with voice commands that still have not become prevalent in user interfaces?

Garbage in Garbage out is the quality of system output is dependent on the quality of the system input. In information theory, this is finding the signal in the noise. If it is all noise then no signal will be found. This cliché might have a new interpretation for business that recycling gives a new place for waste. The business might be extracting the quality from the garbage as in the data analytics tech businesses attempt to do. Think of the enormous amounts of spam email and the attempts to manipulate the search engines and one can see how garbage in creates the conditions for a business to provide value out. The premise of this design is about the amount of energy needed to get quality out of garbage will be much higher than if quality materials were developed at the start.

Hick's Law is the time it takes to make a decision increases as the number of alternatives increases. In business, this is not just the alternatives and includes the variables with each. In a planet of abundance, this may produce many variations on a theme to give an abundance of undifferentiated options to the consumers for products that are not functionally different. The alternatives might just be surface features and the business is stuck on the trivial. Entrepreneurs will figure out how to impose constraints to help solve problems or to redefine them. When too many options exist, it may be necessary to remove them in order to make progress. This is counter intuitive and I have seen entrepreneurs have many false starts by being too entertained with the pursuit of alternatives, each one causing a restart before the previous alternative was not played out enough to determine whether it would make money.

Law of Pragnanz is a tendency to interpret ambiguous images as simple and complete instead of complex and incomplete. This is avoiding the nuances and dynamic nature of complex systems where the emergent patterns cannot be easily anticipated. Over simplifying complex problems can lead to disaster. An example is the potential consequences of global warming. The contrary is dangerous, making simple problems arbitrarily complex thinking that this adds to the perception of value.

Not invented here is a bias against ideas and innovations that originate elsewhere. Businesses do this all the time and sometimes by design to make it easier for the team to identify with being different from the competition. This can be fatal when done with critical aspects of the business where it is not necessary and would have been far better to source a solution from a supplier. Just because the construction crew can bake bricks made on the premises does not mean they should do this. Buy the bricks, do not make them.

Recognition over Recall is memory for recognizing things is better than memory for recalling things. In business, this can be frequently observed when presenting new products to customers and they respond with recognizing a pattern that solves a problem they have. If one was to ask the customer what they wanted, to recall when they had a particular problem and whether an abstract solution would work, the customer cannot tell you, or if they do recall from imagination they are likely making up an answer that is unreliable. This creates a real dilemma for the entrepreneur who might conclude that if they just build the solution then the customers will come once they see the value, which is seldom the case. Designers are well versed in the art of interpreting how customers may perceive an object.. They create objects and services that are easy for the users to recognize and use the recognition to recall a function or behavior that is familiar. When the recognition and recall is not balanced, the business and product may be confusing to the consumers.

Satisficing is defined as, when it is preferable to settle for a satisfactory solution rather than pursue an optimal solution. Businesses need to make money, as soon as possible get to break-even. This causes an entrepreneur to focus on the positive outcomes as they surface through discovery and what becomes important is whether whatever led to the positive outcome can be repeated consistently over time. If it is good enough and makes money, then it wins. It is challenging for tech entrepreneurs who may strive for perfection or optimal solutions and are disturbed by a fickle consumer that responds to marketing messages over actual best technical solution. The best technical solution seldom wins over the solution that is easiest for the buyer to understand that still solves the problems or desire they have.

Scaling Fallacy is a tendency to assume that a system that works at one scale will work at a smaller or larger scale. The new venture business that is doing something innovative may test the market with prototypes and go through co-creation with customers and suppliers. It is not practical to do this with the entire segmented market, therefore a representative portion is part of the experiment. The problem happens when the entrepreneur assumes that if the product works for ten customers that it will work for ten million. Scaling manufacturing production and distribution delivery are major challenges for any business. When these are solved the next level of scaling problems might be how to service the product in the field.

Veblen Effect is a tendency to find a product desirable because it has a high price. This design insight is in effect in every venture finance deal where the company is given an arbitrary high valuation, which is not based on market evidence other than a belief the product will lead the market and easily scale without obstacles. This can be seen in the luxury market where high margins and pricing is a necessity for customer appeal. Customers are willing to ascribe value to high priced items because of artificial scarcity.

Wabi-Sabi are objects and environments that embody naturalness, simplicity, and subtle imperfection to achieve a deeper, meaningful aesthetic. For a successful business, perfection is not the motivation for making money.

The entrepreneur recognizes that representations are approximations and that managing the business takes judgment so that messy workflows can function. The standard accounting practices would have the ledger balance out perfectly. Yet when they are off by a few pennies due to rounding errors it may not be worth spending the time to get a perfect net balance of zero between the credits and debits. Understanding imperfection can be an asset in making rapid progress.

Weakest Link is the use of a weak element that will fail in order to protect other elements in the system from damage. This is counter intuitive and exists in hiring practices where the desire is for everyone to be an A player but a few B and C players are necessary to act as a balance and protection against over stressed growth. By monitoring the weak links, one can assess the level of pressure on the entire staff. This does not mean the weakest link is an underperformer relative to the pool of all talent, but he or she may be weaker than the best employees.

These design patterns are a small sampling of the business lore embedded in the assumptions that are made about correctness and acceptance in the interactions amongst business parties. Many patterns exist with the above list of interpretations offering a starting point of departure for helping young entrepreneurs see them with clarity so they gain experience in reading these social constructs. Practice evaluating each situation on these terms to extract the patterns you are observing and set up the reflective learning process that helps the business grow rapidly.

Exercises

After reading this book, participate in the on-line forums and review the references for further study. Find a peer to practice with since these exercises are best done in small teams.

Instructions: complete the following simple exercises to express your business concept. Write down your answers and practice by presenting them to friends and team mates.

These exercises will seem simplistic until you try to do them in earnest. Write your answers down first. As you tell them to others, gauge their reactions. Are you being clear? Do you sound confused? Can they understand what you are saying? It is common to experience some difficulty on the first try. The exercises may be done as you read the book or you can wait to finish the entire book then reread the sections that help you think about how you would do the exercises.

You may try the exercises first if you like in the spirit of failing fast and learning by doing. I have taught a course that uses a summarized version of the content of this book and have experimented with several teaching methods. I used these exercises one year with little to no lectures and readings and the students got something out of it. If you live in a world of Twitter feeds and Facebook for breakfast and do not have the patience or attention to read a book, then just try the exercises and read the references until you can reclaim your humanity and control your time to focus on your future.

Entrepreneurship requires self-directed learning so you can devise the best learning path for your goals. I would much rather you try something, anything, than nothing. I do not want people to read the book then put it down and do nothing. I hope that if that is the case the person just stops reading in the first few pages and passes the book onto someone else. Not everyone is ready to be an entrepreneur, although my premise is that everyone will be forced to be entrepreneurial to survive, and gaining these skills early can ease the pain and help open up opportunities that otherwise might not have been seen.

The exercises are meant to be fun while challenging. You can make them easy or difficult, when you are ready. If they are too easy and it comes naturally to you then do them repeatedly in different context and with different business concepts. That is the point, entrepreneurship needs to be practiced not read about.

While you can do these exercises looking in the mirror, that would miss the point of the book. Entrepreneurship is what you do with others to create value. Do not be stuck on your ideas or do the exercises as a self-indulgence. Have fun, make it a game, take on the challenge. This is the game of life so get serious and make something happen.

Exercise: Would you hire yourself?

Would you hire yourself as the first employee of your company?

Do you need to be the CEO or President? If so why, if not why not?

Why are you the best person for the job of starting your company?

Could you pursue your passion at another company that shares the same values?

What are you about, your values, what is important to you?

Review the following list of words and pick out a few that represent what is important to you: wealth, order, pressure, take, wisdom, market, personal, pleasure, service, variety, inner, honest, loyalty, part, practice, security, stability, fame, freedom, financial, position, physical, open, serenity, supervising, alone, family, excitement, excellence, integrity, problems, self-respect, time, around, affection, creativity, effectiveness, change, community, democracy, authority, competition, efficiency, competition, cooperation, accountability, arts, development, challenge, competence, growth, country, advancement, achievement, decisiveness, adventure, awareness, caring, close, economic, fast, ethical, job, love, money, freedom, intellectual, harmony, helping, conformity,

EXERCISES

influencing, gain, growth, others, independence, friendship, leadership, knowledge, purity, relationship, status, promotion, responsibility, status, time, supervising, open, public, sophistication, tranquility, truth, work, society, reputation, respect, power, religion, privacy, location, meaningful, living, recognition, quality

List three values that you would not compromise.

List an additional two that are important to you.

As an entrepreneur, it is essential to know yourself first, without being self-absorbed. You need to develop the emotional stamina you will need for the long journey. This is the case if you simply plan to go work for a company but want to progress in a career by doing innovative efforts that may require you to take risk.

Exercise: Personal Branding

For example:

I am Ray Garcia a technology serial entrepreneur with 20 years of innovation experience. I coach new venture firms to launch and grow.

At Buoyant Capital, we acquire funding for emerging market companies by preparing their entities to qualify for private investment.

"Fostering entrepreneurship globally"

What is your personal sales pitch? You have to sell yourself before you can sell your product.

Be yourself, what is your essence, what is your value

Who you are, needs to align with what you do, for consistency.

A unique promise of value is the brand. Volvo = safety for example, it needs to be authentic.

It is not just the image; it needs grounding in the competence.

Ask others to describe you to see how closely the way they would represent you matches how you would represent yourself.

Your personal brand needs to be partly aspirational but mostly based on what you have accomplished and how you want it represented. Anyone who has interviewed successfully for a job would have done this, possibly without realizing it. The interviewer would of asked questions that have you sell yourself to them beyond whether you have the skills for the job but expect you to convince them that you are motivated to create value and that you have examples of applying your competencies.

Exercise: Your Inspiration

Using what you came up with in the previous exercises try to put it together into something coherent that you can state concisely. You can get good at interviewing by interviewing and most people just do not create enough chances to practice this before they have to do it in a real situation that matters to them. This would be like going on stage without a script to tell the story of your life to an audience of one. Write it down and practice it before you get on the stage.

Who are you?

Where did you come from?

What is your business concept?

Why are you the best first person to hire?

How will you start the business?

When will it need a team?

Will it change the world?

Jot down a brief answer to these questions that are consistent with your answers from the previous exercises and find a few people to tell them. In 5 minutes why you would hire yourself or you would make a good hire for the other persons company.

Showing motivation, enthusiasm for the future and your ability to make a difference will leave an impression. The investor or employer wants to understand whether you are curious and self-motivated enough to find your inspirations that will keep you motivated.

Exercise: Generating the ideas

Pick a few broad topics that interest you and one that you are less interested in, then combine them. These can be anything from water resources to food to health, the environment, urban or rural spaces, poverty, education, transportation, communications, financial inclusion, conflict, stopping crime, improving government, or other broad area of problems that you encounter daily or are aware of from your travels or that interest you from being troubled by seeing it in the news. Try to stay with areas that are global and big issues and avoid the common local or trivial issues.

For each area try to combine them, for example, health and education or urban and waste, or transportation and small manufacturing. It can be a hybrid between two areas that is not clearly related, like water and art, or food and nano-science. It creates the space for imagination to work across the boundaries of several areas.

Come up with ideas that are outrageous first, those that might defy laws of physics or seem impossible, then think of what might exist that is close to it already, and finally try and convert it to something that is grounded in the foundations of science and your reality. The last thing you want is a business that becomes a science experiment.

If you are stuck then do the reverse, start with an existing solution, decompose it into parts, and try to reconstruct an improvement that is dramatically better or just different.

Recall from the chapter on ideas, if you are unable to generate hundreds of ideas and rediscover the ideas that others have already pursued then you are unlikely to find a viable business. This is not about novelty; it is about creating value by reframing the problems into solutions that are viable.

Exercise: Selling the Idea = Execution

Part of forming the idea is to constrain it into a market and have a clear focus to drive the attention. Each of the aspects of this selling statement can be changed and shifted to fit into what is available and what is understood. Regardless of what the statement is, one needs to test it on the market. The easiest way to do this is to tell many people the statement and observe the reaction, responses, objections, acceptance, and adjust based on what you learn. For this exercise, keep it to under a minute and address one point for each item.

FOR target customer

WHO HAS customer need,

product name

IS A market category

THAT one key benefit

UNLIKE competition

THE PRODUCT unique differentiation

I have done this exercise with hundreds of students and am amazed at how hard it is. On the first try, many students will take over five minutes to explain what they want to say. It has nothing to do with how brilliant the person is, how well they are able to communicate complex ideas in simple terms. The main issue is that many want to explain how the product works but at this stage resist this tendency.

One business strategy is to pre-sell the product before it exist. This tactic has been used by many entrepreneurs. They make a sale then figure out how to service it quickly. Refer to this as selling the vision and delivering the product. The buyers are often early adopters who have a need they are willing to take risk to address, since not addressing it is more painful than making a purchase and getting it partially solved. In this respect, buyers can act and think entrepreneurial.

Exercise: The Mantra

A three word association of values to be repeated

Authentic athletic performance

Fun, family entertainment

Rewarding everyday moments

Think Differently

Mantra's are the internal associations that everyone in the company uses to help focus on the value and meaning being created. The mantra needs to be repeated and made an integral part of the company culture. This is a creative process and requires many attempts to get to the essence of the company. Start with lots of words that come to mind then find the few that get to the essence of the company and do this by a process of elimination. Simplicity is much harder to do well than complexity.

This is all internal marketing and I find this to be important at the early stages. The reason is the culture is influenced by whatever the mantra is. This is not an easy exercise at all, many books describe forming a vision and mission statement, but I would skip those at this early stage and try to pick three words that embody the values of the company. These are not the only values; they are the primary ones that have the focus.

Exercise: The Tag Lines

Tag lines are for the customers to help them quickly place your company and products into a space of associations that support the branding and marketing of the products.

> *You're Potential. Our Passion.*
>
> *Shoot it. Save it. Share it*
>
> *Runs faster. Costs less. And never breaks.*

If you can get the customers to repeat these tags over time, they start to believe it. By declaring a position, people assume that it must be true.

Exercise: Design the Business

Enroll the team with a big idea to change the world using your mantra

Define your business structure together

Determine your selling strategy

Enroll your resources with your pitch and tag

From the first presentation, use your personal branding statement to explain who you are, what your company is about, and how you want to change the world and what you need in terms of help from people and resources to do it.

We will go through a structured statement that tries to capture concisely the business concept in simple terms. These are the launch points for expanding on the business concepts to create a complete business structure in a 10-page business concept presentation.

Exercise: Business structure formation

Reviewing the business structure generation framework try and come up with preliminary answers to each of the questions. These do not have to be perfect but they should provoke discussion on what they might be. You may need to do quick research on-line to explore unfamiliar areas and come up with the issues.

The value offer is the most important aspect of the business structure and the hardest one to get right. As an entrepreneur, you will find many appealing Customer Groups and many Resources available but until you can find the unique value you are creating, it is not possible to create a product and sell it.

Typical Value Offer questions are: What value do we deliver to the customer? Which one of our customer's problems are we helping to solve? Which customer needs are we satisfying? What bundles of products and services are we offering to each Customer Group?

The business structure covers the following questions. What is the value of the product or service? Who is the customer group that wants that value? How will it get to them through distribution and logistics? How does the business maintain a relationship with the customer? How does the business find these customers and how do those customers find the business? What are the product or services components and sources to supply them? What do you expect are the most important resources and activities? List out the people resources and equipment that may be needed? What is the unit cost of manufacturing and delivery for the product and service? What would you charge for it? How else can you make money from the sale?

[Company Name] is driven by [Customers, Suppliers, Cost, Revenue stream] with our product [Name, an Innovation] we sell [new Value Offer to market] through [Distribution Channel] to [Customer Group (gain)].

Our [Research IP, Activities] solves [Customer Problem (pain)] with [Team, Resources, Partners].

Many variations of this pitch exist. Try to come up with the fewest words first that are self-evident, and then you can expand on this to have a richer explanation. After the pitch, tell a user story to frame it into a context the buyer can relate.

Exercise: State your Sale Strategy

We prospect for sales leads by [Marketing, Direct Calls, Solicitations, Web, Trade Shows, Networking] to engage them in our [Demonstration, Trial, Test, Release].

To acquire customers we convert the prospects after a successful engagement by [Persuasion, Negotiation, Pricing, Discounting, Influencing, Proving with Data ROI, Risk Reduction, Savings].

To keep the customer we will provide [Customer Service, Attention, Follow-up, Free service, Consulting] so they refer us to other prospects.

This is to get you started on the sales process. It is not the only way to sell but it follows the structure we reviewed and helps explain to others how you plan to convert interest into paying customers. This is necessary to build credibility with your team and your partners. The business needs to be well thought out. It will succeed since it is focused on sales and engaging customers.

The funding is below and it will become clear why selling in the early stage is an essential skill.

Exercise: Practice, Practice, Practice

Find an audience to present your business concept, explain your business structure and sales strategy. Practice your pitches until you can explain it in five minutes or less.

Research the industry to find information that validates your assumptions or exposes what you do not yet know. Practice, Practice, Practice on real people

With a learning process, it takes practice, so doing exercises will help codify what was presented.

These exercises are sketches to get you started on the entrepreneurial journey. They can be practiced many times and are language structures to help frame the thoughts around a business concept. The exercises have no correct answer or test; they are guides and therefore should be revised to reflect the needs of your business concept. They are concise treatments of the business. Most businesses will have layers of dimensions needed to understand them so these exercises are of use in the early stages to help activate the action. Put the ideas to words, verbalizing them, selling the concepts to others, and getting the dialog going, so you can shape and develop the ideas into functioning businesses.

The focus of the book has been for high-potential ventures but much of the thinking and actions are equally useful for starting any business. They are of value for people working in a corporate innovation role where they need to generate winning ideas and express them to peers and management to gain support for creating a product to deliver to the market.

Exercise: Social Profile

List five people in your area of expertise you can call on for expertise.

List five people in business areas that you need to use as resources

List five people that you can help

List the industry associations that are valuable for your sector

List the locations of the industry cluster regions in each part of the world

Exercise: Resource Base

List the following for each resource

Met how? Gender, culture, context of Interaction,

Years Known, Topic of Conversation

Resource or Helped – When and for What

List five scenarios where you can access your customer grouping

List five events where you can find customers and resources

Exercise: Social Design

Complete your LinkedIn profile and make the connections with your network

Review your business structure and find what resources are missing. How will you find and access them?

Where will you find your co-founder, business partners, and team?

How do you plan to use your personal brand to enroll others as your resources?

Exercise: Design a Social Strategy.

Pick one from the list that you are likely to find other people who are in the same industry. Notice the list is not restricted to social media; it includes Trade Shows, Events, Conferences, and physical places where you can meet people face to face. Each industry has its own usage pattern for these venues. Use trade journals, industry groups, and what is present on the Internet.

Bookmarking, Apps, Blogs, Conference Speaking, Branding monitoring, Discussion Boards, Banner Ads, Crowdsourcing, Content Aggregation, Email Subscription, Events, Fan Pages, Exhibitions, Groups, Journal Articles, Magazine Articles, New Articles, Microblogging, Forums, Meetups, Online Ads, Online Video, Outreach Programs, Presentation Sharing, Photosharing, Podcasting, Ratings, Print Ads, Public Relations, RSS, Reviews, Tagging, Trade Shows, Voting, Widgets, Wikis, Social Networks, Virtual Worlds, Sponsorships, Personalities

The social strategy is not the same for enrolling resources as it is for acquiring customers. It is likely that your suppliers and customers are not reached through the same social channels; you need to design a strategy for each.

The social strategy is not the same as sales, it might generate leads, but the purpose is to place yourself into the cluster of activities for the industry so that you create a reputation that others can assess and you can leverage to gain access to people through sharing knowledge and contacts.

Make a distinction between Business Development and Sales, business development expands and changes the business structure through new alliances, and partnership, Sales finds customers within the groups and sells the products in the market.

For consumer products, the sales process is primarily marketing communications. Marketing, Press Releases, Brand management are all-necessary and these position your company in the industry. They can be used effectively to signal to customers that your business is stable and your products are worth buying.

The one area not represented in the word cloud is education. This is often necessary for innovative products that extend beyond the gap of current usage and the customer needs to adopt a new behavior or understanding to use the product. These types of innovation are risky and costly to put forth into the market since they have a natural barrier that is expensive to bridge, the company would need to provide training before the customer understands what they are buying and how to use it. The training and educations can be implicit in the marketing material but this is difficult to execute on well.

Exercise: Review your Business Structure

Given your social design strategy, how would you extend your business structure to have a global reach of customers and suppliers?

What new resources would you need?

Adjust the business structure to pursue the largest opportunity

Find the next step to test the business structure

Exercise: Make your Life Style Choices

What are your material expectations?

Work and reward, security and risk

Family, housing, leisure

Household Financial Management

Create your personal financial plan

Exercise: Calculate the Affordable Loss

Create a personal financial plan

Calculate affordable loss in money, time, and reputation

Estimate business break-even and cash flow

Determine your funding sources and uses

The use of funds can be to create the product if you have a valid Patentable invention and have IP protection. You could raise the money for hiring, marketing, office, and general business operating capital. The best position to be in is to create enough value that you can run the company without needing investment and have funded the company through the bootstrap process.

Exercise: Find Funding Sources

List all the potential funding sources that apply to your business.

Create a short spreadsheet with an itemizations of all the cost you will incur to start the business and the potential initial sales revenue.

Create a bootstrapping financial plan

Review your business plan again to adjust for a pragmatic next step to making it real

Exercise: Funding Pitch

Our [Company] is seeking funding of X Euros for % equity in the company

by Y date to sell/distribute [Product]

and will break even by D date with a CAGR of %.

We expect to reach a Billion Euro in P years.

The pre-money valuation is V Euros based on comparable like W company a competitor

When you are looking for funding, you need to ask for the investment. Knowing how to ask for it and what your terms and conditions are shows that you are prepared and understand the issues involved. That kind of signal lets the investor know that you are serious.

Exercise: Finalize the Business Concept presentation

To finalize the business concept you should be ready to present and address each of the following points:

Who are you in relationship to the audience, why are you there presenting and why are they there listening.

What is the problem, frame the pain points and what is the resistance to changes.

Explain why you care about this problem, why does this matter to you.

What is the solution, how do people gain, and what are the forces for this change

Market size and how many people will want this gain

Social good, make sure it does no harm or have unintended consequences, explain how it has a common benefit.

Why now, what are the trends, why is it urgent to fix the problem with this solution.

Competition, who else solves this problem and how do they do it, how is your solution different and better.

How does it make money? What is the business structure that includes the customer group? How will the company find the customers? How will the customers find the company? How will the company maintain a relationship to the customer? How will it distribute the product? What are the logistical challenges? Who are the suppliers and what do they provide? What activities are the most important? What is the unit cost of the product or service? What is the pricing model? What other major cost are incurred? How else can the company make money?

Who is the team, why can it solve this problem?

Milestones, what has been accomplished so far, what is in the plan, specifically what will be delivered that is tangible evidence of accomplishing the milestone.

What are the risks? What might prevent this business from succeeding? Focus on the uncertainty, the challenges with regulations, the degree of competition, the length of the sales cycle, but you have to be ready with a way to mitigate each of these.

Provide financial model summary with the details in an appendix. The model might highlight assumptions and the method used to arrive at the projected financials. Show the cash flow, capital requirements, and break-even point. Remember to have a bootstrapping scenario that minimizes the capital requirements. With investors, you have to show the sources and uses for the money.

If it is high tech business with a novel invention description that captures Intellectual Property, how does it work, what is the science behind it, where does the science go next? Show the functions and structure of the system and how do they behave. This is only relevant if something is very novel and truly a competitive invention that is the basis for a product innovation.

What help do you need to get it done, what have you done to build a support network? Who are the advisors, how many customers have you talked to, have you lined up the suppliers, and are they ready to go?

Reward incentive, what is the return potential when this is solved and the market has adopted the solution?

Next step, who else can they introduce you to that might be helpful?

The follow up, get the contact information and tell them when, how, and why you will reach them?

The above are a sampling of what you may include in a full presentation. This is the summary outline in presentation form of a complete business plan that includes all the research that supports the assertions. Not every item in the list has to be included. It should be relative to audience and the evolution of the business concept. What you are trying to accomplish with the audience? How much time you have with them? You must be ready at all times to pitch the business and speak with confidence and in detail about what the team has done and will do in the coming months.

Be serious about building a business even if you are just doing this as an exploratory exercise in class or for a contest or at work to propose an innovative product, if you are not serious and prepare neither will the audience be and that just defeats the point of the exercise. The mantra for augmented reality gaming is "this is not a game", yet it uses a gaming structure and feels like fun but to simulate reality you need to get into the zone of creating and telling the story by suspending disbelief and acting out the future now.

Exercise: Present the Business Plan

20 slides maximum, 24-point font, use images, graphics, charts, facts, and tell a story

Prepare a 10-minute presentation, 30 seconds each slide, and create a pitch for each slide

Write your pitch in the notes and memorize it

Practice aloud, then with friends and family to sell it.

Record the presentation using video and review it to help you refine your presentation style.

Get ready to present to a business audience or customers, suppliers, and potential investors.

Take the 20 slides and draft a full business plan complete with all the background support in research. Lastly, draft a one page executive summary with the key elements that represent a concise view of the business.

Exercise: Repetition

I have taught hundreds of aspiring entrepreneurs, all highly talented, and have built several companies and consulted for over 40 ventures and without doubt the exercises above apply in all cases and in every stage. They appear to be simplistic, and they are, but repeatedly I find these fundamental patterns persist for mature companies and it is startling how often they are ignored by well-trained MBA professionals. I am equally guilty of this flaw and have to force myself back to basics even when I am confident in the business. As often as I have tried to applied them myself, each new situation presents a twist I had not encountered before. That forces me to re-examine the simplicity again and struggle with whether other tactics exist to improve the outcomes for the entrepreneurs and business that are attempting to grow. It always comes back to these basic communications of the business structure and explaining it to others is the best way to rediscover the issues and the value in what you are doing. So repeated practice will reveal layers of nuance that are not explained fully in the book but using the patterns will help you discover them for yourself.

The last suggestion on repetition as practice is that practicing in the right way, with the right techniques gets results. This is why a coach is so valuable and the top athletes and CEO's know this and hire coaches that can observe and remind them of the right way to practice and to practice the right things so the patterns of failure do not stay stuck in failure but instead lead down a path where success surfaces. Once success is felt, celebrate for one minute then put it behind you quickly and focus on the next achievement to strive for.

Mentoring or Coaching?

The exercises will take a lifetime of practice and as you learn from a business being launched, layers upon layers of things you had no idea existed as problems will surface. Add to this learning how to deal with the range of cultures and personalities that is needed to get anything done is a study that will never be mastered. As discussed in the Social Design chapter, you have to construct a team of people to help get the business launched, selling and growing, and for this to happen more people are needed than the business can reasonably afford to pay. The founding team and staff you hire might be experienced, but since everyone is working in a new business for the first time the relationships have to be negotiated to a productive pattern.

You are unlikely to be able to hire the most experienced people, so how does one avoid the hundreds of easy mistakes that experienced people make so that these are not repeated in a new context? Who will be the objective protagonist that says, "great job, put it behind you now, and get on with doing more"? Finding and creating the environment to thrive will not be easy. The incubators and accelerators are set up for this purpose, to simulate an ecosystem of support and infrastructure to help the entrepreneurs develop the businesses. It can be confusing to try and distinguish between the experience of all the people that might become available in an incubator, so it is helpful to categorize the experience each person brings and how it might help.

Mentoring or Coaching a startup within an incubator

If we were to recognize that aspiring entrepreneurs are at risk, in that the chance of failure is high and therefore fear may set in at any time preventing the entrepreneur from making progress, then we can ask the question: what support would the entrepreneur need to get through this journey? Since fear and failure are perceptions based on cognitive issues, the entrepreneur may benefit from forming trust relationships with people who may help them think clearly about the issues they are confronting. Mentoring or coaching can provide valuable guidance to vulnerable first-time entrepreneurs who are at risk stopping the business formation at the first encounter of a monumental perceived barrier.

Benefits to the entrepreneur:

- Get business information and guidance in launching and growing a company

- Gain and improve leadership skills that come from relationships with experienced professionals

- Set personal and company goals where progress can be tracked and feedback provided

- Discover options and opportunities that otherwise would not have be available

- Prepare for scaling the company and understanding how best to receive help from others

- Reduce the risk of failures that can be avoided

- Increase the chance of success by leveraging the experience of others

Benefits to the mentors or coaches:

- Gain personal satisfaction in other's success

- Develop patience, insight, and understanding in developing talent

- Experience a different cultural, social, economic background different

- Learn or refresh what it takes to innovate as an entrepreneur

- Make an impact on the community and industry

What are differences between coaching and mentoring and why may both be needed? Often coaching and mentoring are the same but they have some distinct differences which make coaching more suitable for aspiring entrepreneurs and mentoring appropriate for those who have launched a business. A mentor believes they are accomplished and have something to offer those who may chart a similar journey as their own, they may think, "be like me" and you will be a success. This is where coaching is different, it would come from the perspective of, "I will help you be whoever you want to be". The coaches will be successful as well but will implicitly understand that it's the team that wins. The mentor may focus on, "it's the CEO that made it all happen". These speak to different value systems but they are not opposing views. They just need to be applied appropriately in the context of the entrepreneur and the stage of the business.

If the entrepreneur is transitioning from the business concept to launching a functioning business, the situation presents a challenge to the entrepreneur seeking guidance. The coaching may not be enough and the entrepreneur may want to find a suitable mentor. An overlap period may be necessary to help the entrepreneur learn how best to receive the mentoring.

Coaching should not be confused with training or teaching. The coach is there while the entrepreneur is going through the phases of getting the business started. The assumption is that the entrepreneur has adequate training and took a few foundational courses to prepare for the many skills they need to start and run a business. The coach might identify deficiencies and suggest additional training or courses but they are focused on performance during the critical startup stage which gets the entrepreneur from a concept to actively launching a business. The coaches may be former teachers, friends and family interested in the members of the team succeeding, hired or volunteer guides that have experience or expertise in the formative stages of business startups, or subject matter experts providing pro bono services. Entrepreneurs are self-directed learners so seeking more training, self study, pushing the boundaries of their knowledge and experience are expected but to be done within the context of launching a business. The learning progresses from reading and listening, to doing, measuring, and improving.

In startups, the company mentors may come from several participants, an experienced co-founder or staff member, the advisors, investors, the board, or industry experts that act in this role. A mentor expects that a viable business exists and that the entrepreneur has adequate training, was coached through the stages of formation, and has the requisite skills to run a business, and recognizes what competencies are needed to create a team.

Differences and similarity between coaches and mentors:

Coaching will:

- Encourage self-motivation, positive attitudes and outlook

- Maximize overall performance results within a person's unique talent

- Help set bold but achievable goals

- Facilitate expanding knowledge and skills

- Maintain free flowing dialog with constructive feedback

- Guide towards solutions and positive outcomes

- Connect personal goals with team entrepreneurial goals

- Be interested in developing talent and increasing competency

Mentor may:

- Provide access to network of relationships in industry

- Share industry domain knowledge

- Share expertise

- Act as person to emulate or imitate by example

- Provide inspiration and encouragement, extrinsic motivation

- Be interested in leaving a legacy in their industry and fueling change

Both coach and mentors:

- Provide trust, time, dialog, sharing

- Are credible, authentic, accomplished

- Stimulate the person to try and overcome hurdles

- Need to be mindful of the person first, be there, be aware, be fair

- Give positive feedback without empty praise

- Abide by a code of ethics

- Are transparent with intentions and purpose

- Not have any conflicts of interest

- Commit time to the relationship.

Neither should:

- Act as a psychologist

- Give criticism without constructive corrective course

- Neither should imply they are angel investors without having invested in the company

- Have intentions to invest in the company which triggers an agenda inconsistent with providing goodwill to the entrepreneur.

- Act as coach and mentor simultaneously without being clear about the role they are speaking from.

- Disparage the entrepreneur or the company

To make coaching or mentoring effective for the startup:

- Commit to try to their full abilities and use the time wisely

- Have integrity, take initiative, be resilient, have a positive attitude, create support teams

- Be honest with themselves

- Abide by a code of ethics

- Coach or mentor others once they have enough experience to develop good judgment

- Pass the goodwill forward to others in the company.

- Understand the incentives of the coach or mentor.

- Share the potential benefits with all that help where appropriate.

Before asking for help, startups should ask themselves:

- Have they done everything they can to learn what they need to be successful?

- Are they fully committed to the business and others who are on the team?

- Do they understand the background of the mentor and coach?

- Are they mature enough to take advice and either act on it or seek to understand it before deciding not to follow through?

- They are willing to say they do not know enough, or understand, or agree with a suggestion?

- They will not hold the mentor or coach liable for the impact on the business for any advice given and be solely responsible for making the final decisions.

- They will not seek conflicting advice from several people which may confuse issues and waste the time of the people trying to help.

Before a mentor or coach helps a startup they should ask:

- Are they willing to commit the time to help?

- Do they have the particular experience that is relevant to the proposed business?

- Are they willing to let the entrepreneur learn from their mistakes?

- Is it clear that they are not to help run the business or direct its operations?

- They do not intent to work for the company if it gets funded.

- They have no intention to invest in the company.

- They will abide by the proprietary and confidentiality of the business discussions and not compete with the company or have any other conflicting interest.

- They are not disclosing proprietary or confidential information from other companies

- They are willing to assign all rights in the solutions that arise from the relationship to the company and will not make claims of ownership of IP.

- They are willing to admit they do not know how to solve a problem or not have an answer to a question avoiding making a suggesting out of context that may have the consequence of the entrepreneur making decisions on advice that was not based on experience.

While it is important to make a distinction for the role someone is in with respect to the company it is possible for a coach to also be a mentor and visa versa. The position the person is taking must be made clear to both parties to be productive. A mentor can easily confuse their role when the company gets into trouble. The mentor may switch to acting as a coach in reacting the an entrepreneur asking for help. With the switch from mentor to coach the person may start to direct the entrepreneur and the consequence is the mentor turned coach does not realize they are interfering and potentially doing long term harm to the company's ability to survive. By giving directions the mentor is acting inappropriate since they are not running the company. This can degrade the effectiveness of the relationship between the entrepreneur and the mentor therefore it requires that the entrepreneur have the professional maturity to manage the people they are seeking help from. Mentors, turned investors, have the greatest risk of confusion and interference, so growing the company includes understanding how to best use all the help that becomes available and clearly establishing how that help is to be received.

Mentoring and coaching can come from the generosity of the person contributing goodwill but it is best to understand the incentives and satisfaction they are seeking. What is it that they are doing that drives them to provide help? What incentives are in place for them to continue? Once the company has investors, then coaches and mentors may be reluctant to continue helping since doing so provides a benefit to others who are not involved to be magnanimous but to have expectations of financial gain. One strategy that has been used to resolve this is to provide a small equity grant to the people who helped get the business launched through their advice and counsel. These are referred to as advisors shares and these may be allocated at any time but it is best to do this early to avoid any potential conflict and to make sure to align all the interest. The entrepreneur may find that someone being helpful may decline the shares but will appreciate that the entrepreneur understands how to manage the people who are helping. Showing appreciation is easy and does not cost much, so be generous with showing it.

The use of the term coach in this context does not refer to "professional executive coaches". Executive coaches are trained to work with experienced business management in workforce development and career advancement or to help an executive achieve personal goals. These types of coaches are expensive, are primarily trained human resource experts or psychologist and are not well suited for young entrepreneurs learning how to start a first business.

The term mentor is often used very loosely and may be associated with a person who has significant experience or achievements that are recognized as outstanding or exceptional. In the context of a startup entrepreneur, a mentor is not an iconic admired figure, it may be someone who has a bit more experience than the entrepreneur, a person a few year older who possibly failed at a venture themselves, or had nominal success in a company. They may simply have something that the entrepreneur deems valuable to share. This latter description is what is prevalent in the tech startup venture community and is what is adopted for the above discussion.

One should not assume that giving help that can be acted on by the entrepreneur is easy and it is just providing an opinion. Being a good coach or mentor requires thoughtful consideration, some training, and a lot of patience and practice and should not be taken for granted. Not everyone makes for a good coach or mentor in all situations. The degree to which the coach and mentor can easily identify and communicate with the entrepreneur matters greatly as to whether it will be effective. Given that both parties have to make a determined investment in time with each other, the personal cost is one that warrants a potential for mutual benefit to both parties even if those benefits are different.

An entrepreneur who learns the skills of receiving help from experienced people may have a huge advantage over the competition through the avoidance of obvious failures. They learn how to manage expertise and this is a valuable skill to acquire when building a company. The relationship sets a pattern of performance, generosity, achievement, and reward. An inability for a young entrepreneur to learn effectively from these kinds of relationships is an early warning sign that they may not be ready for the challenge and it may be best for them to work in a company while they grow professionally.

Implementing the program at an incubator:

Assess need. survey the status of the entrepreneurship team to determine their view on what they need. Determine if they know how to make use of guidance they can get from experienced people. Find out what other programs do and how they work. Start with what is working. Make use of the expertise available and pool resources.

Convene an advisory board. Include all constituents that can help in the mentoring of the teams, from the schools, the alumni, within the startup community, and industry in the vicinity.

Set program goals and objectives. Design strategies to monitor your progress. Whether working to lower the failure rates, improve business performance, enhance business competencies, or teach new skills, be specific and realistic in stating your goals. Don't forget the importance of short-term goals. Even small successes boost morale.

Develop an evaluation plan. As you design your program, you must also design your evaluation strategy. Evaluation will enable you to identify strengths and weaknesses in your program, measure your overall success, and establish a basis for additional funding.

Create an infrastructure for your program. Define the roles and responsibilities for staff and participants. Adequate staffing is essential. Staff provide scheduling, supervision and support and make sure that mentor pairs are meeting regularly.

Assess your resources. Look for funding within your college or university, private foundations, local corporations, business and industry councils, state departments of education, and federal agencies. Look for other forms of support, too, including donations of goods and services to support a project, and recognize hard-working volunteers.

Be knowledgeable about liability and confidentiality. Consult with your college/university risk management office. Be sure to take basic precautions including references for mentors; informed consent for program participation; permission slips for attending special events; and contracts for mentoring and the entrepreneurs.

Hold a mentor orientation meeting. An information/orientation session allows you to present the important components of your program and gives potential mentors an opportunity to evaluate their readiness to volunteer. Mentors should expect to give a commitment for some specified duration and time availability for one-on-one and group activities. Emphasize realistic expectations. Mentors cannot and should not be expected to solve all problems. Remember to present the rewards as well as the responsibilities of mentoring.

Not everyone makes a good mentor. Screen out potential volunteers who don't have the time, commitment, or maturity to be effective.

Take care in selecting the entrepreneur participants. Sometimes an entrepreneur's needs or circumstances may be too problematic for mentoring to be effective.

Match pairs thoughtfully. Matching by race, gender and common interests can facilitate trust and help break the ice. Informal gatherings of mentors and young people can lead to "natural matches."

Prepare young entrepreneurs for the program. just as mentors want and need orientation, young people must also understand the time commitment and requirements of the program.

Mentor training is crucial. Training builds skills, provides new information, and introduces important issues that mentors will encounter. Mentor training should address startup development, communication skills, diversity/ cultural sensitivity, crisis management, conflict resolution.

Mentoring can be hard work. Mentors need support and encouragement throughout. Discussion and support meetings reduce frustration and enhance service by allowing mentors to share and compare experiences and solve problems together. Be sure mentors know when and how to reach program staff in case of a problem and plan regular reflection sessions to review progress. Mentoring programs can rise and fall on the strength of training and support provided for mentors.

Entrepreneurs learn by doing and this is very reminiscent of the way an apprentice learns a craft. They seek out a master of the art and after years of observations, practice, and delivering lesser objects for the master they absorb the patterns and skills and can work independently. The master is both coach and mentor at various stages. Business has lost this apprenticeship means of training the talent and this has to be created somehow by the entrepreneur. One way is to make proper use of coaches and mentors, they might not lead the business and you only have limited time to observe them but they can provide objective opinions where they matter most, the decisions that are not obvious and need perspective of experience.

Teaching and Learning Outline

The book outline is for quick reference to help the reader absorb the context. It is for the entrepreneurship instructor to produce presentation slides to summarize the key points for classroom or online discussion. Although this misses the point of the book, it is available to the student entrepreneur taking a course and wanting to cram for a test. The book started with this outline which I used for several years of teaching the course and tried various presentation tactics. Over five hundred aspiring entrepreneurs influenced the narrative of the book based on feedback from the training and coaching sessions. The outline survived over time as my main teaching instrument. The original references are listed in the bibliography section. The notes of the presentation are the main text of this book. The conversational tone originates from the in-class dialogue that the presentation outline triggers.

For faculty using this book outline, avoid simplistic flash card memorization of the key points placed in a multiple choice test. This would miss the point of the text and exercises. An in-person presentation of the business, with a document for the supporting market research and financials would be a good learning goal. In the European tradition of defending a thesis, the aspiring entrepreneurs present to a mixed panel of judges in a contest format. The judges review the presentation for feasibility, novelty, innovation, risk taking, pragmatism, just as an investor, supplier, and customer would evaluate the business. This would provide a cross section of feedback that may further develop a viable business and motivate the entrepreneurial teams to gain competency and show commitment to making it real. This book came out of reversing the formal education processes, starting with a loose studio format and ended up being a course within an MBA curriculum. The book is still meant to support the business atelier format, a practical studio course challenging the entrepreneurs to launch the business. It is not written for an academic exercise without intentions of students trying to create a business.

The references and recommended books listed in the bibliography strengthen the learning journey and the outline puts them into a context. It places them together in the respective sections for easy access and omits the indexed referencing that are typical of academic textbooks but distract the reader's attention. The book is to be read quickly so the entrepreneur can get to the task of creating the business. The book is a composite of my own experiences and what I found useful as an entrepreneur but it is only one view that comes from coaching and training other successful entrepreneurs.

The entrepreneurial journey takes many years of continuous practice and study therefore I do not make claims of knowing the single path to success neither is this to be inferred. It is also not an exhaustive representation of the large body of knowledge that successful business teams need to gain, therefore the book is an orienting launching pad for those who have a vague desire and need to scope out the journey. The books and references listed in the bibliography may be of enormous value when read and used suitably and only if put into practice. Read and share, discuss with your colleagues, associates, co-founders, employees, mentors and advisers, and build the social contracts needed to scaffold your learning to success.

The Entrepreneurial Spirit

"A dream needs to overcome fear, irrationality, and failure to become reality." - R. Garcia 2011

Human Economic Activity

Advanced economies use prediction to make choices based on their conditioning.

Developing world economies use creative action to overcome their uncertainty out of necessity.

Entrepreneur defined

Desire + Action = Creative Opportunity

An entrepreneur is any person who creates new economic value through business model innovation.

Risk and uncertainty plus social creativity

Entrepreneurs create new value growth in the global economy.

Entrepreneurs Change the World

Is it possible?

Do you believe you can do it?

Is it worth doing?

Do you want to do it?

Sustained desire propels action

Entrepreneurial Action

Abundance of opportunities

Make a difference with a passion

Go into unpredictable markets

Control what can be known

Propensity to act under uncertainty

Like an Artist

Not goal oriented

Start with the means not the end

Use what is available at hand

Find resources, do something with them

Situation aware action focused

The Discovery

Theme, variations, improvise

Cheap failures until successes

Create the market effect then figure out the cause

Use trial & error then repeat

Self determination

We are conditioned to be directed.

Determine the means and the end

Desires are worthless until acted on

Context of Personal Assets

Identity, Competence, Connections

Bias for trust and free exchanges

Making it Happen

Affordable loss

Leveraging contingencies

Bias for action, focus on the next step

Built to Last

Have the value stand on its own merit

Work out the protocol for resolving conflict

Be generous

The Founders

Find a context or create one

Leadership is a myth

Forget the legacy, serve others first

Create a myth but do not believe it

Founders Symptoms

Not coping with the lifestyle choice

Resistance to stopping or pivoting

Not creating value for others

Illusion of grandeur

Irrational Decision Making

Wishful thinking

Confirmation Bias

First alternative found as good enough

Cloudy Thinking

Illusion of Control

Distorted/selective memory

Anchoring

Resisting Change

Status Quo

Prejudice

Peer pressure

Beware of cognitive biases

Failure

To start and act

Expected outcome not met

Failure requires perspective

"Success consists of going from failure to failure without loss of enthusiasm. " - Winston Churchill

Failure Defined

When fear prevents action as a consequence of experience or uncertainty, and the decision to quit is based on irrational influences.

Fear plus irrational thought equals failure

Business Knowledge a Philosophical Position

The epistemology is a phenomenology, or experience, generalized from observation, not theory, or method.

Make Meaning

Mercenaries versus Missionaries

Culture of the Entrepreneur

Flatten the power distance

Face uncertainty, create predictability

Long view, short achievements

Perpetual optimism

Ideas to Execution,
the myths and realities

"Make everything as simple as possible, but not simpler." - Albert Einstein

Wetware

Art ask questions

Design answer questions

Engineering makes things functional

Science explains how it all works

Entrepreneurs create value-using wetware

The Epiphany

Myth: Ideas happen by inspiration and turn into products by magic

Reality: It is just a puzzle/painting you construct within a context and only the last piece feels like an epiphany

Idea Process

Myth: A method for finding good ideas exists that you need to learn.

Reality: Start somewhere, anywhere, and figure it out, do what works, stop doing what does not work.

Need one Idea

Myth: Good ideas are hard to find

Reality: If you cannot generate hundreds of ideas, you are unlikely to find the one that fits the times. It is all about the action not one instance

Best Ideas

Myth: It is all evolution and the best ideas win

Reality: The environment selects the ideas that survive. Suitability of fit is more important than best idea

Novelty

Myth: Ideas need to be unique

Reality: Unless hundreds of others have the exact same idea it won't become a product and be viable in the market. Copy and change.

People like new ideas

Myth: It will work, make money, is a solution for a problem that people did not know they had

Reality: It is the gap between what people do today and what you are asking them to do tomorrow that defines the probability of adoption

It takes a genius

Myth: Sole inventor creates innovations.

Reality: Two heads are better than one. It is all a social construct, genius and leadership are myths and do not exist.

Need for Expertise

Myth: Only one correct path to the solution

Reality: Ideas have a life, need an environment, execution and persuasion is all that matters. They need many paths to pursue. Experts only have one path, the one they followed in the past.

Solutions

Myth: Problems need to be solved

Reality: Problems need to framed, the solution is revealed by the execution by letting it emerge and shift until a framing works

Protecting Ideas

Myth: Ideas need protection and held close

Reality: The idea is not worth anything until you tell as many people as you can about it and let it expand, evolve, and take a shape.

Stability

Myth: Ideas stay the same as you make them real

Reality: What you end up with will look nothing like what you started with

Ownership

Myth: Whoever thought of the idea owns it and the only one who can execute it

Reality: Whoever creates the product, sells it and makes the money

Commitment

Myth: Inventor totally commits to an idea early on

Reality: Inventors commit to an idea only once it works and until then will repurpose, hybridize, morph, and test, many ideas until they become products

Garage Entrepreneurs

Myth: Great companies are born in Garages, Kitchens, basements, dorm-rooms [HP, Apple].

Reality: 90% of companies are started based on prior work situation. Organizational experience builds confidence, gains knowledge, forms social networks, and spots opportunities that are all necessary for starting a venture.

Converting ideas to markets

Generate the Ideas

Create meaning

Sell the idea

Make it a mantra

Brand it with a tag

Act and Learn

Ethnography, Personas, Stories

Themes, Opportunities, Solutions

Product mock-up, Simulated scenarios

Messaging, Field Testing

Empathy Map

What do supporters

Think and feel? Inner workings of their mind, drives, worries, aspirations

See? View of their environment, area, exposure, friends

Listen to? Influence of their environment, who, what communications channels

Say and do? Behavior in public, attitudes, conflicts

Empathy Opportunities

What are the supporters

Pain? Frustrations, obstacles

Gain? Desires, impact, passions

Humanize the customer

Patent the Invention

New/Novel – not made public

Original/Non-obvious – incremental invention not obvious to someone schooled in the art

Useful – the device needs to do something

Commercialize the innovation

Business Structure Formation

Customer Groupings

Value Offer

Distribution and Logistics Channel

Connecting to Customers

Revenue Flows

Access to Resources

Core Activities

Suppliers and Partners

Cost Breakdown

Business structures are messy, focus on finding the winning strategy

Understanding Key Trends

Understanding Key Trends

Political and regulatory

Macro and Socio-economic

Societal and Cultural

Technological

See the big picture

Situation Analysis

Action plan to implement change

Understand the Forces Driving versus Restraining

Value Innovation

All businesses need to create and raise value while eliminating or reducing cost. Only when this spread is dramatically better than what already exist in the market is a business model innovation demonstrated to have achieved its high impact goals.

What are Business Plans for?

The business is alive

Expose what you cannot know

Record what you do know

Become a storyteller

Business Plan Outline

A concise outline for a business plan outline would include, company purpose, problem description, solution demonstration, trends and why now, market size and research, competitive landscape, product and technology IP, business model, team, financial projections, and next steps.

Creating the Team

Find the Sales person

Right size the staff

Under-staff and Outsource everything

Energy and talent over experience

Get evangelist, believers, mantra speaker

Startups require people who act

Hire function over form

Find help within your network

Sales Focus

Sales cycle has four simple phases; prospect by identifying the customers' problem and getting them to respond to an appeal, engage the decision maker with a demonstration and trial, acquire the customer with pricing negotiation so they make a buy decision, keep the customer with a positive experience so they give a referral.

Social by Design

Peopleware

Finding People resources

Enrolling and engaging

Freemium and Crowdsourcing

People are the most expensive resource but they are the cheapest as well.

Social Resource Management

Co-creating the product with customers and key partners requires designing the social interactions that govern the engagements.

Tapping into industry resources requires understanding the implicit social contracts.

What is Social by Design

Design of human systems for social interaction

Business co-generation

Communities of Practice

Serious Social Networks

Co-opetition Partnering

Global sourcing and distribution

Why Social by Design

High-potential entrepreneurs thrive where they can connect to innovation clusters.

Innovation Clusters are locations where industries are in close proximity.

These clusters are now transnational.

Cluster Resources

Customers go to the cluster areas to buy

Suppliers gather around the customers

Talent goes to clusters to find jobs

Schools create supporting programs

Need to use Social Design to tap into the cluster resources

Thriving Tech Clusters

Global interdependent

> New York City to Boston, San Francisco to San Jose, Austin, Hsinchu-Taipei, Bangalore, Tel Aviv, Singapore

Local Social Networks

> Cambridge, Sophia Antipolis, Helsinki, Stockholm, Berlin, Pisa

Tech Cluster Attributes

Start-up Activity

Human Talent

University/R&D Institutes

Global Links

Venture Capital

Low Taxes and Regulations.

Network Economy

Expert Level Workforce

Knowledge generation from R&D

Knowledge transfer between individuals

Entrepreneurial Culture

Source of Risk Capital

Quality of Life

Social Networks build Social Capital

Impact of Social by Design

Comparative Advantages:

Lower cost of available expertise

Raising productivity and performance speed

Creating access to core competencies

Creativity

Challenges:

Generating Intellectual Property ownership

Differentiation

What are Social Networks?

Value from a voluntary group

Communications to form relationships

Commodity of ideas and knowledge

Social Capital is accumulated & convertible

Social Network Design

"Needs organic interactions that build relationships; one on one discussion, civil group discourse, and argumentation, working towards shared goals and outcomes."

Successful Social Design

Define and focus on value

Allow for varying level of participation

Create a pulse for the community

Evolve in response to changing needs

Implications of Social Networks

Global in scope available to everyone

Shared knowledge enables opportunity

Tacit local knowledge disseminated globally

Local business can think and act globally

Social Capital

Network of relationships that facilitate economic vitality

Provide opportunities for knowledge transfer within the network

Modes of Social Capital

Status, familial position

Reputation, peer merit

Authority, formal hierarchy

Building Trusted Social Capital

Establish a common point of introduction

Familiarity through repeated interaction

Calculating reputation through the network

Predictable norms in context

Social Capital in New York

Access large global talent pool of engineers

High labor mobility favor relationships

Social connections transcend company

Information Flow in New York

Quality of information source is highly valued

Trust based on reputation and merit

Free exchange without expectation of short-term return or subject to rational calculation within the network.

Entrepreneurs use Social Design

Tap into the innovation clusters

Enroll the peer experts in business model

Engage the key partners

Design the interactions with customers

Entrepreneurs will do this repeatedly regardless if they succeed or fail at each attempt

NYC Innovation

3 networks facilitate entrepreneurs

Firms, R&D Labs, Universities

VC's, Investment Bankers, Law Firms

Supplier and Customers

The networks are highly diverse and global

Continuous Innovation

Entrepreneurship is disruptive economic dynamism

Breaks old established order

Uncontrolled networks of self-organizing behavior

Performance is the only requirement

Do first ask later attitude

Be different, create the opportunity, have a vision

Take responsibility and risk

Share the rewards

Spread the work to whenever it is best done

Execute with speed

Social Capital to Innovation

Direct path to high tech innovation is through the networks of trusted coordination of knowledge and not through markets or hierarchies.

The absence of an explicit quid pro quo in network enhance the transmission of knowledge which is considered a commodity

Barriers to Social Design

Lack of physical proximity may not foster degree of familiarity needed

Sense of belonging, cross national, cultural, language dimensions

Task focused versus practice based

Overcoming Barriers to Global Relationships

Establish an Identity and Purpose

Open, frequent, exchanges on opportunities, contacts, and developments

Visits to understand cultural factors

Local partner representation

Global ICT Mitigates Cultural Differences

Belief in ICT as an agent of change

Freedom to participation as empowerment

Equal access to information regardless of role

Self organizing networks eliminate power distance

Force of competency over personality or authority

Future uncertainty is adopted as the norm

Risk are managed as a rational choice decisions

Individualism is absorbed into the collective

Time/Space are virtual, continuous, and shifted

Communication skills are computer mediated

Trusted relationships built through network connections

High diversity of roles and cultures to shared outcomes

Funding and Bootstrapping

What do entrepreneurs really do to find source of capital to fund a company?

Funding the Business

Self-fund, build product, get customers, breakeven, get capital, grow fast, then exit, and do it again.

Understanding Money

Personal Net Worth

How much has been in invested in you?

Lucky genes and feelings of entitlement

Repaying a debt to society

Leveraging the investment

Whole life plan

Life Style Choices

Material expectations

Work and reward, security and risk

Family, housing, leisure

Household Financial Management

Values, lifestyle

Entrepreneurial Finance

What is your relationship to money?

What about someone else's money?

Money as a language of business

Money as a unit of measure

The accounting of money

Time value of money

Cost of money

Value is not money

Investment Risk / Return

Personal Investing

Getting to positive net worth

Putting your money to work

Can you do better than the stock market?

Will a job be satisfying and pay enough?

Are you willing to invest in your business?

Think like an investor

Funding in school

Scholarship, Stipend, Sponsorship

University Research

STEM Product research

Patent the IP

Tech Transfer Office licensing to commercial entity

Gov't Grants for Research

Funding through Corporate Sponsors

Corporate Directed Research

Business Plan Competitions are mostly learning experience

Funding while working

Personal Funds (affordable loss)

Cash, credit cards, home loans, revolving credit

Reduce cost of living

Generate more discretionary income

Get two household incomes

Bootstrapping (use resources)

Working off-time to create product, get 1st customer

Funding through consulting

Consulting generates cash

Use cash to reinvest in product

Requires expertise to warrant fees

Use customer to get requirements

Needs contracts to retain IP

Funding the Seed Round

Founders & Family:

Most of the world's economies are family businesses

Jump-start the experience

Friends:

Create environment where they can help

Direct funding or in-kind work

Ask for help

Fools:

Sell a stranger to invest in your idea

Rare and generally not advisable

Funding through Angel Investors

Individual Angels:

High Net worth individuals, family offices

Knowledge of industry with access

Find these in your own network

Angel Groups:

The evaluate deals collectively

Co-invest with each other

Act like VC's but invest pre-revenue

Tend to mentor/coach

Funding Stages

Venture Capitalist: Vary tremendously, look for first round investors

Requires some experience to understand the Term sheet, cost of funds are high

Get something going first

Corporate strategic co-investor

Later Stage VC or Private Equity - Funding only available for growth for companies that are viable and demonstrate real results.

Funding Odds

Excellent for bootstrapping

Very little chance from an investor

They evaluate 100's of plans a year, invest in less than 1% of those they actually look at.

Increasing the Odds

Solid team, extended network

Deliver viable product to market

Growing, Scaling

Fund for growth not survival

Do not wait for funding

Why Bootstrap

No or limited funding options

Desire to retain ownership control

Minimizing exposure to risk

Create an effective business

Increase income and wealth

Stewardship and prudence

Founder Activities

find ways to achieve business goals

Invest in creating the product

minimizing the need for outside financing

maximizing funding impact by entrepreneur

methods for optimizing cash flow

Sell the vision to enroll help

Burn Rate

The rate at which you deplete your funding

Manage fix recurring cost

Match cost to revenue

Overhead matters (G&A/FFE)

Staff is highest recurring cost

Minimize operating costs (T&E)

Know how customers make decisions before marketing

Accounting

Create your metrics

Benchmark

Scorecard

Record and account for activity

Isolate the decisions requiring intuition

Report honestly

Operational control

Cash Flow and Break-even

Compound Annual Growth Rate

CAGR = (end value / beginning value) $^\wedge$ (1 / number of years) − 1

27% = (150.1 Billion / 56.3 Billion) $^\wedge$ (1 / 4) - 1

Funding from Founders, Family, Friends

85% of ventures are funded from F/F/F

Capital structure must be clear

Loans/Equity need formal agreements

Communicate news openly

Bootstrap Culture

Frugality

Creative solutions

"Cash is King"

Stewardship

Funding Negotiations

Know you values

Enroll help from your network

Deal with professional investors

Get a lawyer

Understand the terms

Bootstrap so you own the company

Entrepreneurship Education

Standards Outline

This section is included to help guide the readers' self-study on entrepreneurship and to put this book into an overall context. What will be immediately obvious is that much of the standards outline applies to improving employability for inexperienced talent as well as being useful for workforce development. These are residual benefits of studying and practicing entrepreneurship in that once you have tried to form a business, your appreciation for why it is so difficult and the perspective of the owners and executives who hire talent, will be much better understood. It increases your ability to contribute to the economy by understanding what it takes to create value as an entrepreneur. Educators use standards outline to guide the curriculum development and each course may have a different emphasis.

This book is for aspiring entrepreneurs with a scientific or technical background who may want to commercialize research and learn what does an entrepreneur think and do. It omits material that is readily available in other popular books and free resources related to venture startups. The tech startups are just one class of entrepreneurship that many Universities and Government policy makers are promoting and supporting. Entrepreneurship has many forms and practices and is not exclusive to a technocratic society. Therefore, the material is a bit broader in its representation and characterization of entrepreneurs but still within the realm of what the scientist and technologist are likely to encounter in their early journey.

The standards outline is revised slightly to address some omissions. I indicated what I have tried to address in this book, not directly, using their outline but reoriented to what I thought was most relevant to my students and others like them, either PhD candidates or MBA students in a traditional business program. The book covers topics the standards omit but I consider essential for anyone considering learning entrepreneurship. For example, understanding fear and failure and the role of cognitive biases in decision making under high uncertainty of a startup. The book covers what the standards outline omit which are necessary for new venture creation using technical innovation and has a high degree of market uncertainty but the potential rewards warrant the risk taking.

The standards outline is generic to all small business and focused on what a person would need to know to work in an entrepreneurial business and not on what it takes to start one. Many of the informal startup training and incubator programs have two biases: one is software related businesses, and the second is businesses that are attractive to Venture Capitalist. I come from this experience, and this is where I have had success, but I reject such limiting conditions for the majority of PhD and MBA students who will never fit within this narrow bias. Therefore, most of the startup programs are either pointless for them or a waste of time due to the misalignment of interest. This was one of the motivations for me to start teaching. When I decided to try and teach entrepreneurship I first researched how to teach the subject and if anyone attempted to define a standard for what topics should be included. I used the National Content Standards for Entrepreneurship Education to evaluate what I thought were relevant from my own experience relative to this independent standard that was applicable to the general teaching of entrepreneurship. I consider my value to be a point of view from my own experiences put against the broader standard that was developed by a team of experts with experience in teaching entrepreneurship.

From my own experience as an entrepreneur, many of these topics I learned the hard way, by doing and making mistakes. Through self-examination somehow I found a path forward but this struggle is not necessary. The standards outline appears prescriptive, and I have repeated throughout the book that business is learned by doing it. Business does have a language and some basic expectations for skills the young talent must know to participate. With the extreme specialization that our school systems impose, and the corporate workplace demands, little opportunity exists for people to learn basic business skills. Those in a family business would have a huge advantage in this regard since the family dinner table might discuss all manner of issues relevant to a business. For those not born into a family business situation, the schools do not teach what I consider economic life skills. With this in mind, the standards outline are included for reference and review.

I strongly urge all researchers and faculty who read this book and teach a course, to embedded entrepreneurship into the curriculum within the course content. I do not promote having a separate course on entrepreneurship, which treats it as a separate discipline apart from other topics. This formal academic approach is exactly what makes it so difficult for the youth to absorb the importance of knowing how to make money beyond just getting a job. The topic of entrepreneurship needs to be infused in other courses, even if it is simply asking how something being studied benefits society and the economy. This seemingly trivial question, when I have asked this of researchers, many of them have been stumped and at a loss for a concise answer. Correcting this gap between formal classroom learning and real world practical skills is central to what so many economies struggle with now. If you are faculty, then take on the challenge of innovating education and think entrepreneurially about what you do.

Note: In the outline to follow, an "I" is included where an item or section is addressed in this book, where an "I" is omitted the reader should seek out other books and experiences to help them learn about the topic.

The National Content Standards for Entrepreneurship Education

Copyright © 2004 by the Consortium for Entrepreneurship Education, Columbus, Ohio www.entre-ed.org

	Entrepreneurial Processes
A	**Understands concepts and processes associated with successful entrepreneurial performance**
Discovery	
I	Explain the need for entrepreneurial discovery
	Discuss entrepreneurial discovery processes
	Assess global trends and opportunities
	Determine opportunities for venture creation
	Assess opportunities for venture creation
	Describe idea-generation methods
	Generate venture ideas
	Determine feasibility of ideas
Concept Development	
I	Describe entrepreneurial planning considerations
	Explain tools used by entrepreneurs for venture planning

Assess start-up requirements
Assess risks associated with venture
Describe external resources useful to entrepreneurs during concept development
Assess the need to use external resources for concept development
Describe strategies to protect intellectual property
Use components of a business plan to define venture idea

Resourcing

Distinguish between debt and equity financing for venture creation
Describe processes used to acquire adequate financial resources for venture creation/start-up
Select sources to finance venture creation/start-up
Explain factors to consider in determining a venture's human-resource needs
Describe considerations in selecting capital resources
Acquire capital resources needed for the venture
Assess the costs/benefits associated with resources

Actualization

I	Use external resources to supplement entrepreneur's expertise
	Explain the complexity of business operations
	Evaluate risk-taking opportunities
	Explain the need for business systems and procedures
	Describe the use of operating procedures
	Explain methods/processes for organizing work flow
	Develop and/or provide product/service
	Use creativity in business activities/decisions
	Explain the impact of resource productivity on venture success
	Create processes for ongoing opportunity recognition
	Adapt to changes in business environment
Harvesting	
	Explain the need for continuation planning
	Describe methods of venture harvesting
	Evaluate options for continued venture involvement
	Develop exit strategies
B	**Entrepreneurial Traits/Behaviors**

	Understands the personal traits/behaviors associated with successful entrepreneurial performance
	Leadership
I	Demonstrate honesty and integrity
	Demonstrate responsible behavior
	Demonstrate initiative against adversity
	Demonstrate ethical work habits
	Exhibit passion for goal attainment
	Recognize others' efforts
	Lead others using positive statements
	Develop team spirit
	Enlist others in working toward a shared vision
	Share authority, when appropriate
	Value diversity
	Personal Assessment
I	Describe desirable entrepreneurial personality traits
	Determine personal biases and stereotypes

	Determine interests
	Evaluate personal capabilities
	Conduct self-assessment to determine entrepreneurial potential
Personal Management	
I	Maintain positive attitude
	Demonstrate interest and enthusiasm
	Make decisions under uncertainty
	Develop an orientation to change, improve, and innovate
	Demonstrate problem-solving skills
	Assess risks
	Assume personal responsibility for decisions
	Use time-management principles
	Develop tolerance for ambiguity
	Use feedback for personal growth
	Demonstrate creativity by innovating for improvements
	Set personal goals that are challenging
C	**Business Foundations**

	Understands fundamental business concepts that affect business decision making
Business Concepts	
	Explain the role of business in society
	Describe types of business activities
	Explain types of businesses
	Explain opportunities for creating added value
	Determine issues and trends in business
	Describe crucial elements of a quality culture/continuous quality improvement
	Describe the role of management in the achievement of quality
	Explain the nature of managerial ethics
	Describe the need for and impact of ethical business practices
Business Activities	
	Explain marketing management and its importance in a global economy
	Describe marketing functions and related activities
	Explain the nature and scope of operations management
	Explain the concept of management

	Explain the concept of financial management
	Explain the concept of human resource management
	Explain the concept of risk management
	Explain the concept of strategic management
D	**Communications and Interpersonal Skills** **Understands concepts, strategies, and systems needed to interact effectively with others**
	Fundamentals of Communication
I	Explain the nature of effective communications
	Apply effective listening skills
	Use proper grammar and vocabulary
	Reinforce service orientation through communication
	Explain the nature of effective verbal communications
	Address people properly
	Handle telephone calls in a businesslike manner
	Make oral presentations
	Explain the nature of written communications
	Write business letters

	Write informational messages
	Write inquiries
	Write persuasive messages
	Prepare simple written reports
	Prepare complex written reports
	Use communications technologies/systems (e.g., e-mail, faxes, voice mail, cell phones, etc.)
Staff Communications	
	Follow directions
	Explain the nature of staff communication
	Give directions for completing job tasks
	Conduct staff meetings with an agenda and meeting notes
Ethics in Communication	
	Respect the privacy of others, be transparent in your communications
	Explain ethical considerations in providing information
Group Working Relationships	

I	Treat others fairly at work
	Develop cultural sensitivity and diversity
	Foster positive working relationships
	Participate as a team member
Dealing with Conflict	
	Demonstrate self-control
	Show empathy for others
	Use appropriate assertiveness
	Demonstrate negotiation skills
	Handle difficult customers/clients
	Interpret business policies to customers/clients
	Handle customer/client complaints
	Explain the nature of organizational change
	Describe the nature of organizational conflict
	Explain the nature of stress management
E	**Digital Skills** **Understands concepts and procedures needed for basic computer**

operations

Computer Basics

Use basic computer terminology
Apply basic commands of operating system software
Employ desktop/laptop/tablet operating skills
Determine file organization for documents and all digital assets
Demonstrate system utilities for file management
Compress or alter files
Use reference materials to access information
Use menu systems
Use control panel components
Access data through various computer drives and storage devices

Computer Applications

Demonstrate basic search skills on the Web
Evaluate credibility of Internet resources
Demonstrate file management skills
Communicate by computer

	Solve routine hardware and software problems
	Operate computer-related hardware peripherals
	Explain the nature of e-commerce
	Describe the impact of the Internet on business
	Develop basic website, blog, and social media profile
F	**Economics** **Understands the economic principles and concepts fundamental to entrepreneurship/small to medium business ownership**
Basic Concepts	
	Distinguish between economic goods and services
	Explain the factors of production
	Explain the concept of scarcity
	Explain the concept of opportunity costs
	Describe the nature of economics and economic activities
	Determine forms of economic utility created by business activities
	Explain the principles of supply and demand
	Describe the concept of price
Cost-Profit Relationships	

Explain the concept of productivity
Describe cost/benefit analysis
Analyze the impact of specialization/division of labor on productivity
Explain the concept of organized labor and business
Explain the law of diminishing returns
Describe the concept of economies of scale
Economic Indicators/Trends
Explain measures used to analyze economic conditions
Explain the nature of the Consumer Price Index
Explain the concept of Gross Domestic Product
Determine the impact of business cycles on business activities
Economic Systems
Explain the types of economic systems
Describe the relationship between government and business
Assess impact of government actions on business ventures
Explain the concept of private enterprise

		Assess factors affecting a business's profit
		Determine factors affecting business risk
		Explain the concept of competition
		Describe types of market structures
		Determine the impact of small business/entrepreneurship on market economies
	International Concepts	
	I	Explain the nature of international trade
		Describe small-business opportunities in international trade
		Determine the impact of cultural and social environments on world trade
		Explain the impact of exchange rates on trade
		Evaluate influences on a nation's ability to trade
	G	**Financial Literacy** **Understands personal money-management concepts, procedures, and strategies**
	Money Basics	
		Explain forms of financial exchange (cash, credit, debit, etc.)
		Describe functions of money (medium of exchange, unit of measure,

	store of value)
	Describe the sources of income (wages/salaries, interest, rent, dividends, transfer payments, etc.)
	Recognize types of currency (paper money, coins, banknotes, government bonds, treasury notes, etc.)
	Read and interpret a pay stub
	Explain the time value of money
	Describe costs associated with credit
	Explain legal responsibilities associated with use of money
	Use money effectively
Financial Services	
	Describe services provided by financial institutions
	Explain legal responsibilities of financial institutions
	Explain costs associated with use of financial services
	Select financial institution
	Open account with financial institution
Personal Money Management	
I	Set financial goals

	Develop savings plan
	Develop spending plan
	Make deposits to and withdrawals from account
	Complete financial instruments
	Maintain financial records
	Read and reconcile financial statements
	Correct errors with account
	Explain types of investments
	Invest money
	Develop personal budget
	Build positive credit history
	Improve/repair creditworthiness
H	**Professional Development** **Understands concepts and strategies needed for career exploration, development, and growth**
	Career Planning
I	Evaluate career opportunities based on current/future economy
	Analyze employer expectations in the business environment

	Explain the rights of workers
	Select and use sources of career information
	Determine tentative occupational interest
	Explain employment opportunities in entrepreneurship
Job-Seeking Skills	
	Utilize job-search strategies
	Complete a job application
	Interview for a job
	Write a follow-up letter after job interviews
	Write a letter of application
	Prepare a résumé
	Describe techniques for obtaining work experience (e.g., volunteer activities, internships)
	Explain the need for ongoing education as a worker
	Explain possible advancement patterns for jobs
	Determine skills needed to enhance career progression

	Utilize resources that can contribute to professional development (e.g., trade journals/ periodicals, professional/trade associations, classes/seminars, trade shows, and mentors)
	Use networking techniques for professional growth
I	**Financial Management** **Understands the financial concepts and tools used in making business decisions**
Accounting	
	Explain accounting standards (GAAP)
	Prepare estimated/projected income statement
	Estimate cash-flow needs
	Prepare estimated/projected balance sheet
	Calculate financial ratios
	Determine and deposit payroll taxes
	File tax returns
Finance	
	Explain the purposes and importance of obtaining business credit
	Make critical decisions regarding acceptance of bank cards

Establish credit policies
Develop billing and collection policies
Describe use of credit bureaus
Explain the nature of overhead/operating expenses
Determine financing needed to start a business
Determine risks associated with obtaining business credit
Explain sources of financial assistance
Explain loan evaluation criteria used by lending institutions
Select sources of business loans
Establish relationship with financial institutions
Complete loan application process
Determine business's value
Money Management
Establish financial goals and objectives
Develop and monitor budget
Manage cash flow
Explain the nature of capital investment

	Foster a positive financial reputation
	Implement procedures for managing debt
	Supervise/implement regular accounting procedures and financial reports
J	**Human Resource Management** **Understands the concepts, systems, and strategies needed to acquire, motivate, develop, and terminate staff**
Organizing	
	Develop a personnel organizational plan
	Develop job descriptions
	Develop compensation plan/incentive systems
	Organize work/projects for others
	Delegate responsibility for job tasks
Staffing	
	Determine hiring needs
	Recruit new employees
	Screen job applications/résumés
	Interview job applicants

	Select new employees
	Negotiate new-hire's salary/pay
	Dismiss/Fire employee
Training/Development	
	Orient new employees (management's role)
	Conduct training class/program
	Coach employees
Morale/Motivation	
I	Exhibit leadership skills
	Encourage team building
	Recognize/reward employees
	Handle employee complaints/grievances
	Ensure equitable opportunities for employees
	Build organizational culture
Assessment	
	Assess employee morale
	Provide feedback on work efforts

	Assess employee performance
	Take remedial action with employee
	Conduct exit interviews
K	**Information Management** **Understands the concepts, systems, and tools needed to access, process, maintain, evaluate, and disseminate information for business decision-making**
Record keeping	
	Explain the nature of business records
	Maintain record of daily financial transactions
	Record and report sales tax
	Develop payroll record keeping system
	Maintain personnel records
	Maintain customer records
Technology	
	Explain ways that technology impacts business
	Use Personal Information Management/Productivity applications
	Demonstrate writing/publishing applications

		Demonstrate presentation applications
		Demonstrate database applications
		Demonstrate spreadsheet applications
		Demonstrate collaborative/groupware applications
		Determine venture's technology needs
	Information Acquisition	
		Select sources of business start-up information
		Conduct an environmental scan to obtain marketing information
		Monitor internal records for marketing information
		Determine underlying customer needs/frustrations
L		**Marketing Management** **Understands the concepts, processes, and systems needed to determine and satisfy customer needs/wants/expectations, meet business goals/objectives, and create new product/service ideas**
	Product/Service Creation	
I		Explain methods to generate a product/service idea
		Generate product/service ideas
		Assess opportunities for import substitution

Determine product/service to fill customer need	
Determine initial feasibility of product/service ideas	
Plan product/service mix	
Choose product name	
Determine unique selling proposition	
Develop strategies to position product/service	
Build brand/image	
Evaluate customer experience	
Marketing-information Management	
	Explain the concept of market and market identification
	Describe the role of situation analysis in the marketing-planning process
	Determine market segments
	Select target markets
	Conduct market analysis
	Explain the concept of marketing strategies
	Describe the nature of marketing planning
	Set a marketing budget

	Develop marketing plan
	Monitor and evaluate performance of marketing plan
Promotion	
	Describe the elements of the promotional mix
	Calculate advertising media costs
	Select advertising media
	Prepare a promotional budget
	Develop promotional plan for a business
	Write a news release
	Obtain publicity
	Select sales-promotion options
	Write sales letters
	Manage online (www) activities
	Evaluate effectiveness of advertising
Pricing	
	Calculate breakeven point
	Explain factors affecting pricing decisions

	Establish pricing objectives
	Select pricing strategies
	Set prices
	Adjust prices to maximize profitability
Selling	
	Acquire product information for use in selling
	Analyze product information to identify product features and benefits
	Prepare for the sales presentation
	Establish relationship with client/customer
	Determine customer/client needs
	Determine customer's buying motives for use in selling
	Differentiate between consumer and organizational buying behavior
	Recommend specific product
	Convert customer/client objections into selling points
	Close the sale
	Demonstrate suggestion selling
	Plan follow up strategies for use in selling

	Process sales documentation
	Prospect for customers
	Plan strategies for meeting sales quotas
	Analyze sales reports
	Train staff to support sales efforts
	Analyze technology for use in the sales function
	Manage online sales process
M	**Operations Management** **Understands the processes and systems implemented to facilitate daily business operations.**
Business Systems	
	Plan business layout
	Determine equipment needs
	Document business systems and procedures
	Establish operating procedures
	Develop project plans
	Analyze business processes and procedures
	Implement quality improvement techniques

	Evaluate productivity of resources
	Manage computer-based operating systems
Channel Management	
	Select business location
	Select distribution channels
	Develop and implement order-fulfillment processes
Purchasing/Procurement	
	Explain the buying process
	Describe the nature of buyer reputation and vendor relationships
	Establish company buying/purchasing policies
	Conduct vendor search
	Choose vendors
	Negotiate contracts with vendors
	Place orders
	Barter with vendors
Daily Operations	

	Schedule staff
	Maintain inventory of products/supplies
	Organize shipping/receiving
N	**Risk Management** **Understands the concepts, strategies, and systems that businesses implement and enforce to minimize loss**

Business Risks

Describe types of business risk
Determine ways that small businesses protect themselves against loss
Establish controls to prevent embezzlement/theft
Establish and implement systems to protect customer/employee confidentiality
Determine business's liabilities
Explain ways to transfer risk
Obtain insurance coverage
Develop strategies to protect computer (digital) data
Develop security policies and procedures
Establish safety policies and procedures

	Protect assets from creditors
	Establish parameters for staff responsibility/authority
	Develop continuation plan
Legal Considerations	
	Explain legal issues affecting businesses
	Protect intellectual property rights
	Select form of business ownership
	Obtain legal documents for business operations
	Describe the nature of businesses' reporting requirements
	Adhere to personnel regulations
	Implement workplace regulations (including OSHA, ADA)
	Develop strategies for legal/government compliance
O	**Strategic Management** **Understands the processes, strategies, and systems needed to guide the overall business organization**
Planning	
I	Conduct SWOT analysis
	Conduct competitive analysis

	Evaluate business acquisition options
	Develop company goals/objectives
	Develop business mission
	Forecast income/sales
	Conduct break-even analysis
	Develop action plans
	Develop business plan
Controlling	
	Use budgets to control operations
	Develop expense-control plans
	Analyze cash-flow patterns
	Interpret financial statements
	Analyze operating results in relation to budget/industry
	Track performance of business plan

Bibliography

The bibliography is included as a reference to researchers who may be curious what an entrepreneur reads to validate their own experience and to faculty who may want to use this book in a course or create their own variation. I segment the bibliography by major themes equivalent to the chapters of the book. I do not advocate that the entrepreneur reading this book spend time on this background since much of it is already highly summarized in the text. To learn how to be an entrepreneur requires that one stop reading and start doing. As one is acting on the business I do encourage continuous learning and reflection of which will be a life long effort, so if the entrepreneur is formulating a business and they wish to learn more of the background of many subtopics of the book the bibliography will be useful. I suggest starting with the books which are complete works and leaving the academic papers as snippets of curious attempts at asserting some position. The validity of the book is from my own direct business experience and my interpretation of what I could understand so I can only attest to its usefulness in my own business. As to whether it helps others that is for the reader to try and learn on their own and in 20 years they can write a book about what they experienced.

Entrepreneurial Spirit

"7 Billion And Counting: Can Earth Handle It?" *NPR.org Talk of the Nation*. Accessed October, 2014. http://www.npr.org/2011/01/06/132708954/meeting-the-needs-of-the-booming-global-population.

Backhaus, Jürgen G. *Entrepreneurship, Money and Coordination: Hayek's Theory of Cultural Evolution*. Edward Elgar Publishing, 2005.

Belsky, Gary, and Thomas Gilovich. *Why Smart People Make Big Money Mistakes and How to Correct Them: Lessons from the Life-Changing Science of Behavioral Economics*. Simon and Schuster, 2010.

Bickel, Warren K., and Rudy E. Vuchinich. *Reframing Health Behavior Change With Behavioral Economics*. Psychology Press, 2000.

Birley, Sue. "The Role of Networks in the Entrepreneurial Process." *Journal of Business Venturing* 1, no. 1 (1985): 107–17. doi:10.1016/0883-9026(85)90010-2.

Brad Feld. "Founder's Syndrome and Origin Stories." *Feld Thoughts*. Accessed October, 2014. http://www.feld.com/archives/2014/01/founders-syndrome-origin-stories.html.

Brockhaus, Robert H. *The Psychology of the Entrepreneur*. SSRN Scholarly Paper. Rochester, NY: Social Science Research Network, 1982. http://papers.ssrn.com/abstract=1497760.

Bull, Ivan, and Gary E. Willard. "Towards a Theory of Entrepreneurship." *Journal of Business Venturing*, Special Theoretical Issue, 8, no. 3 (May 1993): 183–95. doi:10.1016/0883-9026(93)90026-2.

Burrowes, Dr Nina. "The Psychology of Entrepreneurship: Have You Got What It Takes?" *The Guardian*, December 5, 2013, sec. Women in Leadership. http://www.theguardian.com/women-in-leadership/small-business-blog/2013/dec/05/psychology-entrepreneurs-starting-new-business.

Camerer, Colin F., George Loewenstein, and Matthew Rabin. *Advances in Behavioral Economics*. Princeton University Press, 2011.

Cornwall, Jeff. "The Importance of Self-Assessment and Self-Reflection." *Dr Jeff Cornwall*. Accessed October, 2014. http://www.drjeffcornwall.com/2004/10/28/the_importance_of_selfassessme/.

David K. Williams. "Great Companies Are Led By Missionaries, Not Mercenaries." *Forbes*. Accessed October, 2014. http://www.forbes.com/sites/davidkwilliams/2013/03/29/great-companies-are-led-by-missionaries-not-mercenaries/.

DeFotis, Dimitra. "IMF On Emerging Markets: 4.4% Growth." *Barrons*. Accessed October, 2014. http://blogs.barrons.com/emergingmarketsdaily/2014/10/08/imf-on-emerging-markets-4-4-growth/.

Dishman, Lydia. "The Science And Psychology Behind What Drives Serial Entrepreneurs." *Fast Company*. Accessed October, 2014. http://www.fastcompany.com/3019350/dialed/the-science-and-psychology-behind-what-drives-serial-entrepreneurs.

Douglas L. Griest. "Entrepreneurs and Personality | Management Psychology Group." Accessed October, 2014. http://www.managementpsychology.com/articles/entrepreneurs-and-personality/.

"Emerging Market Growth Beats US: What Makes Emerging Markets Great Investments?" *Forbes*. Accessed October, 2014. http://www.forbes.com/pictures/eglg45gdjd/emerging-market-growth-beats-us-2/.

Eric Schurenberg. "What's an Entrepreneur? The Best Answer Ever." *Inc.com*. Accessed October, 2014. http://www.inc.com/eric-schurenberg/the-best-definition-of-entepreneurship.html.

"Family Business Survey 2012: Italy." *PwC*. Accessed October, 2014. http://www.pwc.com/it/en/industries/pmi/family-business-survey-2012.jhtml.

Fiet, James O. "The Theoretical Side of Teaching Entrepreneurship." *Journal of Business Venturing* 16, no. 1 (January 2001): 1–24. doi:10.1016/S0883-9026(99)00041-5.

Frese, Michael, and Michael M. Gielnik. "The Psychology of Entrepreneurship." *Annual Review of Organizational Psychology and Organizational Behavior* 1, no. 1 (2014): 413–38. doi:10.1146/annurev-orgpsych-031413-091326.

Gartner, William B. "A Conceptual Framework for Describing the Phenomenon of New Venture Creation." *Academy of Management Review* 10, no. 4 (October 1, 1985): 696–706. doi:10.5465/AMR.1985.4279094.

Gartner, William B. "What Are We Talking about When We Talk about Entrepreneurship?" *Journal of Business Venturing* 5, no. 1 (January 1990): 15–28. doi:10.1016/0883-9026(90)90023-M.

Goss, David. "Schumpeter's Legacy? Interaction and Emotions in the Sociology of Entrepreneurship." *Entrepreneurship Theory and Practice* 29, no. 2 (March 1, 2005): 205–18. doi:10.1111/j.1540-6520.2005.00077.x.

Hagedoorn, John. "Innovation and Entrepreneurship: Schumpeter Revisited." *Industrial and Corporate Change* 5, no. 3 (January 1, 1996): 883–96. doi:10.1093/icc/5.3.883.

Hagen, Everett. "The Entrepreneur As Rebel Against Traditional Society." *Human Organization* 19, no. 4 (December 1, 1960): 185–87.

Hébert, Robert F., and Albert N. Link. "In Search of the Meaning of Entrepreneurship." *Small Business Economics* 1, no. 1 (March 1, 1989): 39–49. doi:10.1007/BF00389915.

Heidi Roizen. "Adventures in Entrepreneurship." *Stanford's Entrepreneurship Corner.* Accessed October, 2014. http://ecorner.stanford.edu/authorMaterialInfo.html? mid=3244,

Hoang, Ha, and Bostjan Antoncic. "Network-Based Research in Entrepreneurship: A Critical Review." *Journal of Business Venturing* 18, no. 2 (March 2003): 165–87. doi:10.1016/S0883-9026(02)00081-2.

Honig, Benson. "Entrepreneurship Education: Toward a Model of Contingency-Based Business Planning." *Academy of Management Learning & Education* 3, no. 3 (September 1, 2004): 258–73. doi:10.5465/AMLE.2004.14242112.

Jessica Bruder. "The Psychological Price of Entrepreneurship." *Inc.com.* Accessed October, 2014. http://www.inc.com/magazine/201309/jessica-bruder/psychological-price-of-entrepreneurship.html.

John Doerr. "Entrepreneurs: Missionaries, Not Mercenaries." *Venture Hacks.* Accessed October, 2014. http://venturehacks.com/articles/missionaries.

John Doerr—. "Mercenaries and Missionaries." *Stanford's Entrepreneurship Corner.* Accessed October, 2014. http://ecorner.stanford.edu/authorMaterialInfo.html? mid=1274.

Jones, Colin, and Jack English. "A Contemporary Approach to Entrepreneurship Education." *Education + Training* 46, no. 8/9 (October 1, 2004): 416–23. doi:10.1108/00400910410569533.

Justin Rosenstein. "Leading Big Visions From the Heart." *Stanford's Entrepreneurship Corner.* Accessed October, 2014. http://ecorner.stanford.edu/authorMaterialInfo.html?mid=3117.

Kevin Ready. "Founders Syndrome: The Third Rail of the Startup World." *Forbes.* Accessed October, 2014. http://www.forbes.com/sites/kevinready/2012/07/10/founders-syndrome-the-third-rail-of-the-startup-world/.

Klyver, Kim, Kevin Hindle, and Thomas Schøtt. "Who Will Be an Entrepreneur?" *Frontiers of Entrepreneurship Research* 27, no. 7 (June 9, 2007). http://digitalknowledge.babson.edu/fer/vol27/iss7/1.

Larry E. Greiner. "Evolution and Revolution as Organizations Grow." *Harvard Business Review.* Accessed October, 2014. http://hbr.org/1998/05/evolution-and-revolution-as-organizations-grow/ar/1.

Leah Busque. "Do Something You Love." *Stanford's Entrepreneurship Corner.* Accessed October, 2014. http://ecorner.stanford.edu/authorMaterialInfo.html?mid=3302.

Levinson, Harry. *Designing and Managing Your Career.* Harvard Business Press, 1989.

Litz, Reginald A. "The Family Business: Toward Definitional Clarity." *Family Business Review* 8, no. 2 (June 1, 1995): 71–81. doi:10.1111/j.1741-6248.1995.00071.x.

"Macroeconomic Insights - 2014 Outlook: Growth Trends in the Emerging Markets."

Goldman Sachs. Accessed October, 2014. http://www.goldmansachs.com/our-thinking/outlook/wilson-2014-outlook/multimedia/02-video.html.

"Macroeconomic Insights - Economic Outlook: Emerging Markets." *Goldman Sachs*. Accessed October, 2014. http://www.goldmansachs.com/our-thinking/outlook/dominic-wilson-emerging-markets-2014-index.html? CID=PS_01_73_07_00_00_00_01.

Marchionatti, Roberto. "On Keynes' Animal Spirits." *Kyklos* 52, no. 3 (August 1, 1999): 415–39. doi:10.1111/j.1467-6435.1999.tb00225.x.

Matthew Herper. "The Psychology Of Success." *Forbes*. Accessed October, 2014. http://www.forbes.com/2002/10/18/1018profile.html.

Noam Wasserman. "The Founder's Dilemmas." Video. *Stanford's Entrepreneurship Corner*. Accessed October, 2014. http://ecorner.stanford.edu/authorMaterialInfo.html? mid=2995.

O'Connor, Kevin. "Nine Psychological Traits of an Entrepreneur: Do You Have What It Takes?" *Huffington Post*, August 26, 2010. http://www.huffingtonpost.com/kevin-oconnor/nine-psychological-traits_b_689058.html.

Paul Gregory. "The Psychology of the Entrepreneur." Accessed October, 2014. http://www.theicehouse.co.nz/the-psychology-of-the-entrepreneur/.

Pinchot, Gifford III. *Intrapreneuring: Why You Don't Have to Leave the Corporation to Become an Entrepreneur*. SSRN Scholarly Paper. Rochester, NY: Social Science Research Network, 1985. http://papers.ssrn.com/abstract=1496196.

"Private Companies Outperform the Economy but Plan to Hire Just a Little." *PwC - Trendsetter Barometer® Q2 2014*. Accessed October, 2014. http://www.pwc.com/us/en/private-company-services/publications/pcs-trendsetter-barometer.jhtml.

Robert Kunzig. "7 Billion." *National Geographic*, January 2011. http://ngm.nationalgeographic.com/7-billion.

Ron Proctor. "Personal Branding." 14:03:35 UTC. http://www.slideshare.net/RonProctor/personal-branding-2390487.

Sapienza, Paola, Luigi Zingales, and Luigi Guiso. *Does Culture Affect Economic Outcomes?*. Working Paper. National Bureau of Economic Research, February 2006. http://www.nber.org/papers/w11999.

Saras Sarasvathy. "Effectuation." Video. *Big Think*. Accessed October, 2014. http://bigthink.com/users/sarassarasvathy.

Schumpeter, Joseph A. *Entrepreneurship as Innovation*. SSRN Scholarly Paper. Rochester, NY: Social Science Research Network, 2000. http://papers.ssrn.com/abstract=1512266.

Simon, Mark, Susan M. Houghton, and Karl Aquino. "Cognitive Biases, Risk Perception, and Venture Formation: How Individuals Decide to Start Companies." *Journal of Business Venturing* 15, no. 2 (March 2000): 113–34. doi:10.1016/S0883-9026(98)00003-2.

Sørensen, Bent Meier. "'Behold, I Am Making All Things New': The Entrepreneur as Savior in the Age of Creativity." *Scandinavian Journal of Management,* Recreating/Recontextualising Entrepreneurship, 24, no. 2 (June 2008): 85–93. doi:10.1016/j.scaman.2008.03.002.

Stewart Jr., Wayne H., Warren E. Watson, Joann C. Carland, and James W. Carland. "A Proclivity for Entrepreneurship: A Comparison of Entrepreneurs, Small Business Owners, and Corporate Managers." *Journal of Business Venturing* 14, no. 2 (March 1999): 189–214. doi:10.1016/S0883-9026(97)00070-0.

"The Generation Game." *The Economist,* March 2, 2000. http://www.economist.com/node/347923/print.

"The Vital Entrepreneur - High-Impact Entrepreneurs: The Ripple Effect." Accessed October, 2014. http://www.ey.com/US/en/Services/Strategic-Growth-Markets/The-vital-entrepreneur--1-High-impact-entrepreneurs--the-ripple-effect.

"The Winklevoss Syndrome: When Founders Are Left Behind." *OPEN Forum.* Accessed October, 2014. https://www.americanexpress.com/us/small-business/openforum/articles/the-winklevoss-syndrome-when-founders-are-left-behind/.

"The World's Fastest Growing Markets." *EY Emerging Markets Center.* Accessed October, 2014. http://emergingmarkets.ey.com.

Tomas Chamorro-Premuzic. "Personality and Entrepreneurship: Why Are Some People More Entrepreneurial than Others, and Why Should You Care?" Accessed October, 2014. http://www.psychologytoday.com/blog/mr-personality/201010/personality-and-entrepreneurship-why-are-some-people-more-entrepreneurial.

Ward, John L. "Growing the Family Business: Special Challenges and Best Practices." *Family Business Review* 10, no. 4 (December 1, 1997): 323–37. doi:10.1111/j.1741-6248.1997.00323.x.

Wennekers, Sander, and Roy Thurik. "Linking Entrepreneurship and Economic Growth." *Small Business Economics* 13, no. 1 (August 1, 1999): 27–56. doi:10.1023/A:1008063200484.

Wood, John Cunningham. *Karl Marx's Economics: Critical Assessments.* Taylor & Francis, 1993.

Zahra, Shaker A., James C. Hayton, and Carlo Salvato. "Entrepreneurship in Family vs. Non-Family Firms: A Resource-Based Analysis of the Effect of Organizational Culture." *Entrepreneurship Theory and Practice* 28, no. 4 (June 1, 2004): 363–81. doi:10.1111/j.1540-6520.2004.00051.x.

Ideas to Execution

"12 Shocking Ideas That Could Change the World." *WIRED*. Accessed November, 2014. http://archive.wired.com/techbiz/people/magazine/17-10/ff_smartlist.

"25 Ideas to Change the World," Accessed November, 2014, http://www.forbes.com/2010/06/15/forbes-india-25-ideas-to-change-the-world-ideas-10_land.html.

Adams, Errol A., J.D., M.L.S., on September 26, and 2012 at 12:24 Am Said. "10 Important Resources on the WIPO Website for IP Professionals." *The Intellogist Blog*. Accessed October 14, 2014. http://intellogist.wordpress.com/2012/09/19/10-invaluable-resources-on-the-wipo-website-for-ip-professionals/.

Allen, Thomas J. *Managing the Flow of Technology: Technology Transfer and the Dissemination of Technological Information Within the R&D Organization*. MIT Press Books. The MIT Press, 1984. https://ideas.repec.org/b/mtp/titles/0262510278.html (https://ideas.repec.org/b/mtp/titles/0262510278.html).

Audia, Pino G., and Christopher I. Rider. *A Garage and an Idea: What More Does an Entrepreneur Need?*. SSRN Scholarly Paper. Rochester, NY: Social Science Research Network, 2005. http://papers.ssrn.com/abstract=1501554.

Bercovitz, Janet, and Maryann Feldman. "Entreprenerial Universities and Technology Transfer: A Conceptual Framework for Understanding Knowledge-Based Economic Development." *The Journal of Technology Transfer* 31, no. 1 (January 1, 2006): 175–88. doi:10.1007/s10961-005-5029-z.

Berkun, Scott. *The Myths of Innovation*. O'Reilly Media, Inc., 2010.

Bock, Gee W., and Young-Gul Kim. "Breaking the Myths of Rewards: An Exploratory Study of Attitudes about Knowledge Sharing." *Information Resources Management Journal* 15, no. 2 (32 2002): 14–21. doi:10.4018/irmj.2002040102.

Bray, Michael J, and James N Lee. "University Revenues from Technology Transfer: Licensing Fees vs. Equity Positions." *Journal of Business Venturing* 15, no. 5–6 (September 2000): 385–92. doi:10.1016/S0883-9026(98)00034-2.

Breen, Bill. "The 6 Myths of Creativity." *Fast Company* 89 (2004): 75.

Chaudhuri, Saabira. "10 Ideas That Could Change The World." *Fast Company*. Accessed November, 2014. http://www.fastcompany.com/720286/10-ideas-could-change-world.

Christopher Mims. "World Changing Ideas." *Scientific American*, December 2009. http://www.scientificamerican.com/article/world-changing-ideas/.

Davila, Tony, Marc Epstein, and Robert Shelton. *Making Innovation Work: How to Manage It, Measure It, and Profit from It, Updated Edition.* FT Press, 2012.

Debra Kaye. "To Patent or Not: What to Learn from Rainbow Loom's Battle." *Inc.com.* Accessed November, 2014. http://www.inc.com/debra-kaye/patent-rainbow-loom.html.

Denning, Peter J., and Robert Dunham. *The Innovator's Way: Essential Practices for Successful Innovation.* MIT Press, 2010.

Farnworth, Demian. "A Complete Guide to Crawling Inside Your Customer's Head With Empathy Maps." *Copyblogger.* Accessed November, 2014. http://www.copyblogger.com/empathy-maps/.

Frankelius, Per. "Questioning Two Myths in Innovation Literature." *The Journal of High Technology Management Research* 20, no. 1 (2009): 40–51. doi:10.1016/j.hitech.2009.02.002.

Girotra, Karan, Christian Terwiesch, and Karl T. Ulrich. "Idea Generation and the Quality of the Best Idea." *Management Science* 56, no. 4 (February 24, 2010): 591–605. doi:10.1287/mnsc.1090.1144.

Harmon, Steve. *Zero Gravity: Riding Venture Capital from High-Tech Start-up to Breakout Ipo.* Bloomberg Press, 1999.

"How to Use Empathy Maps to Make Your Message Relevant." *CauseVox.* Accessed November, 2014. http://www.causevox.com/blog/making-your-message-relevant-empathy-maps/.

"Inventing the Future: An Introduction to Patents for Small and Medium-Sized Enterprises." World Intellectual Property Organization, n.d. http://www.wipo.int/edocs/pubdocs/en/sme/917/wipo_pub_917.pdf.

"Is Your Business Idea Patentable? A Guide to What Entrepreneurs Can Patent." *Small Business Association.* Accessed November, 2014. http://www.sba.gov/blogs/your-business-idea-patentable-guide-what-entrepreneurs-can-patent.

Leonard, Dorothy, and Walter Swap. "Gurus in the Garage," January 2, 2001. http://hbswk.hbs.edu/item/1864.html.

Lockett, Andy, Mike Wright, and Stephen Franklin. "Technology Transfer and Universities' Spin-Out Strategies." *Small Business Economics* 20, no. 2 (March 1, 2003): 185–200. doi:10.1023/A:1022220216972.

Loyalka, Michelle Dammon. "When Do You Really Need a Patent?" *Business Week: Small_business,* January 31, 2006. http://www.businessweek.com/stories/2006-01-31/when-do-you-really-need-a-patent.

Markham, Stephen K., and Lynda Aiman-Smith. "Product Champions: Truths, Myths and Management." *Research-Technology Management* 44, no. 3 (May 1, 2001): 44–50.

McMullen, Jeffery S., and Dean A. Shepherd. "Entrepreneurial Action And The Role Of

Uncertainty In The Theory Of The Entrepreneur." *Academy of Management Review* 31, no. 1 (January 1, 2006): 132–52. doi:10.5465/AMR.2006.19379628.

Michalko, Michael. *Thinkertoys: A Handbook of Creative-Thinking Techniques.* 2 edition. Berkeley, Calif: Ten Speed Press, 2006.

Neck, Heidi M. "Idea Generation." In *The Portable MBA in Entrepreneurship*, edited by William D. Bygrave DBA and Andrew Zacharakis, 27–52. John Wiley & Sons, Inc., 2009. http://onlinelibrary.wiley.com/doi/10.1002/9781118256121.ch2/summary.

Nijstad, Bernard A., and Wolfgang Stroebe. "How the Group Affects the Mind: A Cognitive Model of Idea Generation in Groups." *Personality and Social Psychology Review* 10, no. 3 (August 1, 2006): 186–213. doi:10.1207/s15327957pspr1003_1.

O'Shea, Rory P., Thomas J. Allen, Arnaud Chevalier, and Frank Roche. "Entrepreneurial Orientation, Technology Transfer and Spinoff Performance of U.S. Universities." *Research Policy*, The Creation of Spin-off Firms at Public Research Institutions: Managerial and Policy Implcations, 34, no. 7 (September 2005): 994–1009. doi:10.1016/j.respol.2005.05.011.

Passuello, Luciano. "Creative Problem Solving with SCAMPER." *Litemind.* Accessed July 29, 2014. http://litemind.com/scamper/.

"Patents." Accessed November, 2014. http://www.uspto.gov/inventors/patents.jsp.

Paulus, Paul B, and Huei-Chuan Yang. "Idea Generation in Groups: A Basis for Creativity in Organizations." *Organizational Behavior and Human Decision Processes* 82, no. 1 (May 2000): 76–87. doi:10.1006/obhd.2000.2888.

Pérez Pérez, Manuela, and Angel Martínez Sánchez. "The Development of University Spin-Offs: Early Dynamics of Technology Transfer and Networking." *Technovation* 23, no. 10 (October 2003): 823–31. doi:10.1016/S0166-4972(02)00034-2.

"PEST Analysis," n.d. http://www.netmba.com/strategy/pest/.

Pui, Jasmine. "10 Myths On How To Patent An Idea Or Invention." *Entrepreneur.* Accessed November, 2014. http://www.entrepreneur.com/article/48746.

Rietzschel, Eric F., Bernard A. Nijstad, and Wolfgang Stroebe. "Productivity Is Not Enough: A Comparison of Interactive and Nominal Brainstorming Groups on Idea Generation and Selection." *Journal of Experimental Social Psychology* 42, no. 2 (March 2006): 244–51. doi:10.1016/j.jesp.2005.04.005.

Sarasvathy, Saras D. *Effectuation: Elements of Entrepreneurial Expertise.* Edward Elgar Publishing, 2009.

Shane, Scott A. *The Illusions of Entrepreneurship: The Costly Myths That Entrepreneurs, Investors, and Policy Makers Live By.* Yale University Press, 2008.

Siegler, M. G. "One Year Later, Google's Project 10^100 Lives! But Overwhelmed Google Needs Your Help." *TechCrunch.* Accessed November, 2014. http://techcrunch.com/2009/09/24/one-year-later-googles-10100-project-lives-but-overwhelmed-google-needs-your-help/.

"Six Ideas That Will Change the World." *Esquire* Accessed November, 2014. http://www.esquire.com/features/best-brightest-2007/sixideas1207.

Sosik, John J., Surinder S. Kahai, and Bruce J. Avolio. "Transformational Leadership and Dimensions of Creativity: Motivating Idea Generation in Computer-Mediated Groups." *Creativity Research Journal* 11, no. 2 (April 1, 1998): 111–21. doi:10.1207/s15326934crj1102_3.

Tan, Kay. "20+ Tools to Create Your Own Infographics." Accessed July 29, 2014. http://www.hongkiat.com/blog/infographic-tools/.

Technology, Copyright © Massachusetts Institute of, and 1977-2014 All rights reserved. "The 5 Myths of Innovation." *MIT Sloan Management Review*. Accessed November, 2014. http://sloanreview.mit.edu/article/the-5-myths-of-innovation/.

"Ten Ideas to Change the World." Accessed November, 2014. http://www.cnn.com/2010/LIVING/08/23/10.simple.things/index.html.

Wind, Yoram (Jerry) R., and Colin Crook. *Does It Feel Right? Develop the Intuition to Act Quickly.* Pearson Education, 2010.

Business Structure Formation

Alan Chapman. "SWOT Analysis Methods and Analysis," n.d. http://www.businessballs.com/swotanalysisfreetemplate.htm.

Andrew Burke, André van Stel, and Roy Thurik. "Blue Ocean vs. Five Forces." *Harvard Business Review*. Accessed November 2, 2014. http://hbr.org/2010/05/blue-ocean-vs-five-forces.

Bennis, Warren, and Patricia Ward Biederman. *Organizing Genius: The Secrets of Creative Collaboration*. 1 edition. Reading, Mass.: Basic Books, 1998.

Blank, Steve, and Bob Dorf. *The Startup Owner's Manual: The Step-by-Step Guide for Building a Great Company*. K&S Ranch, Incorporated, 2012.

Bridgeland, David M., and Ron Zahavi. *Business Modeling: A Practical Guide to Realizing Business Value*. Morgan Kaufmann, 2008.

Brinckmann, Jan, Dietmar Grichnik, and Diana Kapsa. "Should Entrepreneurs Plan or Just Storm the Castle? A Meta-Analysis on Contextual Factors Impacting the Business Planning–performance Relationship in Small Firms." *Journal of Business Venturing* 25, no. 1 (January 2010): 24–40. doi:10.1016/j.jbusvent.2008.10.007.

Bygrave, William D., and Andrew Zacharakis. *Entrepreneurship*. John Wiley & Sons, 2011.

Chesbrough, Henry. *Open Services Innovation: Rethinking Your Business to Grow and Compete in a New Era*. John Wiley & Sons, 2010.

Chesbrough, Henry, and Richard S. Rosenbloom. "The Role of the Business Model in Capturing Value from Innovation: Evidence from Xerox Corporation's Technology Spin-off Companies." *Industrial and Corporate Change* 11, no. 3 (June 1, 2002): 529–55. doi:10.1093/icc/11.3.529.

Clay Christensen. "Reinventing Your Business Model." *Harvard Business Review*. Accessed November 2, 2014. http://blogs.hbr.org/2008/11/harvard-business-ideacast-122/.

Cunningham, Ian. "Disentangling False Assumptions about Talent Management: The Need to Recognize Difference." *Development and Learning in Organizations: An International Journal* 21, no. 4 (July 3, 2007): 4–5. doi:10.1108/14777280710758781.

Delmar, Frédéric, and Scott Shane. "Does Business Planning Facilitate the Development of New Ventures?" *Strategic Management Journal* 24, no. 12 (December 1, 2003): 1165–85. doi:10.1002/smj.349.

Eric Ries. *The Lean Startup: How Today's Entrepreneurs Use Continuous Innovation to Create Radically Successful Businesses*. First Edition edition. New York: Crown Business, 2011.

Fisher, Roger, William L. Ury, and Bruce Patton. *Getting to Yes: Negotiating Agreement Without Giving In.* Penguin, 2011.

Francis, June. *When in Rome? The Effects of Cultural Adaptation on Intercultural Business Negotiations.* SSRN Scholarly Paper. Rochester, NY: Social Science Research Network, September 1, 1991. http://papers.ssrn.com/abstract=1806127.

Graham, John L. *The Influence of Culture on the Process of Business Negotiations: An Exploratory Study.* SSRN Scholarly Paper. Rochester, NY: Social Science Research Network, March 1, 1985. http://papers.ssrn.com/abstract=1786265.

Hanson. "Preparing an Effective Case Analysis." Cengage, n.d. http://www.cengage.com/resource_uploads/downloads/0170186288_243672.pdf.

Honig, Benson. "Toward a Model of Contingency-Based Business Planning." *Academy of Management Learning & Education* 3, no. 3 (September 1, 2004): 258–73. doi:10.5465/AMLE.2004.14242112.

Joan Magretta. "Why Business Models Matter." *Harvard Business Review.* Accessed December, 2014. http://hbr.org/2002/05/why-business-models-matter.

Johannisson, Bengt. "Business Formation — a Network Approach." *Scandinavian Journal of Management* 4, no. 3–4 (1988): 83–99. doi:10.1016/0956-5221(88)90002-4.

Johnson, Mark W. *Seizing the White Space: Business Model Innovation for Growth and Renewal.* Harvard Business Press, 2013.

Johnson, Ralph A. *Negotiation Basics: Concepts, Skills, and Exercises.* SAGE, 1993.

Kaufman, Josh. *The Personal MBA: Master the Art of Business.* Penguin, 2010.

Lance A. Bettencourt, and Anthony W. Ulwick. "The Customer-Centered Innovation Map." *Harvard Business Review.* Accessed December, 2014. http://hbr.org/2008/05/the-customer-centered-innovation-map.

Lewis, Robert E., and Robert J. Heckman. "Talent Management: A Critical Review." *Human Resource Management Review,* The New World of Work and Organizations, 16, no. 2 (June 2006): 139–54. doi:10.1016/j.hrmr.2006.03.001.

Matthew J. Eyring, Hari Nair, and Mark W. Johnson. "New Business Models in Emerging Markets." *Harvard Business Review.* Accessed December, 2014. http://hbr.org/2011/01/new-business-models-in-emerging-markets.

Mauro F. Guillén, and Esteban García-Canal. "Execution as Strategy." *Harvard Business Review.* Accessed December, 2014. http://hbr.org/2012/10/execution-as-strategy/.

Maurya, Ash. *Running Lean: Iterate from Plan A to a Plan That Works.* O'Reilly Media, Inc., 2012.

McRae, Brad. *Negotiating and Influencing Skills: The Art of Creating and Claiming Value.* SAGE, 1998.

Morris, Michael, Minet Schindehutte, and Jeffrey Allen. "The Entrepreneur's Business Model: Toward a Unified Perspective." *Journal of Business Research,* Special Section:

The Nonprofit Marketing Landscape, 58, no. 6 (June 2005): 726–35. doi:10.1016/j.jbusres.2003.11.001.

Mullins, John, and Randy Komisar. *Getting to Plan B: Breaking Through to a Better Business Model*. Harvard Business Press, 2013.

Oakes, Leslie S., Barbara Townley, and David J. Cooper. "Business Planning as Pedagogy: Language and Control in a Changing Institutional Field." *Administrative Science Quarterly* 43, no. 2 (June 1998): 257. doi:10.2307/2393853.

Osterwalder, Alexander, and Yves Pigneur. *Business Model Generation: A Handbook for Visionaries, Game Changers, and Challengers*. John Wiley & Sons, 2013.

"Pitch Training Material." *Seed Forum*, n.d. http://www.seedforum.org/seed-forum-pitch-training-material.

Ramon Casadesus-Masanell, and Joan E. Ricart. "How to Design a Winning Business Model." *Harvard Business Review*. Accessed December, 2014. http://hbr.org/2011/01/how-to-design-a-winning-business-model.

Robert S. Kaplan, and David P. Norton. "Using the Balanced Scorecard as a Strategic Management System." *Harvard Business Review*. Accessed December, 2014. http://hbr.org/2007/07/using-the-balanced-scorecard-as-a-strategic-management-system.

"SWOT Analysis II: Looking Inside for Strengths and Weaknesses." *Harvard Business Review*. Accessed December, 2014. http://hbr.org/product/swot-analysis-ii-looking-inside-for-strengths-and-weaknesses/an/5535BC-PDF-ENG.

Tarique, Ibraiz, and Randall S. Schuler. "Global Talent Management: Literature Review, Integrative Framework, and Suggestions for Further Research." *Journal of World Business*, Global Talent Management, 45, no. 2 (April 2010): 122–33. doi:10.1016/j.jwb.2009.09.019.

The Five Competitive Forces That Shape Strategy, 2008. http://www.youtube.com/watch?v=myF2_FBCvXw&feature=youtube_gdata_player.

Triandis, Harry C., Peter Carnevale, Michele Gelfand, Christopher Robert, S. Arzu Wasti, Tahira Probst, Emiko S. Kashima, et al. "Culture and Deception in Business Negotiations: A Multilevel Analysis." *International Journal of Cross Cultural Management* 1, no. 1 (April 1, 2001): 73–90. doi:10.1177/147059580111008.

Venkatraman, N. "Strategic Orientation of Business Enterprises: The Construct, Dimensionality, and Measurement." *Management Science* 35, no. 8 (August 1, 1989): 942–62. doi:10.1287/mnsc.35.8.942.

Verstraete, Thierry, and Estele Jouison-Laffitte. *A Business Model for Entrepreneurship*. Edward Elgar Publishing, 2011.

W. Chan Kim, and Renée Mauborgne. "Blue Ocean Strategy." *Harvard Business Review*. Accessed November 2, 2014. http://hbr.org/2004/10/blue-ocean-strategy.

"Writing a Business Plan." *Grove by Sequoia Capital.* Accessed December, 2014. http://www.sequoiacap.com/grove/posts/6bzx/writing-a-business-plan.

Zott, Christoph, and Raphael Amit. "Business Model Design: An Activity System Perspective." *Long Range Planning*, Business Models, 43, no. 2–3 (April 2010): 216–26. doi:10.1016/j.lrp.2009.07.004.

Social by Design

Akerlof, George A., and Robert J. Shiller. *Animal Spirits: How Human Psychology Drives the Economy, and Why It Matters for Global Capitalism*. Princeton University Press, 2010.

Albors, J., J. C. Ramos, and J. L. Hervas. "New Learning Network Paradigms: Communities of Objectives, Crowdsourcing, Wikis and Open Source." *International Journal of Information Management* 28, no. 3 (June 2008): 194–202. doi:10.1016/j.ijinfomgt.2007.09.006.

Alesina, Alberto, and George-Marios Angeletos. *Fairness and Redistribution: U.S. versus Europe*. Working Paper. National Bureau of Economic Research, February 2003. http://www.nber.org/papers/w9502.

Arthur, W. Brian. "'Silicon Valley' Locational Clusters: When Do Increasing Returns Imply Monopoly?." *Mathematical Social Sciences* 19, no. 3 (June 1990): 235–51. doi:10.1016/0165-4896(90)90064-E.

Baba, Yasunori. "The Dynamics of Continuous Innovation in Scale-Intensive Industries." *Strategic Management Journal* 10, no. 1 (January 1, 1989): 89–100. doi:10.1002/smj.4250100108.

Botsman, Rachel. "Welcome to the New Reputation Economy." *Wired UK*. Accessed July 29, 2014. http://www.wired.co.uk/magazine/archive/2012/09/features/welcome-to-the-new-reputation-economy.

Boyd, Danah M., and Nicole B. Ellison. "Social Network Sites: Definition, History, and Scholarship." *Journal of Computer-Mediated Communication* 13, no. 1 (October 1, 2007): 210–30. doi:10.1111/j.1083-6101.2007.00393.x.

Brabham, Daren C. *Crowdsourcing*. MIT Press, 2013.

Burrows, Edwin G., and Mike Wallace. *Gotham: A History of New York City to 1898*. Oxford University Press, 1998.

Burt, Ronald S. *Structural Holes: The Social Structure of Competition*. Harvard University Press, 2009.

Centola, Damon. "The Spread of Behavior in an Online Social Network Experiment." *Science* 329, no. 5996 (September 3, 2010): 1194–97. doi:10.1126/science.1185231.

Chiu, Chao-Min, Meng-Hsiang Hsu, and Eric T. G. Wang. "Understanding Knowledge Sharing in Virtual Communities: An Integration of Social Capital and Social Cognitive Theories." *Decision Support Systems* 42, no. 3 (December 2006): 1872–88. doi:10.1016/j.dss.2006.04.001.

Cooke, Philip N., and Luciana Lazzeretti. *Creative Cities, Cultural Clusters and Local Economic Development*. Edward Elgar Publishing, 2008.

Cross, Robert L., and Andrew Parker. *The Hidden Power of Social Networks: Understanding How Work Really Gets Done in Organizations*. Harvard Business Press, 2004.

Delgado, Mercedes, Michael E. Porter, and Scott Stern. "Clusters and Entrepreneurship." *Journal of Economic Geography* 10, no. 4 (July 1, 2010): 495–518. doi:10.1093/jeg/lbq010.

Drath, Wilfred H., and Charles J. Palus. *Making Common Sense: Leadership as Meaning-Making in a Community of Practice*. Center for Creative Leadership, 1994.

Duguid, Paul. "'The Art of Knowing': Social and Tacit Dimensions of Knowledge and the Limits of the Community of Practice." *The Information Society* 21, no. 2 (April 1, 2005): 109–18. doi:10.1080/01972240590925311.

Estellés-Arolas, Enrique, and Fernando González-Ladrón-de-Guevara. "Towards an Integrated Crowdsourcing Definition." *Journal of Information Science* 38, no. 2 (April 1, 2012): 189–200. doi:10.1177/0165551512437638.

Gallivan, Michael J. "Striking a Balance between Trust and Control in a Virtual Organization: A Content Analysis of Open Source Software Case Studies." *Information Systems Journal* 11, no. 4 (October 1, 2001): 277–304. doi:10.1046/j.1365-2575.2001.00108.x.

Granovetter, Mark. *Getting a Job: A Study of Contacts and Careers*. University of Chicago Press, 1995.

Granovetter, Mark. "The Strength of Weak Ties." *American Journal of Sociology* 78, no. 6 (1973): 1360–80. doi:10.2307/2776392.

Gray, Bette. "Informal Learning in an Online Community of Practice." *Journal of Distance Education* 19, no. 1 (January 2004): 20–35.

Greengard, Samuel. "Following the Crowd." *Commun. ACM* 54, no. 2 (February 2011): 20–22. doi:10.1145/1897816.1897824.

Hendriks, Paul. "Why Share Knowledge? The Influence of ICT on the Motivation for Knowledge Sharing." *Knowledge and Process Management* 6, no. 2 (1999): 91–100. doi:10.1002/(sici)1099-1441(199906)6:2%3C91::aid-kpm54%3E3.0.co;2-m.

Howe, Jeff. "The Rise of Crowdsourcing." *Wired* 14, no. 6 (June 2006). http://www.wired.com/wired/archive/14.06/crowds.html.

Huber, Franz. "Social Capital of Economic Clusters: Towards a Network-Based Conception of Social Resources." *Tijdschrift Voor Economische En Sociale Geografie* 100, no. 2 (April 1, 2009): 160–70. doi:10.1111/j.1467-9663.2009.00526.x.

Ipe, Minu. "Knowledge Sharing in Organizations: A Conceptual Framework." *Human Resource Development Review* 2, no. 4 (December 1, 2003): 337–59. doi:10.1177/1534484303257985.

James, Aaron. *Fairness in Practice: A Social Contract for a Global Economy*. Oxford University Press, 2012.

Kempe, David, Jon Kleinberg, and Éva Tardos. "Maximizing the Spread of Influence Through a Social Network." In *Proceedings of the Ninth ACM SIGKDD International Conference on Knowledge Discovery and Data Mining*, 137–46. KDD '03. New York, NY, USA: ACM, 2003. doi:10.1145/956750.956769.

Kenney, Martin. *Understanding Silicon Valley: The Anatomy of an Entrepreneurial Region*. Stanford University Press, 2000.

Kenney, M., and U. von Burg. "Technology, Entrepreneurship and Path Dependence: Industrial Clustering in Silicon Valley and Route 128." *Industrial and Corporate Change* 8, no. 1 (March 1, 1999): 67–103. doi:10.1093/icc/8.1.67.

Kittur, Aniket, Boris Smus, Susheel Khamkar, and Robert E. Kraut. "CrowdForge: Crowdsourcing Complex Work." In *Proceedings of the 24th Annual ACM Symposium on User Interface Software and Technology*, 43–52. UIST '11. New York, NY, USA: ACM, 2011. doi:10.1145/2047196.2047202.

Lampe, Cliff A.C., Nicole Ellison, and Charles Steinfield. "A Familiar Face(Book): Profile Elements As Signals in an Online Social Network." In *Proceedings of the SIGCHI Conference on Human Factors in Computing Systems*, 435–44. CHI '07. New York, NY, USA: ACM, 2007. doi:10.1145/1240624.1240695.

Lesser, Eric L. *Knowledge and Social Capital: Foundations and Applications*. Elsevier, 2000.

Levin, Daniel Z., and Rob Cross. "The Strength of Weak Ties You Can Trust: The Mediating Role of Trust in Effective Knowledge Transfer." *Management Science* 50, no. 11 (November 1, 2004): 1477–90. doi:10.1287/mnsc.1030.0136.

Lewis, Michael. *The New New Thing: A Silicon Valley Story*. W. W. Norton & Company, 1999.

Lin, Nan. *Social Capital: A Theory of Social Structure and Action (Structural Analysis in the Social Sciences)*. Cambridge University Press, 2002.

McSweeney, Brendan. "Hofstede's Model of National Cultural Differences and Their Consequences: A Triumph of Faith - a Failure of Analysis." *Human Relations* 55, no. 1 (January 1, 2002): 89–118. doi:10.1177/0018726702551004.

Miles, Raymond E., Grant Miles, and Charles Curtis Snow. *Collaborative Entrepreneurship: How Communities of Networked Firms Use Continuous Innovation to Create Economic Wealth*. Stanford University Press, 2005.

Moran, Robert T., Neil Remington Abramson, and Sarah V. Moran. *Managing Cultural Differences*. Routledge, 2014.

Patti, Anthony L. "Economic Clusters and the Supply Chain: A Case Study." *Supply Chain Management: An International Journal* 11, no. 3 (May 1, 2006): 266–70. doi:10.1108/13598540610662176.

Pitelis, Christos. "Clusters, Entrepreneurial Ecosystem Co-Creation, and Appropriability: A Conceptual Framework." *Industrial and Corporate Change*, March 24, 2012, dts008. doi:10.1093/icc/dts008.

Poetz, Marion K., and Martin Schreier. "The Value of Crowdsourcing: Can Users Really Compete with Professionals in Generating New Product Ideas?" *Journal of Product Innovation Management* 29, no. 2 (March 1, 2012): 245–56. doi:10.1111/j.1540-5885.2011.00893.x.

Porter, Michael E. *Competitive Advantage of Nations: Creating and Sustaining Superior Performance*. Simon and Schuster, 2011.

Porter, Michael E. "Location, Competition, and Economic Development: Local Clusters in a Global Economy." *Economic Development Quarterly* 14, no. 1 (February 1, 2000): 15–34. doi:10.1177/089124240001400105.

Rosenfeld, Stuart A. "Bringing Business Clusters into the Mainstream of Economic Development." *European Planning Studies* 5, no. 1 (February 1, 1997): 3–23. doi:10.1080/09654319708720381.

Saxenian, Annalee, and Jinn-Yuh Hsu. "The Silicon Valley–Hsinchu Connection: Technical Communities and Industrial Upgrading." *Industrial and Corporate Change* 10, no. 4 (December 1, 2001): 893–920. doi:10.1093/icc/10.4.893.

Schonfeld, Erick. "SCVNGR's Secret Game Mechanics Playdeck." *TechCrunch*. Accessed July 29, 2014. http://techcrunch.com/2010/08/25/scvngr-game-mechanics/.

Szeman, Imre, and Timothy Kaposy. *Cultural Theory: An Anthology*. John Wiley & Sons, 2010.

"The 39 Best Pieces of Sales Advice You'll Hear This Year." Accessed July 29, 2014. http://firstround.com/article/The-39-Best-Pieces-of-Sales-Advice-Youll-Hear-This-Year.

Tonnessen, Tor. "Continuous Innovation through Company Wide Employee Participation." *The TQM Magazine* 17, no. 2 (April 1, 2005): 195–207. doi:10.1108/09544780510583254.

Woodward, Douglas, Octávio Figueiredo, and Paulo Guimarães. "Beyond the Silicon Valley: University R&D and High-Technology Location." *Journal of Urban Economics* 60, no. 1 (July 2006): 15–32. doi:10.1016/j.jue.2006.01.002.

Yang, Shih-Hsien. "Using Blogs to Enhance Critical Reflection and Community of Practice." *Educational Technology & Society* 12, no. 2 (January 2009): 11–21.

Funding

Aldridge, Alan. "Habitus and Cultural Capital in the Field of Personal Finance." *The Sociological Review* 46, no. 1 (February 1, 1998): 1–23. doi:10.1111/1467-954X.00087.

Bates, Timothy. "Self-Employment Entry across Industry Groups." *Journal of Business Venturing* 10, no. 2 (March 1995): 143–56. doi:10.1016/0883-9026(94)00018-P.

Bhide A. "Bootstrap Finance: The Art of Start-Ups." *Harvard Business Review* 70, no. 6 (December 1991): 109–17.

Brush, C. G., and Candida G. Brush. *Growth-Oriented Women Entrepreneurs and Their Businesses: A Global Research Perspective.* Edward Elgar Publishing, 2006.

Carter, Richard B., and Howard Van Auken. "Bootstrap Financing and Owners' Perceptions of Their Business Constraints and Opportunities." *Entrepreneurship & Regional Development* 17, no. 2 (March 1, 2005): 129–44. doi:10.1080/08985620500067548.

Christina Farr. "Venture Capital Picks up the Moneyball Strategy." *VentureBeat.* Accessed July 29, 2014. http://venturebeat.com/2012/11/09/startup-algorithm/.

DeGennaro, Ramon P. "Angel Investors: Who They Are and What They Do; Can I Be One, Too?" *The Journal of Wealth Management* 13, no. 2 (July 1, 2010): 55–60. doi:10.3905/jwm.2010.13.2.055.

Denis, David J. "Entrepreneurial Finance: An Overview of the Issues and Evidence." *Journal of Corporate Finance*, Venture Capital, Initial Public Offerings, and Entrepreneurial Finance, 10, no. 2 (March 2004): 301–26. doi:10.1016/S0929-1199(03)00059-2.

De Noble, Alex F. "Raising Finance from Business Angels." *Venture Capital* 3, no. 4 (October 1, 2001): 359–67. doi:10.1080/13691060010024719.

Doyle, Kenneth O. "Toward a Psychology of Money." *American Behavioral Scientist* 35, no. 6 (July 1, 1992): 708–24. doi:10.1177/0002764292035006007.

Ebben, Jay, and Alec Johnson. "Bootstrapping in Small Firms: An Empirical Analysis of Change over Time." *Journal of Business Venturing* 21, no. 6 (November 2006): 851–65. doi:10.1016/j.jbusvent.2005.06.007.

Ekanem, Ignatius. "'Bootstrapping': The Investment Decision-Making Process in Small Firms." *The British Accounting Review* 37, no. 3 (September 2005): 299–318. doi:10.1016/j.bar.2005.04.004.

Freear, John, Jeffrey E. Sohl, and William E. Wetzel. "Angels: Personal Investors in the

Venture Capital Market." *Entrepreneurship & Regional Development* 7, no. 1 (January 1, 1995): 85–94. doi:10.1080/08985629500000005.

Carman, C. Thomas, and Raymond Forgue. *Personal Finance*. Cengage Learning, 2011.

Gianforte, Greg, and Marcus Gibson. *Bootstrapping Your Business: Start and Grow a Successful Company with Almost No Money*. Avon, Mass.: Adams Media, 2005.

Harrison, Richard T., and Colin M. Mason. "Does Gender Matter? Women Business Angels and the Supply of Entrepreneurial Finance." *Entrepreneurship Theory and Practice* 31, no. 3 (May 1, 2007): 445–72. doi:10.1111/j.1540-6520.2007.00182.x.

Ibrahim, Darian M. "(Not So) Puzzling Behavior of Angel Investors, The." *Vanderbilt Law Review* 61 (2008): 1405.

Jeng, Leslie A., and Philippe C. Wells. "The Determinants of Venture Capital Funding: Evidence across Countries." *Journal of Corporate Finance* 6, no. 3 (September 1, 2000): 241–89. doi:10.1016/S0929-1199(00)00003-1.

Jones, Oswald, and Dilani Jayawarna. "Resourcing New Businesses: Social Networks, Bootstrapping and Firm Performance." *Venture Capital* 12, no. 2 (April 1, 2010): 127–52. doi:10.1080/13691061003658886.

Kerr, William R., Josh Lerner, and Antoinette Schoar. "The Consequences of Entrepreneurial Finance: Evidence from Angel Financings." *Review of Financial Studies* 27, no. 1 (January 1, 2014): 20–55. doi:10.1093/rfs/hhr098.

Koen, Peter A. *Cognitive Mechanisms: Which Ones Allow Corporate Entrepreneurs to Obtain Startup Funding*, n.d.

Lam, Wing. "Funding Gap, What Funding Gap? Financial Bootstrapping." *International Journal of Entrepreneurial Behaviour & Research* 16, no. 4 (June 15, 2010): 268–95. doi:10.1108/13552551011054480.

Manalo, Marivic V., and Scott Brandley. *Basic Accounting: Service Business Study Guide*. eBookIt.com, 2013.

Marcketti, Sara B., Linda S. Niehm, and Ruchita Fuloria. "An Exploratory Study of Lifestyle Entrepreneurship and Its Relationship to Life Quality." *Family and Consumer Sciences Research Journal* 34, no. 3 (March 1, 2006): 241–59. doi:10.1177/1077727X05283632.

Mason, Colin M. "Informal Sources of Venture Finance." In *The Life Cycle of Entrepreneurial Ventures*, edited by Simon Parker, 259–99. International Handbook Series on Entrepreneurship 3. Springer US, 2007. http://link.springer.com/chapter/10.1007/978-0-387-32313-8_10.

Morris, Kenneth M., and Virginia B. Morris. *The Wall Street Journal Guide to Understanding Money & Investing*. Simon and Schuster, 2004.

Morrissette, Stephen G. "A Profile of Angel Investors." *The Journal of Private Equity* 10, no. 3 (January 1, 2007): 52–66. doi:10.3905/jpe.2007.686430.

Payne, William H., and Matthew J. Macarty. "The Anatomy of an Angel Investing Network: Tech Coast Angels." *Venture Capital* 4, no. 4 (October 1, 2002): 331–36. doi:10.1080/1369106022000024950.

Prasad, Dev, Garry D. Bruton, and George Vozikis. "Signaling Value to Businessangels: The Proportion of the Entrepreneur's Net Worth Invested in a New Venture as a Decision Signal." *Venture Capital* 2, no. 3 (July 1, 2000): 167–82. doi:10.1080/13691060050135064.

Schueth, Steve. "Socially Responsible Investing in the United States." *Journal of Business Ethics* 43, no. 3 (March 1, 2003): 189–94. doi:10.1023/A:1022981828869.

Smith, David. "Financial Bootstrapping and Social Capital: How Technology-Based Start-Ups Fund Innovation." *International Journal of Entrepreneurship and Innovation Management* 10, no. 2 (January 1, 2009): 199–209. doi:10.1504/IJEIM.2009.025182.

Souitaris, Vangelis, Stefania Zerbinati, and Andreas Al-Laham. "Do Entrepreneurship Programmes Raise Entrepreneurial Intention of Science and Engineering Students? The Effect of Learning, Inspiration and Resources." *Journal of Business Venturing* 22, no. 4 (July 2007): 566–91. doi:10.1016/j.jbusvent.2006.05.002.

Steier, Lloyd, and Royston Greenwood. "Newly Created Firms and Informal Angel Investors: A Four-Stage Model of Network Development." *Venture Capital* 1, no. 2 (April 1, 1999): 147–67. doi:10.1080/136910699295947.

Tyson, Eric. *Personal Finance For Dummies*. John Wiley & Sons, 2006.

Van Auken, Howard, and Lynn Neeley. "Evidence of Bootstrap Financing among Small Start-Up Firms." *The Journal of Entrepreneurial Finance* 5, no. 3 (December 1, 1996): 235–49.

Williams, Colin C. "A Lifestyle Choice? Evaluating the Motives of Do-it-yourself (DIY) Consumers." *International Journal of Retail & Distribution Management* 32, no. 5 (May 1, 2004): 270–78. doi:10.1108/09590550410534613.

Wilson Sonsini. "Plain Preferred Term Sheet." *Docstoc.com*. Accessed January, 2014. http://www.docstoc.com/docs/10303638/FFI---Plain-Preferred-Term-Sheet.

Wiltbank, Robert, and Warren Boeker. *Returns to Angel Investors in Groups*. SSRN Scholarly Paper. Rochester, NY: Social Science Research Network, November 1, 2007. http://papers.ssrn.com/abstract=1028592.

Wiltbank, Robert, and Robert Wiltbank. "Angel Investors Do Make Money, Data Shows 2.5x Returns Overall." *TechCrunch*. Accessed July 29, 2014. http://techcrunch.com/2012/10/13/angel-investors-make-2-5x-returns-overall/.

Winborg, Joakim. "Use of Financial Bootstrapping in New Businesses: A Question of Last Resort?" *Venture Capital* 11, no. 1 (January 1, 2009): 71–83. doi:10.1080/13691060802351248.

Winborg, Joakim, and Hans Landström. "Financial Bootstrapping in Small Businesses: Examining Small Business Managers' Resource Acquisition Behaviors." *Journal of*

Business Venturing 16, no. 3 (May 2001): 235–54. doi:10.1016/S0883-9026(99)00055-5.

Winton, Andrew, and Vijay Yerramilli. "Entrepreneurial Finance: Banks versus Venture Capital." *Journal of Financial Economics* 88, no. 1 (April 2008): 51–79. doi:10.1016/j.jfineco.2007.05.004.

Wong, Andrew Y. *Angel Finance: The Other Venture Capital*. SSRN Scholarly Paper. Rochester, NY: Social Science Research Network, January 1, 2002. http://papers.ssrn.com/abstract=941228.

Business Lore

Chai, Kah-Hin, Jun Zhang, and Kay-Chuan Tan. "A TRIZ-Based Method for New Service Design." *Journal of Service Research* 8, no. 1 (August 1, 2005): 48–66. doi:10.1177/1094670505276683.

Fog, Klaus, Christian Budtz, Philip Munch, and Stephen Blanchette. "Storytelling in Business." In *Storytelling*, 49–58. Springer Berlin Heidelberg, 2010. http://link.springer.com/chapter/10.1007/978-3-540-88349-4_3.

Georgeff, Michael, Barney Pell, Martha Pollack, Milind Tambe, and Michael Wooldridge. "The Belief-Desire-Intention Model of Agency." In *Intelligent Agents V: Agents Theories, Architectures, and Languages*, edited by Jörg P. Müller, Anand S. Rao, and Munindar P. Singh, 1–10. Lecture Notes in Computer Science 1555. Springer Berlin Heidelberg, 1999. http://link.springer.com/chapter/10.1007/3-540-49057-4_1.

Kashima, Yoshihisa, Allison McKintyre, and Paul Clifford. "The Category of the Mind: Folk Psychology of Belief, Desire, and Intention." *Asian Journal of Social Psychology* 1, no. 3 (December 1, 1998): 289–313. doi:10.1111/1467-839X.00019.

Lidwell, William, Kritina Holden, and Jill Butler. *Universal Principles of Design, Revised and Updated: 125 Ways to Enhance Usability, Influence Perception, Increase Appeal, Make Better Design Decisions,*. Rockport Publishers, 2010.

Maclean, Mairi, Charles Harvey, and Robert Chia. "Sensemaking, Storytelling and the Legitimization of Elite Business Careers." *Human Relations* 65, no. 1 (January 1, 2012): 17–40. doi:10.1177/0018726711425616.

Mancuso, James C. "Constructionism, Personal Construct Psychology and Narrative Psychology." *Theory & Psychology* 6, no. 1 (February 1, 1996): 47–70. doi:10.1177/0959354396061004.

Martin, Roger L. *The Design of Business: Why Design Thinking Is the Next Competitive Advantage*. Harvard Business Press, 2009.

O'Connor, Ellen. *Storytelling to Be Real: Narrative, Legitimacy Building and Venturing*. SSRN Scholarly Paper. Rochester, NY: Social Science Research Network, 2004. http://papers.ssrn.com/abstract=1497283.

Ratcliffe, Matthew. *Rethinking Commonsense Psychology: A Critique of Folk Psychology, Theory of Mind and Simulation*. Palgrave Macmillan, 2007.

Epilogue

Closing remarks

At the start of this the book I mentioned the University of Pisa PhD Plus program which began in 2011. Since that time it has improved each year, experimenting with various formats, topics and speakers. In 2014 the team that I worked with closely, and listed in the acknowledgement section, was awarded a grant by the European Union (Erasmus+ Knowledge Alliances) to collaborate with other E.U. Universities. The team will adopt and combine the PhD Plus program with other initiatives to generalize its methods and make them broadly available throughout the E.U.. The program continues to innovate and use entrepreneurship to teach entrepreneurship.

Every author needs to ask themselves why are they writing a book and the answer I came up with is that I have a strong point of view that I want to share with others. Since this book came out of the course I taught for five years, I concluded that with all my experiments in teaching entrepreneurship, using action learning and hybrid classrooms, from blogging to showing movies, giving short lectures, lots of projects, the students still asked for a traditional format, a book and a test. As much as I tried to resist this and think it is not the way to learn business I have to give them what they asked for and not think that I have a better way until I have tried the traditional methods. Therefore, the book is a vanity and exposure of vulnerability, or the reverse in that it is an admission of the failures of previous attempts at innovating the teaching and learning of entrepreneurship. The resignation that to demonstrate my own ego, my over confidence, my own cognitive biases, I have to resort to a vanity, the notion that what I have to say has value to someone, and if not, that I can impose my views onto the future students, thinking I know better how to guide their futures than they do. Therefore, with the vulnerability, the fear of writing, and with much humility, I add one book to the thousands that are published each year. My hope is that it helps someone open the possibilities for self-determination. It is my current challenge and act of entrepreneurship.

Get prepared for the long journey, reclaim your economic self-determination, and recognize good fortune when it is presented while overcoming all the obstacles along the way, create value in everything you do and be fully human connecting to others on planet earth.

Dedication

This book is dedicated to all who may benefit from it by jolting their entrepreneurial spirit into action.

To the rector, vice-rectors, faculty, staff, researchers, and students, entrepreneurs, at the University of Pisa, Italy, who created, supported, and participated in the PhD Plus and International MBA program, their success and failures respectively initiated the creation of this book.

To the faculty, staff, students, and board members of the Field Center for Entrepreneurship at Baruch College, New York City. They provided the forum for my explorations into understanding what drives my own entrepreneurial spirit and expanded my knowledge of the broader range of entrepreneurial pursuits.

To my wife, mother and father, family, associates, and all those who I learned from simply by listening, watching, and imitating what they do. My brother Bill who taught me the value of social ventures and my brother Bob who showed me the value of living a creative life, and my cousin Henry Galiano who showed me how science, commerce, and personal interest can enrich one's life and help to educate the next generation while making money.

Acknowledgements

Many entrepreneurs have contributed indirectly to this book. By working with these associates, I learned patterns that I absorbed into my work and used it to propel my own modest success. They are all inspirations that framed my understanding of what works and what does not.

I wish to thank the following team members of University of Pisa, PhD Plus program; Gualtiero Fantoni, Antonella Magliocchi, Gabriele Montelisciani, Leonello Trivelli, Giacomo Tazzini, Donata Gabelloni, Marco Tonsini, Daniele Mazzei, Felipe Belo, Davide Cecchini, Riccardo Paterni, and many invited speakers from 2011 to 2015.

Paolo Ferragina, PhD, Vice Rector for Innovation and Research, University of Pisa, he gave me the opportunity to get involved in a unique innovation of including entrepreneurship in the PhD programs of the University.

Marco Allegrini, PhD, Professore Ordinario in "Economia Aziendale", in 2012 as the Director of the International MBA program he invited me to teach entrepreneurship and be the coordinator for its curriculum.

Monica Rivera Dean, Administrative Director, Field Center for Entrepreneurship, Baruch College, her invitation to get involved with the programs at Baruch were an inspiration for me to attempt to teach what I have experienced as an entrepreneur.

Lindsay Siegel, Executive Director, Zahn innovation Center, Grove School of Engineering, City College of New York, showed me how social entrepreneurship is not different from tech startups and shares a value system of fairness, responsibility, collaborative sharing, problem solving and the pursuit of creating value.

Matt Tucker, the entrepreneur who executes. His insight can figure out what I mean when it does not make sense to everyone else. He showed me how tolerance for poor languages skills can uncover the value in the message.

Giovanni Battistini, the entrepreneur who thinks globally. A business partner, perpetual innovator, and marathon runner in truest sense.

Jeff Carter, the entrepreneur who deconstructs the future into reality, co-conspirator of our magnanimous subversions. He gave me the opportunity to learn why corporations and the great cathedrals of academia are so broken and no longer fit the needs of humanity.

Manny Ohonme, a social entrepreneur who inspired me to volunteer my experiences in the service of the next generation of entrepreneurs doing good to fix the many problems we have in the world.

Ashok Kamal and Nik Seet, the next generation, co-founders of sivi.com (2014) for creating a social venture for supporting entrepreneurs and in so doing allowed me to learn that ultimately a true entrepreneur creates the space for other entrepreneurs.

Camille Santistevan, freelance editor and writing consultant. Without her proofreading and basic copyediting I would have never finished this book.

Disclaimer

I have worked and been a consultant to over fifty companies and clients in the past twenty five years. In the last five years I have had over five hundred students in my course lectures with at least a hundred teams presenting businesses that I coached or mentored. During that journey, I have encountered a wide variety of business situations. Being an entrepreneur and working as a corporate executive, I have been privy to confidential information and discussions that afford me a view into the inner decision-making processes of an entrepreneurial team. Resemblance to a particular company, product, process, or individual in this book is purely coincidental. The description of situations is a composite, aggregate of my experience and included for illustrative purposes. They are portions of real business scenarios with challenges, as all new ventures and innovations come with many risk and hurdles to being commercially realized. The descriptions are abstracted and generalized to apply to a broader range of common challenges that entrepreneurs will encounter. Each new venture has challenges and what I found is that common patterns do exist, so former clients, co-founders, investors, and employees, may read this book and recognize their situation without realizing that my consulting and coaching was simply highlighting issues they thought were unique to them but were obvious recurring problematic patterns.

About the Author

Ray Garcia is the managing director of Buoyant Capital, a global peer advisory think tank addressing the growth challenges of small to medium sized enterprises. The firm coordinates its team of experts to help its clients improve competitiveness through talent management, global market expansion partnership access, technology asset management, capital investment and restructuring. Buoyant Capital was founded in 2000 in New York City and has helped launch several start-up companies and works as an advisory to company founders, CEO's, and their investors. Ray has over 20 years of experience as a technology entrepreneur, as company CTO co-founder, for four venture-backed companies. Earlier in his career, he worked as an executive for major banks including, Citicorp, Republic National Bank (now HSBC), Bank of America, and as a technology consultant to several large U.S. multi-national corporations. In 2008, he was elected to serve as an executive in resident at MIT Media Lab. Since 2010 he serves on the advisory board of Baruch College Field Center for Entrepreneurship. From 2011 to 2014, he taught an accelerated course in entrepreneurship at the University of Pisa, Italy, School of Economics, to PhD candidates and International MBA executives with a focus on innovation, technology transfer and venture spin-offs. In 2015 he is serving as a business expert to E.U. Commission Horizon 2020 SME innovation instrument where he will evaluate commercialization grant proposals of technology ventures.

www.ingramcontent.com/pod-product-compliance
Lightning Source LLC
Chambersburg PA
CBHW070923210326
41520CB00021B/6774